The Fun Seeker's Toronto

THE ULTIMATE GUIDE TO ONE
OF THE WORLD'S HOTTEST CITIES

THE FUN SEEKER'S TRAVEL SERIES

...t guide. We accept no payment of any ...sion in this book. **We welcome your views** ...k@greenlinepub.com.

... checked as rigorously as possible before going to press. The publisher acc... ...sponsibility for any changes that may have occurred since, or for any other variance of fact from that recorded here in good faith.

No part of this book may be reproduced in any form without permission in writing from the publisher, except by a reviewer who wishes to quote brief passages for a published review. For information regarding permission to reproduce sections from this book, contact: Greenline Publications, P.O. Box 590780, San Francisco, CA 94159-0780.

This publication is a creative work fully protected by all applicable copyright laws, as well as by misappropriation, trade secrets, unfair competition, and all other applicable laws. The authors and editors of this work have added value to the underlying factual material herein through one or more of the following: unique and original selection, coordination, expression, arrangement, and classification (including the itineraries) of the information.

Distributed in the United States and Canada by National Book Network (NBN).
First Edition. Printed in the United States. 100% postconsumer content.
All rights reserved.
Copyright © 2005 Greenline Publications, Inc.
ISBN: 0-9759022-3-7

Credits

Executive Editor	Alan S. Davis
Series Editor	Christina Henry de Tessan
Copy Editor	Gail Nelson Bonebrake
Maps	Chris Gillis
Production	Samia Afra

Back Cover Photo Credits: The Boiler House (left) photo by Lucas Digital Art; Scaramouche (center) photo by Interior Images; Caribana Festival (right) photo by TonyEno.com.

Special Sales

For information about bulk purchases of Greenline books (ten copies or more), email us at bookorders@greenlinepub.com. Special bulk rates are available for charities, corporations, institutions, and online and mail-order catalogs, and our books can be customized to suit your company's needs.

GREENLINE PUBLICATIONS
Extraordinary Guides for Extraordinary Travelers
P.O. Box 590780
San Francisco, CA 94159-0780

THE FUN SEEKER'S TRAVEL SERIES

The Fun Seeker's Toronto

THE ULTIMATE GUIDE TO ONE
OF THE WORLD'S HOTTEST CITIES

Anya Wassenberg

GREENLINE PUBLICATIONS

ABOUT THE AUTHOR

Anya Wassenberg has been a freelance writer of short stories and non-fiction articles for several years. Her eclectic interests have led her to cover a wide range of topics, from Canadian football to lifestyle, the arts, and travel features, and her work has appeared in a variety of media from print to web to radio. Her short fiction has appeared in magazines and anthologies throughout North America, as well as in the U.K.

To Our Readers:

One of my college summer jobs was to escort tour groups around Europe and evaluate them for my parents' tour company. I've had the travel bug ever since. But it was only as I got older did I realize how important it is to recognize that *time is precious ... and so is fun*. That is why ten years ago I "retired" and set out on a journey to find the 100 most fun places to be in the world at the right time. The difficulty in finding, qualifying and getting the most out of these events—from the Opera Ball in Vienna to the Calgary Stampede—led me to write a guidebook.

The success of my book, *The Fun Also Rises*, named after Ernest Hemingway's *The Sun Also Rises*, which helped popularize what has become perhaps the most thrilling party on earth (Pamplona's Fiesta de San Fermín, also known as the Running of the Bulls), persuaded me of the need for a different approach to travel book publishing—one that focused on peak experiences.

Greenline Publications—*extraordinary guides for extraordinary travelers*—was launched at the end of 2002 with *The 25 Best World War II Sites: Pacific Theater*, the first book in the **Greenline Historic Travel Series**. We now also have in the series *The 25 Best World War II Sites: European Theater* and *The 25 Best Civil War Sites*.

The **Fun Seeker's** series of city guides was launched in 2003, and will include eleven titles by the end of 2005. The guides are designed for singles and couples, who, like me, know that the night is as important as the day. It is for those who want to experience the best that a city has to offer—hotels, restaurants, nightlife and attractions that are exciting without the stuffiness.

Greenline's guiding principle is simple: never settle for the ordinary. We hope that a willingness to explore new approaches to guidebooks, combined with meticulous research, provides you with unique and significant travel experiences.

Please let me know if our guides fail to meet your expectations in any way. To reach me, or for updated information on all Greenline books, please visit our website at **www.greenlinepub.com**.

Wishing you extraordinary travels,

Alan S. Davis
Publisher

We Take Fun Seriously.

Seeking Fun

Travel should include all of a destination's peak experiences: an amazing museum, a unique spa, a spectacular view. But travel also should be fun—specifically, urban grown-up fun, the kind that thrives by night as well as by day. Fun is a hip nightclub or a trendy restaurant. It is finding a great beach with lots of other fun people, not escaping from them. It is not lonely planet; it is LIVELY planet.

Choosing the Right Place, Right Time

At the restaurants we recommend, food is important, but so is the scene. The hotel selections, which tend to be 4- or 5-star properties, make their guests feel special. At our wide range of nightlife choices you won't find kids with fake IDs. And the attractions must be remarkable. But experienced travelers know these criteria do not on their own guarantee fun. Going to a restaurant can be a totally different (and less fun) experience at 7 p.m. than at 9 p.m.; a champagne boat cruise might be ordinary in the afternoon but spectacular at sunset. With these considerations in mind, we construct our itineraries.

Striving for Perfection

Your time is precious. That is why our executive editor, editors, and writers (locals who are in touch with what is great—and what is not) have spent more than a thousand hours researching, writing, and debating selections for each guide. In *The Perfect Toronto* we have chosen the best of the best in 33 categories that highlight what is great about the city. Because fun comes in many colors, we've divided *The Toronto Experience* into four distinct thematic approaches to exploring Toronto, each with its own three-day itinerary to provide an unbeatable fun time.

Of course, all the information you need is at your fingertips to fashion your own perfect visit. *The Toronto Black Book* lists all the hotels, restaurants, nightlife (we include here drinking and entertainment even if it is not at night), and attractions that appear in *The Perfect Toronto* and *The Toronto Experience* chapters, with contact information and page references.

Our goal is to provide information that is easy for you to use to create an extraordinary trip. Please let us know if we have succeeded. We review and value all feedback from our readers. **Please contact us at feedback@greenlinepub.com.**

Table of Contents

INTRODUCTION 10

Greater Toronto Map 14

HIT THE GROUND RUNNING 15
City Essentials 16
Conventioneers 26
The Cheat Sheet: The Very Least You Ought to Know About Toronto 29
(Neighborhoods, Performing Arts Venues, City Parks, Streets, Retail Centers, Pro-Sport Teams, Sports Stadiums, Area Codes, Expressways, Tower)

THE PERFECT TORONTO 35
Best Always-Hot Restaurants 36
Best Asian Restaurants 37
Best Brunches 38
Best Canadian Cuisine 39
Best Celeb Sitings 40
Best Chic Museums 41
Best Cigar Lounges 42
Best Clubs for Live Music 43
Best Cool Art Spaces 44
Best Dance Clubs 45
Best Ethnic Dining 46
Best Fine Dining 47
Best Gay Bars 48
Best Gay Dance Clubs 49
Best Guided Tours 50
Best Historic Buildings 51
Best Jazz Clubs 52
Best Late-Night Eats 53
Best Late-Night Hangouts 54
Best Martinis 55
Best Meet Markets 56
Best Only-in-Toronto Attractions 57
Best Romantic Rendezvous 58

Best Scene Bars ... 59
Best Seafood Restaurants ... 60
Best Sexy Lounges ... 61
Best Spas ... 62
Best Summer Patios ... 63
Best Swanky Hotel Bars ... 64
Best Trendy Restaurants ... 65
Best Views ... 66
Best Ways to Enjoy a Sunny Day ... 67
Best Ways to Escape a Rainy Day ... 68

THE TORONTO EXPERIENCE ... 69
Hot & Cool Toronto ... 70
The Itinerary ... 71
The Hotels ... 75
The Restaurants ... 77
The Nightlife ... 86
The Attractions ... 94
Arts & Entertainment Toronto ... 98
The Itinerary ... 99
The Hotels ... 103
The Restaurants ... 105
The Nightlife ... 115
The Attractions ... 120
Hipster Toronto ... 124
The Itinerary ... 125
The Hotels ... 129
The Restaurants ... 131
The Nightlife ... 140
The Attractions ... 146
Classic Toronto ... 152
The Itinerary ... 153
The Hotels ... 157
The Restaurants ... 159
The Nightlife ... 170
The Attractions ... 175

Toronto Region Map 180

LEAVING TORONTO 181
Overnight Trips
    Cottage Country 182
    Niagara Falls 184
    Niagara-on-the-Lake 186
    Stratford 188
    Thousand Islands 190
Day Trips
    Hamilton and Burlington. 192
    Kleinburg 193
    St. Jacobs 194

THE TORONTO CALENDAR 195

THE TORONTO BLACK BOOK 203
The Toronto Black Book by Best Category 218
The Toronto Black Book by Neighborhood 220

Toronto Area Map 223

Introduction

Toronto: What It Was, What It Is

Toronto is the Huron word for "meeting place," and there's no better name for this bright modern city of 2.5 million on the shores of Lake Ontario. Recent census figures show that fully half the population of Canada's largest city was born outside the country and represents over 90 nationalities and ethnic groups who speak over 100 languages—no surprise, then, that the UNESCO named it the world's most multicultural city. In a very real sense, the world meets here.

But back up a century or two, and Toronto's roots are first with the aboriginal peoples who used the area as a place to congregate and trade with other settlements. Then came the Europeans, the first French fur traders, who came into contact with the Huron Nation from 1615 onward. Friction between the fur traders and native people led to the creation of Fort Rouillé on the present-day site of the city in 1749. Further friction between the French and the English, and then the War of 1812, delayed the area's development as a residential center until hostilities ceased in 1814. The city of Toronto (previously known as York) was incorporated soon after in 1834.

Innovations in travel, including lake steamers and the Canadian National Railroad, contributed to the city's growth throughout the 19th century. Toronto became a bustling center for commerce and manufacturing, with much of its waterfront taken up by industry and warehousing. While Victorian-era Toronto was the scene of some surprising liberalism for the period—like mixed-race marriages between proper Victorian ladies and escaped slaves—its once prevailing reputation as an uptight, prim, and Waspy town was well on the way to being established. Growth continued, with a huge spike in the Second World War era due to the city's advantageous position with respect to transportation and proximity to raw materials.

The postwar period saw an influx of some 400,000 European immigrants in its immediate aftermath, and this is when the Waspy old lady that was Toronto began to acquire her more cosmopolitan air. This period saw the beginnings of Little Italy and Greektown, sidewalk cafes and patios, and sunnier cuisine to heat up the dining scene. The city boasts the largest Italian-speaking population outside Italy, and the largest Greek ethnic neighborhood outside the Mediterranean. Since the 1970s, changes to Canada's immigration policy have brought in a steady wave of newcomers from all parts of the globe. Many of the city's most successful citizens are first-generation immigrants, and Torontonians pride themselves on the peaceful coexistence of so many different nationalities and ethnicities. In fact, ethnic is cool in this town, and you'll find some of the hippest places to eat and let down your hair in the ethnic 'hoods. That famously polite Toronto tolerance extends to its gay community, which is second in size only to San Francisco's. Pride Week and the fabulous parade that ends the celebrations have become as much a city tradition as the annual spirited Caribana Festival celebrating Caribbean heritage.

While the city's population was growing and diversifying by leaps and bounds, the economic engine that propels the nation forward was building itself into the slick modern model of efficiency it is today. Canada's financial markets are based in Toronto's Bay Street, and the Toronto Stock Exchange (TSE) is third in volume in North America after the NYSE and NASDAQ. The city's now familiar skyline of gleaming glass towers—along with the world's tallest freestanding structure, the CN Tower—began to take shape around the core of solid Victorian architecture. Renowned social historian Jane Jacobs called Toronto "the city that works," and you'll very likely agree with that characterization once you've witnessed rush hour and the transformation of the city from workday office land to evening hot spot. The people took back the waterfront from its industrial beginnings, and today it's divided between pricey condominiums and public-use spaces like the popular Harbourfront Centre for the Arts. Along the way, Toronto shed its old proper and bland image for one of cosmopolitan liberalism, combined with enough hustle to keep the financial wheels rolling.

Much of Toronto's most recent boom, begun over the last decade or so, is due to burgeoning creative industries like television and film, design and the arts. Entire neighborhoods of old warehouses and industrial buildings have been retrofitted into cool studio space. Once-rough inner-city neighborhoods, with their fair share of inner-city problems, are going condo, the yuppies moving in and bringing good restaurants and designer home-furnishing shops with them. Historic renovations of an old tavern in the city's west end, and

> **Fully half the population of Canada's largest city was born outside the country and represents over 90 nationalities and ethnic groups who speak over 100 languages—no surprise then, that it was named the world's most multicultural city.**

an old distillery complex just east of downtown, have sparked waves of urban renewal. The vision of a few impresarios decades ago has led to a thriving performing-arts scene, with international-caliber venues that have made it the third-largest center for theater in North America (after Los Angeles and New York). The future promises even bigger and better things in the Theatre District. In 2006, the Mirvish Brothers (www.mirvish.com) will host a $27 million world premiere of the musical stage version of *The Lord of the Rings* at the Princess of Wales Theatre.

Along with the business have come the beautiful people, the international glitterati who are now regular fixtures on the Toronto streetscape, either pausing for makeup during a shoot or partying down in the Entertainment District. Film and television shoots have become so commonplace all over town they're rarely greeted with anything other than passing curiosity. The Toronto Film Festival has grown into a celebration of film second only to Cannes, bringing more waves of sophisticated visitors—and the nightlife scene to cater to their tastes. Canadian actors have often complained of the lack of a "star" system in Canada, but it's the very lack of hype that proves to be so attractive to the international celeb set. For years, the Rolling Stones have begun their world tours by coming to Toronto to rehearse for a few months, drawn by the same laid-back attitude that makes the Film Festival so popular with both fans and stars.

If Toronto at heart is a Waspy old lady, she's let down her hair and gone a little wild. There are over 7,000 restaurants and eateries in the Greater Toronto Area, proving the city's insatiable appetite for variations in cuisine. The restaurant and nightclub scene in town has truly exploded over the last five to ten years and created a highly competitive market. The Entertainment District includes "Clubland," a stretch of several blocks of upscale nightclubs, restaurants, and lounges, but it's only one of many. There's hip and fashionable Little Italy, wealthy Yorkville, and cool Greektown, among others, each with its own particular style. Between indoor waterfalls, designer martinis, and great spots for pasta at 5 a.m., you'll find something for every taste—and then some.

The rest of Canada looks at Toronto with a mixture of admiration and bemusement, and a smattering of jealousy in having to live in the shadow of the behemoth. Outsiders see the downtowner habit of dressing entirely in black as a pseudo-Manhattan affectation; Canadians see it as a Toronto affectation, but one that's entirely in keeping with the city's image. Richmond Street just wouldn't be the same without a couple of reed-thin design-studio denizens, impeccably turned out in head-to-toe black and scurrying down the sidewalk for a shoot or lunch in a chic bistro. Toronto's famous for its "center of the universe" attitude—if it's not here, it's simply not worth having. Typically, however, you'll find the majority of Torontonians friendly to a fault.

Decades ago the city was known as "Toronto the Good," and while the accuracy of that moniker has faded with the onset of typical urban problems, the city's murder rate (between 60 and 65 over the last few years in a population of 2.5 million) is still well below those of comparable U.S. centers, *Places Rated Almanac* ranks it as the safest large metropolitan area in North America. The downtown area is clean and generally safe.

> **Toronto's famous for its center of the universe attitude—if it's not here, it's simply not worth having. Typically, however, you'll find the majority of Torontonians friendly to a fault.**

Though you'll find the city full of cool indoor spaces to stay, eat, and play, Torontonians love the outdoors. Just about every restaurant with the space has a patio, and you'll find hardy Torontonians flooding the patios from late May until early September at least, and ringing in the New Year outdoors at Nathan Phillips Square.

And it's a city of festivals, with something going on virtually every week during high season and even during the winter months. The locals love their city, and turn out in droves for its many festivals and events. You won't want to miss a moment of the fun, so book your ticket and join the cosmopolitan crowds who have discovered that Toronto is indeed one of the most fun cities on the planet.

Welcome to fabulous Toronto...

GREATER TORONTO

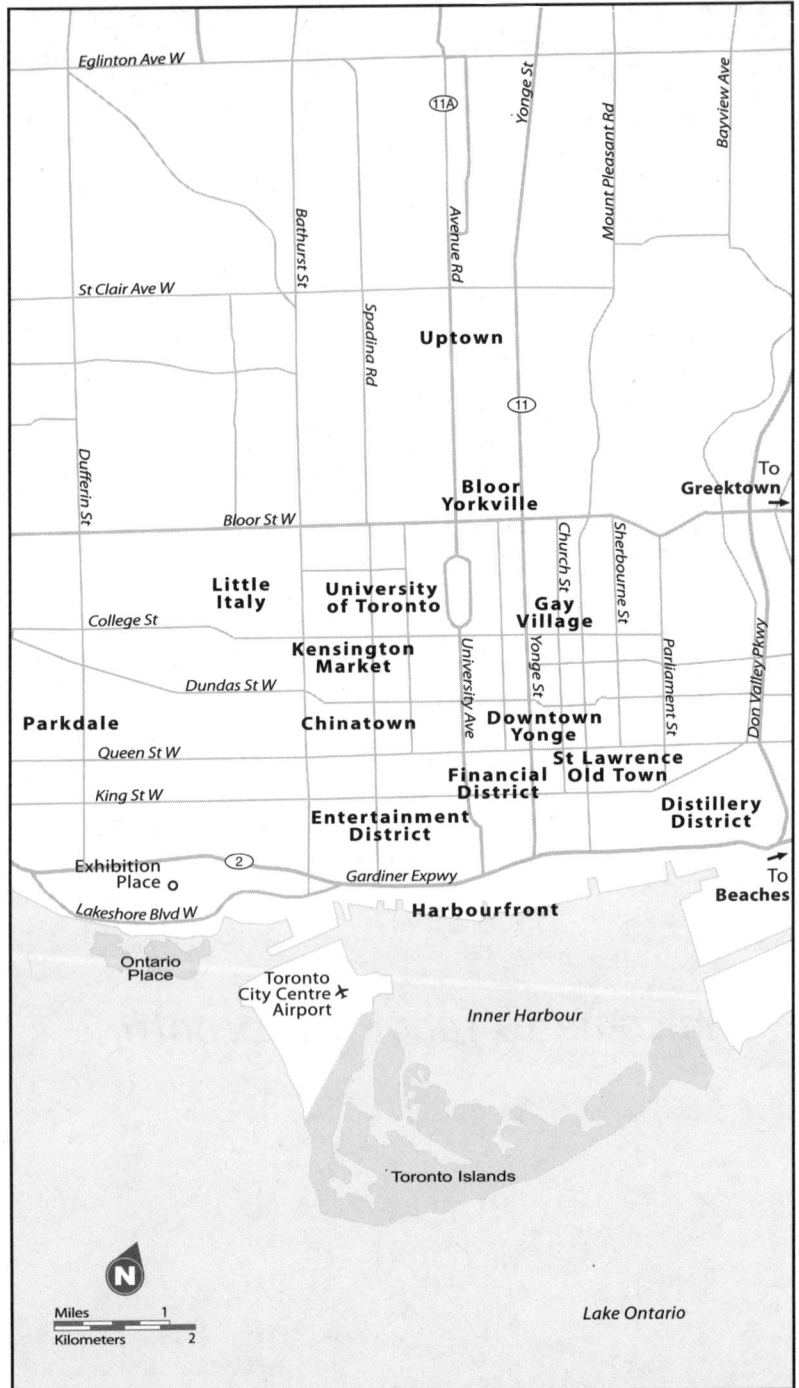

Hit the Ground Running

See and do Toronto like a native. Here's everything you'll need to know as you plan your trip—from what to wear and how to get around to when to go and what resources are available once you're there. You'll also find tips for making business trips a pleasure, and you'll impress a local with your knowledge of a few surprising facts.

City Essentials

Getting to Toronto

By Air: Lester B. Pearson International Airport—or YYZ, its call letters—is located 21 miles, or 34 kilometers, west of downtown Toronto, and is easily accessible from highways 401, 409, and 427. Named after a former prime minister and Nobel Peace Prize winner, Pearson is Canada's busiest airport, currently handling traffic of about 26 million passengers a year and projected to handle almost twice as many by 2020. YYZ is the first airport in North America to receive certification to the ISO 14001 international environmental standard, awarded by SGS International Certification Services Canada.

While Canadians love to hate the busy terminals of Pearson, the facilities, although sprawling, are organized to keep passenger traffic flowing. One very long walk leads you in a single continuous movement from aircraft through customs, then baggage claim, and the exit toward your chosen transportation downtown. But even with the crowds, it's hard to take a wrong turn. Travelers flying to the U.S. will pass through U.S. Customs directly at Pearson, so be sure to allow extra time. The airport is organized into three terminals—Terminal 3 is a few years old, and Terminal 1 was completely renovated recently, so expect decent food and tasty cocktails in the new lounges. Travel and airport information are available on the radio at 1280 AM. For further details, check the airport's website at www.gtaa.com.

From the airport: Flat-rate limo or cab fares to downtown are about C$40. Toronto Transit Commission (TTC) combined bus and subway fare is C$2.25. Pacific Western/Toronto Airport Express Bus to Union Station/Royal York Hotel and some downtown hotels (www.torontoairportexpress.com) leave every 20 to 30 minutes for the downtown hotels for C$14.95.

Flying to Toronto

From	Time (hours)
Boston	1.5
Chicago	1.5
London	7.0
Los Angeles	5.5
Miami	3.5
Montreal	1.0
New York	1.5
San Francisco	5.0
Vancouver	5.0
Washington D.C.	1.5

- Pacific Western/Toronto Airport Express, 905-564-3232 / 800-387-6787
- Aerofleet Limousine Services, 905-678-7077 / 800-268-0905

CITY ESSENTIALS

Airlines Serving Pearson International Airport

Airlines	Website	Phone Number	Terminal
Aeroflot Russia	www.aeroflot.com	416-642-1653	3
Aeromexico	www.aeromexico.com	800-237-6639	3
Air Canada	www.aircanada.ca	888-247-2262	1
(International and domestic)			
(Transborder flights to United States)			2
Air Canada Jazz	www.flyjazz.ca	800-315-1390	
(Transborder flights to United States)			2
(Domestic flights only)			1
Air France	www.airfrance.us	800-667-2747	3
Air Jamaica	www.airjamaica.com	800-523-5585	1
Alitalia	alitalia.ca	800-361-8336	1
All Nippon Airways	www.fly-ana.com	800-235-9262	1
America West Airlines	www.americawest.com	800-235-9292	3
American Airlines	www.aa.com	800-433-7300	3
Austrian Airlines	www.austrianair.com	888-817-4444	1
British Airways	www.britishairways.com	888-334-3448	3
BWIA West Indies Airways	www.bwee.com	800-538-2942	3
Cathay Pacific	www.cathaypacific.com	888-338-1668	3
Continental Airlines	www.continental.com	800-784-4444	3
		800-231-0856	
Cubana Airlines	www.cubana.cu	416-967-2822	3
Czech Airlines	canada.csa.cz/en/northamerica/us_home.htm	416-363-3174	3
Delta	www.delta.com	800-221-1212	3
EL AL	www.elal.co.il	800-361-6174	3
Finnair	www.finnair.com	800-950-5000	3
Iberia Airlines	www.iberia.com	800-772-4642	3
Japan Airlines	www.japanair.com	800-525-3663	3
KLM	www.klm.com	905-612-0556	3
Korean Air	www.koreanair.com	800-438-5000	3
LOT Polish Airlines	www.lot.com	800-668-5928	3
Lufthansa	www.lufthansa.com	800-563-5954	1
Mexicana	www.mexicana.com	905-612-8250	1
Northwest Airlines	www.nwa.com	800-441-1818	3
Olympic Airlines SA	www.olympicairlines.com	905-676-4841	3
Pakistan International	www.piac.com.pk	905-677-9479	3
Qantas	www.qantas.com	800-227-4500	3
SAS Scandinavian Airlines	www.sas.se	800-221-2350	1
Singapore Airlines	www.singaporeair.com	800-387-0038	1
Swiss Air Lines	www.swiss.com	877-359-7947	3
Thai Airways	www.thaiairways.com	800-426-5204	1
United Airlines	www.united.com	800-241-6522	2
US Airways	www.usairways.com	800-943-5436	3
Zoom Airlines	www.flyzoom.com	866-359-9666	3

HIT THE GROUND

By Car: Highways 2 and 401 and the Queen Elizabeth Way (QEW) enter Toronto from the west. The QEW connects to New York State through Niagara, and Highway 401 connects to Michigan in the west through Windsor and Sarnia, and to the east to New York State at various points. Of the three, Highway 2 is the most scenic route, running directly along the shores of Lake Ontario. Highway 401 is part of the TransCanada Highway, and runs from the Atlantic to the Pacific coasts. The QEW and Highway 403 (which connects to the QEW west of Toronto) also connect at various points with Highway 407, a toll road. The 407 runs north of Highway 401, so it's not a good way to get downtown but can be an excellent alternative for getting to the airport. Your license plate will be read electronically as you enter the toll portion of the road, and a bill will then be mailed to your registered address. As an alternative to the often congested 401 or QEW, it can't be beat, but the 407 has the dubious distinction of being the most expensive toll road in the continent. A ride from its western end to Pearson International Airport will run you about C$10.

Rental Cars

If you're picking up a car at Pearson Airport, you can do so on the first and/or the basement level of the Terminal 1 parking garage, and/or on the ground level of the parking garages in Terminal 2 and Terminal 3.

Agency	Website	800 Number
Alamo Car Rental	www.alamo.com	800-462-5266
Avis	www.avis.com	800-879-2847
Budget	www.budgettoronto.com	800-561-5212
Discount and ACE	www.discountcar.com	800-259-1638
Dollar/Thrifty Canada	www.dollar.com or www.thrifty.com	800-667-2925
Enterprise Rent-A-Car	www.enterprise.com	800-736-8222
Hertz Canada	www.hertz.com	800-263-0600
National Car Rental	www.nationalcar.com	800-227-7368

Luxury

The Car Rental Place, 3219 Dufferin St., 416-787-0209, www.carrentalplace.com
For Jaguar, Porsche, Corvette, and BMW.

GTA Exotics, 1049 The Queensway, 416-253-2180, www.gtaexotics.ca
For Porsche, Ferrari, Lamborghini, motorcycles, and more.

CITY ESSENTIALS

By Train: Toronto is served by the VIA Rail System (www.viarail.ca), with connections to the Amtrak system through Niagara Falls to New York City. Union Station is located on Front Street, between Bay and University. The station is connected to Toronto's subway line and GO Transit services.

By Water: Toronto offers docking facilities and complete services for boaters. For information on harbor facilities, call the Toronto Port Authority at 416-863-2000.

Driving to Toronto

From	Distance (miles/km)	Time (hours)
Boston	550/885	9
Chicago	540/870	8
Los Angeles	2,577/4,145	40
Miami	1,530/2,460	24
Montreal	335/540	6
New York	495/800	8
Vancouver	2,780/4,475	43
Washington D.C.	560/900	9

Additional Airports in the Toronto Area:

Toronto City Centre Airport 416-203-6942, www.torontoport.com/Airport.asp
Located on the western tip of the Toronto Islands, the island airport handles scheduled, private, and corporate flights. Major airlines include Air Ontario, Trans Capital Airlines, and Grand Aviation.

Toronto Buttonville Airport 2833 16th St., Markham, 905-477-8100, www.torontoairways.com
Buttonville Airport is used mainly for flight training, but you can also arrange spectacular aerial sightseeing tours.

Getting Around Toronto

By Car: Over a million people come into the city of Toronto each weekday to work, leaving for the suburbs by the dinner hour. You can check out the city of Toronto's traffic cams at any time at www.city.toronto.on.ca/rescu. If you're still mad enough to want to drive around the city, here's a quick lowdown. The speed limit on city streets is 50 kilometers per hour, or 30 miles per hour, unless otherwise noted. Be forewarned that many of the streets that run east-west are one way. In principle, right turns are allowed on red lights, but you'd be wise to check the signage indicating which turns are restricted. It is common for most corners to be restricted downtown. You can follow the streetcars, but be careful to observe the no-passing rule while the doors are open. A provincial law requires motorists to yield the right of way to a public transit vehicle that is changing lanes.

By Taxi: There are several cab companies that service the downtown area and well beyond. You can hail a cab from virtually any downtown street. Taxis typically congregate around the hotels, and will be lined up on Front Street in front of Union Station. Rates are metered and non-negotiable, but be sure to check out your "Passengers' Bill of Rights," which should be clearly posted. These cab companies routinely serve the downtown area:

- Beck Taxi, 416-449-6911
- Diamond Taxi, 416-366-6868

By Public Transit: The Toronto Transit Commission (TTC; www.city.toronto.on.ca/ttc) offers reliable and frequent transport around the city in three different forms—subway, bus, and streetcar. In an integrated network, one fare of C$2.50 can take you from subway to streetcar to bus and back, all the way from the lakeshore to north of Highway 401, from Etobicoke to Scarborough, with transfers beyond to suburbia. Subways run from about 6 a.m., bus and streetcar from about 5 a.m., seven days a week, with service until 1:30 a.m. six days a week and reduced services on Sundays. The Blue Night Network, marked at stops with reflective blue bands, runs all night from 1:30 a.m. until 5 a.m. A day pass is C$8, or five tokens for C$10.

By Train: The Toronto area is served by an excellent commuter train service—the GO (www.gotransit.com)—with conjoining bus service that serves areas well beyond the city limits. Lakeshore service runs from Hamilton in the west to Pickering in the east, with buses from Union Station to Newmarket and parts farther north. Most trips originate from downtown Union Station.

Other Practical Information

Emergency: Call 911 for any emergency to contact police, the fire department, paramedics, or an ambulance. The call is toll free from any pay phone. There are several hospitals in the downtown area, including the four listed below, which operate 24-hour emergency departments:

- Mount Sinai Hospital, 600 University Ave. (between College and Dundas), 416-596-4200
- St. Joseph's Health Centre, 30 The Queensway (west end of town), general information 416-530-6000; after-hours clinic 416-530-6377
- St. Michael's Hospital, 30 Bond St. (right downtown near the Eaton's Centre), 416-360-4000
- Toronto Hospital General Division, 200 Elizabeth St. (near College and University), 416-340-3111

Currency and Taxes

Canadian currency uses the dollar, but U.S. dollars are accepted at most businesses, with change typically returned in Canadian funds. You'll find currency exchange houses all over the downtown area, but you'll get the best rates at any one of Canada's five chartered banks.

Taxes are levied on goods and services at two levels of government, 8 percent at the provincial level and an additional 7 percent in a federal tax called the GST. The good news is that foreign visitors to Canada can apply for a rebate on the GST that is paid on accommodations of up to 30 nights per visit, and on goods purchased in Canada and taken out of the country within 60 days of the purchase. Be sure to keep your receipts, as you'll need to have them validated by Canada Customs at the airport or border crossing when you leave.

For more information about the visitors' tax refund and to obtain an application form, check out the website at www.cra.gc.ca/visitors or call 800-668-4748 (within Canada) or 902-432-5608 (from outside Canada).

Tax Rebate Services

These companies can facilitate the tax rebate process for a fee, so that you can arrange to receive a cash refund before you leave Canadian soil.

Forex House, 416-850-2142, www.forexhouse.ca
Global Refund, 905-791-9089, www.globalrefund.ca
Premiere Tax-Free Services (Canada), 905-270-2702, www.taxfree-services.ca

There's a 24-hour Shopper's Drugmart Pharmacy in the Lucliff Place building at 700 Bay St., 416-979-2424, which is within easy reach of all the downtown hotels.

The following numbers may also help out in an unforeseen situation:

- Assaulted Women's Helpline, 416-863-0511
- Distress Center (Toronto), 416-598-1121 / 416-486-1456
- Poison Information, 800-268-9017
- Toronto Rape Crisis Centre, 416-597-8808

The Travellers' Aid Organization, 416-366-7788, www.travellersaid.ca, can provide community and travel information, as well as offer help in emergencies. Its administration offices are located at Union Station. At Pearson, Travellers' Aid booths are located at the Arrivals level in each terminal:

- Terminal 1, 905-676-2868
- Terminal 2, 905-626-2869
- Terminal 3, 416-776-5890

These are open daily (except Christmas) 10 a.m.–10 p.m., with emergency pager service available through any booth locations and the phone numbers listed above.

Safety: Toronto is one of the safest big cities you'll ever visit, anywhere in the world, but a commonsense approach is nonetheless advisable. Use caution in the downtown area, and avoid deserted streets. With its burgeoning nightlife scene, Toronto has also seen an increase in violent incidents on the weekends, typically centered around closing time at the clubs, so take extra care when you go out for the evening.

Gay Travel: With an urban gay, lesbian, bisexual, and transgender population second only to San Francisco's, Toronto has become a favorite spot for gay travelers, and you'll find a wealth of gay-friendly nightclubs and venues well beyond the Gay Village area (centered around Church and Wellesley Streets), particularly in Little Italy. Pick up a copy of *Fab*, the city's gay lifestyle magazine, and pay a visit to the publishers—who also own Hair of the Dog Pub. Toronto's Pride Week is a huge tourist draw for both gays and straights, a veritable city institution along with Caribana and the Santa Claus Parade. Downtown crowds are very mixed, and you'll find Toronto's much-vaunted tolerance in full force—former Police Chief Julian Fantino was cover boy on *Fab* in late 2004. Check out www.gaytorontotourism.com for the inside scoop.

Weather: It's said that in Toronto, there's winter, and then there's patio season—and it's true that you'll find hardy Torontonians sitting outdoors as soon as the ice begins to melt. But to be perfectly honest, winter is cold in this Canadian city. You can expect the first snowfall in December, and January and February are typically the coldest months. Summers are hot, and the Great Lakes climate typically means high levels of humidity as well. You can count on good summer weather from the end of May until mid-September. In between the two extremes, the weather can vary widely. Early autumn is typically balmy and pleasant, but can also be rainy, and November can see both warm weeks and snowstorms. Spring is similarly unpredictable, varying between snow and suntanning weather. On the whole, unpredictability characterizes the region's weather at any time of year, and you can find warm temperatures in February or snow in April. Plan accord-

CITY ESSENTIALS

ingly and bring layers.

Torontonians love to get out no matter what the weather, and you can access most of the downtown area and Financial District through PATH, an underground network consisting of more than 27 kilometers of trails that connect major hotels, shopping centers, and office complexes. Just look for the PATH signs at street level. The white hallways are pleasantly lit—and you may even forget that you're underground. While there are many entrances, try to enter from the Royal York Hotel, surely the most posh, with a spiraling marble staircase that descends from the lobby.

Average Monthly Temperatures

Month	Fahrenheit High/Low	Celsius High/Low	Rainfall in.	Rainfall cm.
January	30/17	1/-8	2.0	5
February	30/16	1/-9	2.0	5
March	37/25	3/-4	2.4	6
April	52/36	11/2	2.5	6
May	63/45	17/7	2.6	7
June	73/55	23/13	2.7	7
July	79/61	26/16	2.7	7
August	77/59	25/15	3.2	8
September	70/52	21/11	3.0	8
October	57/41	14/5	2.4	6
November	45/32	7/0	2.8	7
December	34/22	1/-6	2.9	7

Attire: Its lakeside location means Toronto's weather is variable, so layers are advisable no matter what time of year you visit. In summer, the heat may be scorching during the day, but evenings can be cool, so always bring a sweater. In the winter, make sure you have proper footwear, including weatherproof boots, and bundle up in layers along with gloves, hat, and scarf if you plan to be outside for any length of time. Spring and fall are the most variable seasons, and it's essential that you at least have a good rain jacket and umbrella on hand.

Torontonians' dress habits depend largely on the neighborhood. Canadians in general are fairly casual in dress, and often sport jeans and T-shirts. But downtown, you'll find a distinct emphasis on fashion, whether it's in the form of conservative but classy designer suits in the Financial District or chic head-to-toe black on Richmond Street West. High-end restaurants may have a "casual" dress code, but if so, the jeans are $500 designer duds, not department-store specials. On Queen Street West, the black uniform often includes black hair dye and fingernails, and funky, artsy accessories. The Entertainment District is designer hip during the day and competitive Clubland at night, so dress to the nines in your clubby best. And definitely dress up a bit in stylish Little Italy. From the Old Town to the groovy Beaches, the city east of Yonge is more casual in tone. But uptown to the Bloor/Yorkville area, it's all about being chic and fashionable—and flaunting it.

Media: Torontonians are served by no fewer than four daily newspapers, two city and two national, all of which are published in the city. The *Toronto Star* (www.torontostar.com) is venerable and slightly left-leaning, with an emphasis on city politics and meaty culture and arts sections even during the week. The *Toronto Sun* (www.torontosun.com) is its tabloid and right-leaning counterpart, heavy on entertainment, sports, and slightly salacious features. The *Globe & Mail* (www.globeandmail.com) is a weighty national rag, considered conservative and business-oriented, with the *National Post* (www.nationalpost.com) a more recent challenger to its absolute authority in the financial pages. All four produce thick weekend editions both Saturdays and Sundays.

In addition, there are two tabloid-style weeklies that specialize in entertainment and alternative news reporting, *NOW* magazine (www.nowtoronto.com) and *eye* magazine (www.eye.net). Both contain extensive arts and entertainment listings, including current schedules for live music and nightclubs, galleries, and shows, along with restaurant reviews and city news.

Toronto Life (www.torontolife.com) is a stylish lifestyle magazine that takes a high-brow look at the city, its people, its dining and entertainment scene, and much more.

General Information for Visitors

Toronto Convention & Visitors Association / Tourism Toronto
207 Queens Quay W., 416-203-2600 / 800-499-2514,
www.tourismtoronto.com
This agency can provide information about member events, attractions, transportation services, and entertainment.
Open Mon.–Fri. 8:30 a.m.–6 p.m., Sat. 10 a.m.–4 p.m.

Toronto Board of Trade
Downtown Centre, 1 First Canadian Pl., 416-366-6811, www.bot.com
Founded in 1845, the Board of Trade is Canada's largest local chamber of commerce, serving over 10,000 members and operating the World Trade Centre Toronto.
Open Mon.–Fri. 10 a.m.–5 p.m.

CITY ESSENTIALS

Legal Drinking Age: The legal drinking age in the Province of Ontario is 19, although you'll find some clubs with a "mature clientele" policy restricting entrance to those 25 and older. Smoking by-laws currently permit smoking in a separately ventilated area, and access to those areas, whether in a restaurant or nightclub, is also restricted to those 19 and over.

Shopping Hours: Standard shopping hours are Mon.–Wed. 10 a.m.–5 p.m.; Thurs.–Fri. 10 a.m.–9 p.m.; Sat. 10 a.m.–6 p.m.; Sun. noon–5 p.m. —most retail and specialty outlets are open on Sundays.

Time Zone: Toronto falls within the Eastern Standard Time Zone (EST).

Radio Stations (a selection)

FM Stations

88.5	CKDX	Unforgettable Hits (Sinatra to Rod Stewart)
88.9	CIRV	Multicultural/Dance Mix
91.1	CJRT	Jazz
91.7	CFUK	Country
92.5	CKIS	Eclectic Hits
93.5	CFXJ	Hip-hop, R&B
94.1	CBLT	(Radio 2) Classical (Public Broadcaster)
96.3	CFMX	Classical
97.3	CJEZ	Soft Rock
98.1	CHFI	Soft Rock
99.1	CBCS	(Radio One) Public Broadcaster, Various
99.9	CKFM	Contemporary Hits
102.1	CFNY	Alternative Rock
103.5	CIDC	Rock
104.5	CHUM	Adult Contemporary
107.1	CILQ	Classic Rock

AM Stations

590	CJCL	Sports
680	CFTR	All News
740	CHWO	Nostalgia
1010	CFRB	Talk
1050	CHUM	Talk, Oldies
1280	CFYZ	Travel and Airport Information
1540	CHIN	Multinational, Multilingual

Conventioneers
Making Business a Pleasure

Even if you're in town on business, for a trade show or convention, there's no need to limit your options to generic hotels and standard business-class dining or entertaining. You'll find that dozens of night clubs and restaurants are packed within areas of a few blocks—like the Entertainment District and Yorkville, as well as the Financial District itself—and most are within walking distance of major hotels and convention facilities. As the main financial engine that drives the country, Bay Street is rich not only in high-powered CEOs but in upscale restaurants and watering holes that compete for their business.

Addresses to Know

Convention Centers

Metro Toronto Convention Centre
255 Front St. W., Toronto, ON M5V 2W6
416-585-8000 • www.mtcc.com

Toronto Congress Centre
650 Dixon Rd., Etobicoke, ON M9W 1J1
416-245-5000 • www.torontocongresscentre.com

International Centre
6900 Airport Rd., Mississauga, ON L4V 1E8
905-677-6131 • www.internationalcentre.com

City Information

City of Toronto
100 Queen St. W., Toronto, ON M5H 2N2
416-338-0338 • www.city.toronto.on.ca

Toronto Convention & Visitors Association
P.O. Box 126, 207 Queens Quay W., Toronto, ON M5J 1A7
416-203-2600 or 800-499-2514 • www.torontotourism.com

Business and Convention Hotels

These business hotels are conveniently located near the convention centers.

Airport Strip

Sheraton Gateway Hotel Toronto International Airport Terminal 3, 905-672-7000
Upscale hotel with modern décor, located in Terminal 3 of Pearson Airport. $$$$

Toronto Airport Hilton 5875 Airport Rd., Mississauga, 905-677-9900
Reliable quality with modern, comfortable, and ergonomic business furnishings. $$$

Wyndham Bristol Place 950 Dixon Rd., Etobicoke, 416-675-9444
Contemporary and comfortable, with high-end dining on site. $$$

Downtown

Cambridge Suites 15 Richmond St. E. (Yonge St.), 416-368-1990
Refined, classy business hotel in the Financial District. $$$

Marriott Bloor 90 Bloor St. E. (Park St.), 416-961-8000
Luxury hotel with all the amenities and chic uptown location near Yorkville. $$$$

CONVENTIONEERS

Renaissance Hotel at Skydome 1 Blue Jays Way (John St.), 416-341-1700
Polished hotel with some rooms that look right into the Skydome arena itself. $$$
Sheraton Centre 123 Queen St. W. (University Ave.), 416-361-1000
Large upscale hotel near City Hall and Financial District. $$$

Business Entertaining

Need to impress a client or network over drinks? These places will help seal the deal.
Bistro 990 (p. 77), 990 Bay St. (St. Joseph's Dr.), 416-921-9990
French bistro with a touch of Hollywood stardust in the Financial District. $$$$
Bistro Restaurant & Diamonds Bar, Renaissance Hotel at Skydome, 1 Blue Jays Way (John St.), 416-341-5045
Continental cuisine in a swanky hotel bar that overlooks the field at Skydome. $$$$
Bymark (p. 161), 66 Wellington St. W. (Bay St.), 416-777-1144
Elegant dining room and sexy lounge, where Bay Street comes to play. $$$$
Jump Cafe & Bar (p. 108), 1 Wellington St. W. (Yonge St.), 416-363-3400
Deceptively low-key, stylish bar and restaurant popular with movers and shakers. $$$
Oro (p. 81), 45 Elm St. (Bay St.), 416-597-0155
Superb cuisine and stunning private dining rooms for the ultimate meeting place. $$$$
Trader's Bar & Grill, Sheraton Centre, 123 Queen St. W. (University Ave.), 416-361-1000
Live feeds from the TSE and Bay Street ambience for the Financial District crowd. $$$
Zachary's, Wyndham Bristol Pl., 950 Dixon Rd. (Etobicoke), 416-675-9444
High-brow and much acclaimed continental cuisine in the airport strip. $$$$

Also see: **Best Fine Dining** (p. 47)
Best Swanky Hotel Bars (p. 64)

Ducking Out for a Half Day

All work and no play can't be good for you, so try one of these liberating pursuits.
Allan Gardens Conservatory (p. 94), 19 Horticulture Ave. (Jarvis St.), 416-392-1111
Lavish indoor gardens in manicured setting for a green escape near downtown.
Art Gallery of Ontario (p. 120), 317 Dundas St. W. (McCaul St.), 416-979-6648
Huge permanent collection, blockbuster traveling shows, and an elegant restaurant. $$
Toronto Islands (p. 179), Toronto Harbourfront, 416-392-8193
Escape the city altogether and catch a ferry to Centre Island. $$

Also see: **Best Spas** (p. 62)
Best Ways to Enjoy a Sunny Day (p. 67)

Gifts to Bring Home

Don't leave Toronto without a fabulous souvenir. Check out these places for the best of the lot.
Queen's Quay Terminal (p. 178), 207 Queen's Quay W. (Bay St.), 416-203-0510
Historic lakeside center offering art, crafts, and other Canadiana.
Textile Museum Gift Shop (p. 96), 55 Centre St. (Bay St.), 416-599-5321
Fab gift shop with artisan scarves, purses, and more.

Party Conversation: A Few Surprising Facts

• Yonge Street, the heart of Toronto's downtown, is the longest street in the world. First laid out in 1796, it now measures 1,896 km or roughly 1,178 miles.

• Considered "Hollywood North" by the film industry, Toronto ranks fourth in North American TV and film production. Among the more noteworthy films shot here were *Chicago* (in the Distillery District), *John Q*, and *Assault on Precinct 13*. *Queer as Folk* is filmed here—Fly nightclub stands in for a New York dance club.

• Toronto is the fifth-largest city in North America.

• The Toronto Blue Jays were the first Major League Baseball team to win the World Championship consecutively in 1992 and 1993.

• The Caribana parade is the biggest single-day happening and largest Caribbean festival in North America.

• One-quarter of Canada's population is located within 160 km (100 miles) of Toronto, or to look at it another way, about eight percent of Canada's population lives within the city limits, on six one-hundred-thousandths of its land.

• Toronto is located at the same latitude as Northern California.

• Some of the world's favorite comedians hail from Toronto. Mike Myers based his *Wayne's World* shtick on his teenage years in Scarborough in the city's East End. Superstar Jim Carrey hails from just west of the city limits, and legendary *Saturday Night Live* producer Lorne Michaels is a Toronto native.

• PATH, Toronto's underground network, is the world's biggest underground shopping complex.

• Michael Ondaatje (Booker Prize, 1992) taught at York University for many years, and still lives in Toronto. The late Carol Shields (Pulitzer Prize, 1995) was a long-time Torontonian, as is Timothy Findley. You might find celebrated author Margaret Atwood at Crush Wine Bar.

• Ernest Hemingway freelanced for the *Toronto Star* just after WWI, and he was on assignment for the *Star* when he returned to Europe in 1921.

The Cheat Sheet
The Very Least You Ought to Know about Toronto

It's always good to know a bit about the place you're going. Here's a countdown of the most essential facts you need to avoid looking like a tourist.

Ten Neighborhoods

The Beaches The Beaches is Toronto's laid-back antidote to the hustle and bustle of downtown and the Financial District. This neighborhood is defined by Queen Street East, a charming and quirky strip of shops and restaurants, as well as the pebbly beaches of Lake Ontario. In the summer, you'll see the locals out in force, walking dogs or congregating at streetside cafes. There are miles to explore, all the way to the park at the Scarborough Bluffs.

Bloor/Yorkville This neighborhood is centered around the intersection of Bloor and Avenue Road, though the chic designer boutiques stretch all the way east along Bloor to Yonge Street. In the 1970s, Yorkville was the epicenter of Toronto's hippie culture. It's since become the place to get designer clothing. It's where the world's celebrities stay and play when they come to Toronto, and you'll find a slew of hot clubs, restaurants, shopping opportunities, and fine hotel rooms all right here.

Chinatown and Kensington Market These two areas thrive side by side west of downtown, and both are constantly bustling with activity. Chinatown is full of Asian restaurants and stores offering a dizzying array of imported clothing and other items, along with fresh food markets streetside. Just to the north, Kensington Market has been the gateway to Toronto for immigrants for over a century, and today is a colorful neighborhood of markets, bakeries, and eclectic shops.

Downtown The heart of Toronto is centered along Yonge Street. In the 1970s, it had degenerated into a sleazy run of strip bars, peep shows, and a few hardy retailers. But the sleaze was cleaned out and the big-name retailers moved in, anchored by the huge Eaton's Centre. Others followed, including the flagship Hudson's Bay department store and the HMV music store. Today it is a thriving area of stores, restaurants, offices, and the glittering glass towers of the Financial District centered along Bay Street. Yonge-Dundas Square is now an outdoor multimedia concert and event venue.

Entertainment District/Clubland/Theatre District Back in the 1980s, a few impresarios saw the potential for live theater in the city. In 1993, the Mirvish empire constructed the Princess of Wales Theatre to show what seemed like an endless run of *Phantom of the Opera*. It began the transformation of the area west of Yonge Street into the entertainment hub it is today. The performing arts thrive at the Royal Alexandra and Roy Thompson Hall, and the nightclub scene has blossomed to accommodate Torontonians' insatiable thirst for a good time. Richmond Street West, now known as "Clubland," is a strip where you can club-hop from one joint to the next.

Greektown Centered along Danforth Avenue between Chester and Jones Avenues, Greektown is the largest Greek ethnic neighborhood in North America. Like the West End's Little Italy, Greektown has evolved over the years from ethnic 'hood to night clubbers' haven, featuring a strip of clubs and restaurants with Mediterranean warmth and flair. While the clubs are busy year-round, the neighborhood really comes alive in the summer, when the proliferation of sidewalk patios will have you wondering which continent you've stumbled onto. The Taste of the Danforth, a long weekend that celebrates Greek culture and food, is a hugely popular city event.

Harbourfront Toronto's waterfront was at one time home to industrial and utilitarian uses, and the people's reclamation of the city's beautiful natural setting on Lake Ontario is still a work in progress. Theme park Ontario Place really established the Harbourfront as a people-friendly place. You can catch a ferry to the Toronto Islands or hop on a tour boat. There's always something going on at the Harbourfront Centre for the Arts. The area is also home to mega-entertainment complexes the Guvernment and the Docks.

Little Italy This area became a distinct part of the city in the early 1950s, when waves of European immigrants arrived after World War II. With them came a little warmth to Toronto's cool Wasp culture—and the city's first sidewalk cafes. For many years, however, College Street was primarily a nondescript area of ethnic retail shops. In the late 1980s, prescient restauranteurs and club owners invested in venues that dazzle the eyes and created menus that charm the senses. The result today is a neighborhood of hip clubs and restaurants where the beautiful people come to play.

St. Lawrence/Old Town/Cabbagetown East of downtown, the venerable St. Lawrence Market has been feeding hungry Torontonians for two centuries. The city grew up around this landmark, and you'll find traces of Victorian and even pre-Victorian architecture, as well as some of the city's best restaurants and clubs. This once-neglected area has seen a transformation into the yuppie haven that it is today. The Distillery District, a restored historic area east of Parliament, has sparked the renaissance. In addition to upscale condos, you'll find designer furniture showrooms and casting and production facilities that have sprung up to accommodate the area's busy filming schedule.

West Queen West Queen Street West has its own funky appeal starting at the first blocks west of Yonge Street, but it's the area west of Bathurst, dubbed West Queen West, that's really hip. Anchored by the fabulous renovation of the Drake Hotel and the Gladstone, Queen West is home to art galleries and artists' studios, eclectic vintage and designer clothing stores, and clubs and bohemian restaurants. Hobnob with the artsy set, who love this street and come out in droves to create a hopping nightlife scene. Wear head-to-toe black and you'll never be out of place here.

Nine Performing Arts Venues

Buddies in Bad Times Theatre A historic building that has undergone a funky renovation, Buddies in Bad Times is home to one of the world's biggest and most respected gay and lesbian theater companies, offering two stages of innovative and often challenging theater.
12 Alexander St., Gay Village, 416-975-8555,
www.buddiesinbadtimestheatre.com

Canon Theatre A plush historic 2,200-seat venue for theater and the performing arts.
244 Victoria St., Downtown, 416-364-4100, www.mirvish.com

Elgin/Winter Garden Theatre A gorgeous and historic double-decker theater that's been packing in the audiences since the days of vaudeville.
189 Yonge St., Downtown, 416-597-0965, www.heritagefdn.on.ca

Hummingbird Centre An elegant 3,100-seat multipurpose venue that hosts performances from ballet to opera to jazz.
1 Front St. E., Downtown, 416-393-7469, www.hummingbirdcentre.com

Massey Hall The grand old lady of Toronto concert halls, still used today as a venue mainly for musical performances and a favorite of the artists for its intimate atmosphere.
178 Victoria St., Downtown, 416-872-4255, www.masseyhall.com

Molson Amphitheatre A huge outdoor concert venue that's part of the lakeside festivities at Ontario Place.
909 Lakeshore Blvd. W., Harbourfront, 416-260-5600,
www.ontarioplace.com/en/amphitheatre/amphitheatre.html

Princess of Wales Theatre A striking modern venue for theatrical performances, decorated in murals by noted contemporary artist Frank Stella.
300 King St. W., Entertainment District, 416-872-1212, www.mirvish.com

Royal Alexandra Built in 1907 and saved from the wrecking ball by Toronto legend Ed Mirvish, the Royal Alex is now home to popular theatrical performances like *Mamma Mia*.
260 King St. W., Entertainment District, 416-872-1212, www.mirvish.com

Roy Thompson Hall A glittery and impressive concert and performance hall, featuring Canada's Walk of Fame on the sidewalk, including impressions from celebrity greats like Jim Carrey and Shania Twain.
60 Simcoe St., Entertainment District, 416-872-4255, www.roythompson.com

Eight City Parks

Ashbridge's Bay Consisting of 300 acres of waterfront, Ashbridge's Bay is located on Lakeshore Boulevard east of Coxwell Avenue, and includes a mile or so of hiking trails, beaches, fishing, and the Boardwalk Bistro.

Cloud Forest Conservatory Located on Richmond Street at Temperance (just west of Yonge), this large indoor garden conservatory is open year-round Mon.–Fri. 10 a.m.–3 p.m.

High Park Consisting of 400 acres of tree-filled parkland at Bloor Street West and Parkside Drive in the West End, this park is home to the historic Colborne Lodge and hosts Shakespeare in the Park and the Scream Literary Festival in the summer.

Kew Gardens Located right in the heart of the Beaches neighborhood at 2075 Queen Street East, this lovely park hosts the lively Beaches Jazz Festival during the summer months.

Marilyn Bell Park This park follows the shoreline of Lake Ontario in the city's West End and was named after the first person to swim the lake from New York State to Toronto in 1954. You can enter by vehicle or public transit only from Lakeshore Boulevard, then park and stroll the shoreline for about half a mile.

Roundhouse Park A historic patch of green on Bremner Blvd., in the shadow of the CN Tower and home to the Steamwhistle Brewing Company.

Toronto Island Park There are 569 acres of beaches and green parklands on the Toronto Islands, with bicycle and boat rentals available.

Trinity Square West of the Eaton's Centre on Yonge Street and south of Dundas, this urban park contains Toronto's only labyrinth, 77 feet in diameter and created as a millennium project.

CHEAT SHEET

Seven Streets

Bathurst Street The official dividing line to the city's West End, Bathurst is home to Toronto's Jewish community, particularly in the area from St. Clair Avenue north all the way beyond the city limits to Thornhill and Vaughan.

Bay Street This is the heart of the city's bustling Financial District, replete with glass towers and a scene of upscale restaurants for the CEO set.

Bloor Street The chic dividing line between downtown and uptown, home to designer boutiques and fab Yorkville.

Danforth Avenue Known to locals as simply "the Danforth," it's the home of Greektown and a legendary restaurant and nightclub scene.

Queen Street The coolest street in Toronto, from its laid-back beginnings east at the Beaches, to its west end of art galleries and nighttime hot spots.

Richmond Street By day, Richmond is the busy center for fashion and design businesses, and by night it becomes the center of Clubland.

Yonge Street The world's longest street and the heart of downtown.

Six Retail Centers

Atrium on Bay The atrium draws natural light from the height of this skyscraper to the galleria of 50 shops, services, and restaurants.
20 Dundas W., Financial District, 416-595-1957, www.atriumonbay.com

BCE Place Includes the airy Allen Lambert Galleria and a second floor devoted to dining establishments and more than 30 shops and services.
161–181 Bay St., Financial District, 416-777-6480, www.bceplace.com

Chinatown Centre A shopping mall with an Asian flavor, where you can buy all manner of imported Chinese goods.
222 Spadina Ave., Chinatown, 416-599-8877

Eaton's Centre A huge landmark shopping center, featuring the famous sculptures of Canada geese, along with more than 285 shops and services.
220 Yonge St., Downtown, 416-598-8700, www.torontoeatoncentre.com

Hazelton Lanes Canada's most expensive mall, rife with designer boutiques and high-end goodies, where you may bump into Hollywood royalty.
55 Avenue Rd., Bloor/Yorkville, 416-968-8680, www.hazeltonlanes.com

Vaughan Mills Mall Canada's largest outlet mall, located north of the city in Vaughan, with an entertainment complex offering movie theaters.
1 Bass Pro Mills Dr., Vaughan, 905-879-2110, www.vaughanmills.com

Five Pro-Sport Teams

Argonauts Canadian Football League, 416-341-2700, www.argonauts.ca

Blue Jays Major League Baseball, 416-341-1000, www.bluejays.ca

Maple Leafs National Hockey League, 416-872-5000, www.torontomapleleafs.com

Raptors National Basketball Association, 416-366-3865, www.nba.com/raptors

The Rock National Lacrosse League, 416-596-3075, www.torontorock.com

Four Sports Stadiums

Air Canada Centre 40 Bay St., Entertainment District, 416-815-5500, www.theaircanadacentre.com

Ricoh Coliseum 100 Princes Blvd., Exhibition Place, Harbourfront, 416-263-3001, www.ricohcoliseum.com

SkyDome/Rogers Centre 1 Blue Jays Way, Entertainment District, 416-341-3034, www.rogerscentre.com

Varsity Stadium 275 Bloor St. W., University of Toronto, 416-946-5125

Three Area Codes

The Toronto area has three area codes. Once, all of Southern Ontario used **416**. When the proliferation of phone numbers necessitated a split, Toronto retained 416, while **905** was given to the outlying areas. To this day, to call someone a "905-er" is to relegate him or her to the uncool world beyond city limits. Now, even 416 isn't big enough, resulting in the creation of **647**.

Two Expressways

The Gardiner Expressway enters the city from the west roughly along the lakeshore, connecting to the QEW (Queen Elizabeth Way) from the west.

The Don Valley Expressway connects to the Gardiner's east end, continuing north to Highway 401 and eventually turning into Highway 404.

One Tower

The CN Tower, the structure that defines Toronto's skyline, is the world's tallest freestanding structure.

The Perfect Toronto

When you're on a trip, you don't want a city with all its flaws and inconsistencies. You want the perfect city. With 33 categories that represent all of Toronto's most outstanding features, *The Perfect Toronto* puts all the hottest, hippest places right at your fingertips. Here are the very best places to eat, drink, dance, lounge, shop, see and be seen, catch sightings of the stars, and make the most of a city that's all about cosmopolitan fun. Listings that also appear in *The Toronto Experience* chapter are noted so that you can easily combine your choices with other activities.

 # Always-Hot Restaurants

Toronto's restaurant scene just gets more enticing by the minute, populated by star chefs like Susur Lee who've received accolades by the bucketful from all over the world. The result is a dining scene where you can expect the food, presentation, and décor to be second to none—and to find yourself among an attractive crowd of trend-setters vying for the best table.

Coco Lezzone Grill and Porto Bar
602 College St. W., Little Italy, 416-535-1489 • Hot & Cool

The Draw: Creative Mediterranean cuisine served in a grand dining room with Little Italy cool and Hollywood cred.

The Scene: Dark wood fixtures, crystal-dripping chandeliers, dark red drapes, tall doorways, and baroque moldings serve as an elegant backdrop to the fashionable crowd. The menu is Mediterranean, with beef carpaccio, grilled octopus, and loads of seafood, and the crowd buzzing. If you're looking to see and be seen and to dine sublimely, this is the place for you. *Open daily for dinner 4 p.m.–2 a.m.* $$$

Hot Tip: This is a stylish place, so dress the part to fit in with the well-dressed locals and chic celebs.

Susur
601 King St. W., Entertainment District, 416-603-2205 • Hot & Cool

The Draw: Polished elegance and food artistry from one of the world's top chefs.

The Scene: The trendy and cosmopolitan diners of Toronto can't get enough of their hometown star chef and flock here for masterpieces of Pan-Asian fusion in streamlined and modern surroundings. Known for expert service and over-the-top plating served at a leisurely pace to an elegant crowd, Susur promises to deliver a magical evening. Reserve far in advance. *Open for dinner Mon.–Sat. 6–10 p.m.* $$$$

Hot Tip: Put yourself in the hands of a master and order the highly recommended seven-course tasting menu.

Xacutti
503 College St. W., Little Italy, 416-323-3957 • Hot & Cool

The Draw: Modern elegance in chocolate tones highlights the trendy and beautiful people who flock here in droves for the Indian-fusion cuisine.

The Scene: High style meets high-concept cuisine at this sexy establishment, where servers record your choice on a device that's read automatically as they enter the kitchen. The menu is Indian fusion by Toronto chef Brad Moore, made with local and seasonal ingredients and enhanced with flavors of the South Pacific. The results are nothing short of fabulous—as are the attractive guests who come to sample the innovation and bask in the stylish ambience. *Open for dinner Mon.–Fri. 6:30 p.m.–1 a.m.; for lunch and dinner Sat. 10:30 a.m.–2 a.m.; Sun. brunch 10:30 a.m.–3 p.m.* $$$$

Hot Tip: Pronounce it "sha-KOO-tee," and you'll be considered someone in the know.

THE PERFECT TORONTO

Best — Asian Restaurants

The Asian population of Toronto has been growing by leaps and bounds for decades. When it comes to dining, it means you'll find great Asian cuisine in virtually every neighborhood in town. These places not only serve up fine cuisine, but an appealing ambience and stylish scene as well.

Banzai Sushi
134 Peter St., Entertainment District, 416-341-0404 • Hot & Cool

The Draw: Super-slick space-age style meets gourmet Japanese cuisine in the heart of the Entertainment District.

The Scene: Stylish clubbers who've come for dinner before the night's dancing mix with an upscale crowd up front at the gleaming sushi bar. Banzai offers a fusion of Japanese dining, music, and art—all in a happening locale. The Japanese menu is characterized by clean flavors and artful plating, and has high-tech touches like touch-screen menus that dispense advice on wine pairings. In-house art is supplied by graffiti artist Duro the Third in the form of a 100-foot wall mural, inspired by traditional Japanese tattoo art and graffiti. *Open daily for dinner 5 p.m.–2 a.m.* $$$

Hot Tip: Try the techie toys that allow you to chat with other diners.

Bright Pearl Seafood
346–348 Spadina Ave., Chinatown, 416-979-3988 • Classic

The Draw: Authentic Chinese right where Kensington Market melts into Chinatown.

The Scene: A bright yellow and green building with red lettering announces the Bright Pearl, a perennial local and media favorite with a delectable all-day dim sum menu that keeps aficionados coming in droves. There's a bustling Chinatown ambience and a mixed crowd of hipsters, foodies, and tourists. Your choices are prepared Cantonese style, with its characteristically simple, fresh flavors. *Open daily for breakfast, lunch, and dinner 9 a.m.–11 p.m.* $$

Hot Tip: Although Bright Pearl is best known for seafood, the Peking duck is superb.

Lai Wah Heen
Metropolitan Hotel, 108 Chestnut St., 2nd Fl., Chinatown, 416-977-9899
• Arts & Entertainment

The Draw: Cantonese in an elegant dining room served with continental flair.

The Scene: In a dramatic contrast to Lai's location on the edge of colorful Chinatown, the décor features pale neutrals accented by sleek black-lacquer chairs. Savvy foodies join the droves of Financial District types here for gourmet Cantonese fare served with artistic flair. The menu includes delicacies like shark fin and abalone. *Open for lunch daily 11:30 a.m.–2:30 p.m.; dinner from 5 p.m.* $$$$

Hot Tip: According to tradition, Lai's delectable dim sum is served only at lunch.

Best Brunches

After a late night out on the town, Torontonians love to come out to refuel on Sundays. With so many restaurants offering a decadent brunch, it can be hard to choose. Here's a look at the places that offer a lively scene and beautiful setting in addition to delicious cuisine.

Cafe Victoria
Le Meridien King Edward Hotel, 37 King St. E., St. Lawrence, 416-863-4125 • Arts & Entertainment

The Draw: A perennially popular brunch in an elegant historic dining room.

The Scene: The Cafe Victoria has an opulent air that's made it a favorite with both locals and visiting dignitaries. Floor-to-ceiling windows and ornate plasterwork create the perfect setting for power breakfast and lunch meetings among the movers and shakers. Brunch has been voted the city's favorite many times. *Open for breakfast, lunch, and dinner Mon.–Thurs. 6:30 a.m.–11 p.m.; Fri.–Sat. 11 a.m.–1 a.m.; Sun. 9:30 a.m.–11 p.m.; Sun. Brunch 10 a.m.–3 p.m.* $$$$

Hot Tip: Check out the other tables carefully—this hotel and swank cafe have played host to the world's royalty as well as international celebrities.

Mildred Pierce
99 Sudbury St., Parkdale, 416-588-5695 • Hipster

The Draw: A grand dining room and the superb offerings of a star chef.

The Scene: In a nondescript location, Food Network chef Donna Dooher has created a bright oasis of good taste. Glassware sparkles against white linens, highlighting the real stars, dishes that change seasonally. Brunch is a Toronto tradition here and draws people from all over town. The crowd includes a good quotient of foodies, along with hip urbanites sipping Bloody Marys and waiting for one of the highly coveted tables. *Open for lunch Mon.–Fri. noon–2 p.m.; Sat. 11 a.m.–3 p.m.; dinner Sun.–Thurs. 5:30 p.m.–10 p.m.; Fri.–Sat. 5:30 p.m.–11 p.m.; Sun. brunch 10 a.m.–3 p.m.* $$$$

Hot Tip: Sunday brunch is the only time Mildred doesn't take reservations, so take a tip from the locals and bring reading material for your wait in line.

Sassafraz Cafe
100 Cumberland St., Bloor/Yorkville, 416-964-2222 • Hot & Cool

The Draw: Jazz and celebrity-rich crowds in a bright airy setting with a trendy address.

The Scene: Both the garden, with its glass ceilings and fountain, and the sun-kissed interior deliver Cali-flavored ambience that's echoed in the Cali-French fusion cuisine rich with the tastes of saffron and tangerine. On Sundays, stylish Yorkville types come in droves for gourmet classics enjoyed to live jazz. *Open daily 11:30 a.m.–2 a.m.* $$$$

Hot Tip: Reservations are an absolute must, especially when tourists are in town for the Toronto Film Festival and celeb-seeking crowds fill the neighborhood.

Best — Canadian Cuisine

What is Canadian cuisine? It relies on local, seasonal, and regional ingredients, and prepares them in classic continental style, with results that are both inventive and delicious. Toronto's hottest chefs were among the first to develop and celebrate this unique variation on classic cuisine, with outstanding results.

Canoe Restaurant & Bar
66 Wellington St. W., 54th Fl., Financial District, 416-364-0054 • Classic

The Draw: A stunning view of the Toronto Islands from atop a Financial District tower, along with cuisine that is sure to impress.

The Scene: The view from the 54th floor of the Toronto-Dominion Tower, along with the elegant décor, will seduce you even before the menu arrives to win you over completely. Some of the finest examples of inventive Canadian cuisine emerge from this kitchen. The crowd is upscale, with a solid expense-account component. This is the place for that impressive business lunch or dinner, or for a drink in high style. *Open daily for lunch 11:30 a.m.–2:30 p.m.; for dinner from 5 p.m.* $$$$

Hot Tip: Reservations are always recommended, especially on weekends when the main dining room is often booked for private functions.

Drake Dining Room and Raw Bar
1150 Queen St. W., Parkdale, 416-531-5042 / 866-372-5386 • Hipster

The Draw: Whiz kid of the Toronto restaurant scene, exec chef David Chrystian fashions imaginative creations in hip surroundings.

The Scene: The crowd is as fashionable as the décor, which includes a gleaming raw bar and plush dining room. Artists and actors, film and television professionals, savvy local politicians and designers lounge on the green cushions waiting for Chrystian's fiendishly unique creations as house plays from the lounge. The hepcat ambience proves that "Canadian" can be the coolest ethnicity of all. *Open daily for breakfast, lunch, and dinner 6 a.m.–11 p.m.; Sun. brunch 10:30 a.m.–2:30 p.m.* $$$$

Hot Tip: Dinner can be your ticket to get ahead of the line for après-dinner drinks in the ever-popular lounge.

Splendido
88 Harbord St., University of Toronto, 416-929-7788 • Classic

The Draw: Consistently high marks for inventive cuisine for a discerning crowd.

The Scene: The mood here is one of quiet elegance—this is a special-occasion restaurant, where diners are well dressed and distinctly upscale. The internationally recognized cuisine evolves constantly with the flavors of each season, and friendly service enhances the entire experience. *Open for dinner Tues.–Sun. 5–11 p.m.* $$$$

Hot Tip: Every month, the chef and sommelier team up to put together a multicourse menu paired with wine choices to please any oenophile.

Best Celeb Sightings

With so many productions filming on Toronto's streets and a steady stream of international sports teams and touring shows hitting town, celebrity sightings have themselves become a favorite sport of locals. But the world of Hollywood and world-class celebrities is fairly small, and the word about where to go in Toronto gets around quickly—here's where you'll have a good chance of catching up with them.

Hemingway's
142 Cumberland St., Bloor/Yorkville, 416-968-2828 • Classic

The Draw: Fun-loving ambience in chic Yorkville that's a hit with locals and visiting celebs alike.

The Scene: Toronto's only heated year-round rooftop patio boasts a fine view of Yorkville's main drag, and an indoor bar and summertime streetside patio that have been perennial favorites since Hemingway's opening. The casual menu features typical bar items, but the crowds come for the friendly party ambience—crowds that can include Hollywood royalty and pro-sports figures. This is a casual, perfectly located pub where the A-listers come to let down their hair. *Open daily 11 a.m.–2 a.m.* $$

Hot Tip: If you need to catch that one game while you're on vacation, this is the place to see it in style.

This Is London
364 Richmond St. W., Entertainment District, 416-351-1100 (entrance off Peter Street) • Hipster

The Draw: Elite Brit-pop cool bar for wealthy over-thirty club kids.

The Scene: This exclusive theme bar boasts stylists in the ladies' room and authentic British-music memorabilia. Room 364, the celebrity-rich VIP area, takes posh partying to its highest level. The large main floor is all dancing go-go boots and minis, the second floor overlooks the gyrating action below, and includes plenty of cozy nooks where you can retire for more intimate conversation. The third floor houses the extravagant ladies' room and spa. *Open Sat. 10 p.m.–3 a.m.* $$

Hot Tip: Calling ahead to get on the guest list is a must if you want to be sure of getting in; ask how to get in ultra-exclusive Room 364.

Trattoria Giancarlo
41 Clinton St., Little Italy, 416-533-9619 • Arts & Entertainment

The Draw: Traditional Italian cuisine in a chic neighborhood.

The Scene: One of the pioneers that transformed Little Italy from ethnic neighborhood to one of Toronto's premier hot spots, Giancarlo remains to this day a place to see and be seen. Sophia Loren loved it, and her three-hour lunch there is still talked about. Watch the mother-and-son chef team prepare your meal in an open kitchen as you enjoy the European ambience. *Open for dinner Tues.–Sun. 6–10 p.m.* $$$

Hot Tip: The streetside summer patio is just the spot for premium people-watching.

THE PERFECT TORONTO

Best — Chic Museums

"Museum" isn't a word that typically conjures up notions of fashion or design. But here in Toronto, you'll find gems that take a look at the unusual in ways that will surprise, excite, and maybe even educate you.

Bata Shoe Museum
327 Bloor St. W., Bloor/Yorkville, 416-979-7799 • Hot & Cool

The Draw: A glittery and fascinating collection of shoes through the ages.

The Scene: The building itself is a work of art, designed on five levels to resemble a shoebox. Some exhibits look at the strictly decorative aspects of shoes, while others put them in historical and social context. Intriguing facts—and numerous celebrity shoes—abound. *Open Tues.–Wed. 10 a.m.–5 p.m.; Thurs. 10 a.m.–8 p.m.; Fri.–Sat. 10 a.m.–5 p.m.; Sun. noon–5 p.m.* $

Hot Tip: Check the website (www.batashoemuseum.ca) for special events, especially Thursday evenings for live music, demonstrations, and more.

Design Exchange
234 Bay St., Financial District, 416-363-6121 • Hipster

The Draw: A museum and exhibition space devoted to the principles of design.

The Scene: The Design Exchange aims to elevate the importance of design in contemporary life. To that end, the Exchange offers educational programs in addition to a variety of theme-based exhibits, such as plastic (materials) or home appliances (functional design). The main exhibition hall is 3,500 square feet and features changing shows, while the Chalmers Design Centre operates in collaboration with other organizations to showcase the work of graduating design classes, competition winners, and the latest innovations. *Open Tues.–Fri. 10 a.m.–6 p.m.; Sat.–Sun. noon–5 p.m.* $

Hot Tip: Be sure not to miss the retro-fun mid–twentieth century furnishings and appliances in the permanent collection.

Gardiner Museum of Ceramic Art
111 Queen's Park, University of Toronto, 416-586-8080
• Arts & Entertainment

The Draw: The world's only museum devoted entirely to ceramic art, where the motto is "Clay comes to life in fire."

The Scene: The museum's permanent collection features 2,700 pieces from Europe, Asia, and the Americas. Major exhibits look at ceramic traditions in both a historic and contemporary context, and have included traveling shows of masters like Picasso. An education program offers classes, and the shop has been a favorite of Torontonians since its opening in 1984. *Open Sat.–Thurs. 10 a.m.–6 p.m.; Fri. 10 a.m.–9 p.m.* $$

Hot Tip: The Gardiner's permanent home is under renovation until the summer of 2005—check the website (www.gardinermuseum.on.ca) or call to confirm exhibit times and locations.

Best | # Cigar Lounges

Trendy Torontonians love a good cigar lounge. Here's where to go for that fine cigar and a nicely aged after-dinner drink to finish off a great meal.

Club 22
Windsor Arms Hotel, 18 St. Thomas St., Bloor/Yorkville, 416-971-9666 • Hot & Cool

The Draw: A posh lounge with a fashionable crowd.

The Scene: White leather stools at the bar highlight the beautiful people, complete with celebrity quotient. From a sleek, sexy lounge where the DJs and live music play, enter a separately ventilated and opulent wood-paneled cigar lounge. Private humidors are available here. Potted greenery and a lengthy list of cognacs, ports, and Scotches complete the old boys' club effect. *Open as club-lounge Wed.–Sat. 5 p.m.–2 a.m.* $$

Hot Tip: There's live music in the lounge, featuring piano from 5 p.m., then other musical entertainment from 9:30 p.m. on—if you go on Fridays you'll catch the after-work rush and miss Saturday's cover charge.

The Easy
225 Richmond St. W., Entertainment District, 416-979-3005 • Classic

The Draw: Live jazz lounge with walk-in humidors.

The Scene: Downstairs at the Easy, the piano plays jazz and the pool tables beckon, as do the inviting white leather couches. Walk-in humidors are available in a privately ventilated cigar-smoking area. The mood is refined, the crowd designer-clad, and the tasting menu sumptuous. And upstairs, the Fifth offers one of Toronto's finest dining experiences. It's the perfect night out—fine dining, cigars and drinks, and a sensual evening of music—all at one address. *Cigar lounge open Thurs. 8–10 p.m.; Fri. & Sat. 9 p.m.–2 a.m.; dining room open daily 6 p.m.–2 a.m.* $$

Hot Tip: On Thursdays, the lounge comes with a complimentary buffet of cocktail hors d'oeuvres. Dinner reservations are a must any day of the week.

2 Cats Cocktail Lounge
569 King St. W., Entertainment District, 416-204-6261 • Hot & Cool

The Draw: A swank Manhattan-style setting where the martinis are tops.

The Scene: Enter the quiet lounge area, where the music plays softly and banquettes are lined with beautiful people. Make your way to the well-stocked bar at the back, which converges with the DJ booth, where the beats are louder and the décor darker and more sultry. The separately ventilated area for sampling fine cigars has comfortable seating for the trendy crowds who come to enjoy a cigar in style. *Open Tues.–Fri. 5 p.m.–2 a.m.; Sat. 8 p.m.–2 a.m.* $$

Hot Tip: This has become a favorite spot to congregate for after-midnight cocktails.

Best

Clubs for Live Music

Long before the advent of Clubland, Toronto was known for its live music scene, boasting plenty of clubs where international luminaries played. If it's live music you're after, these clubs will deliver the goods—great music and a crowd that loves to party.

Healey's
178 Bathurst St., Entertainment District, 416-703-5882 • Classic

The Draw: Blind blues-guitar legend opens bar dedicated to delivering that live rock 'n' roll experience.

The Scene: The décor is classic rock cave, complete with funky, if murky, lighting; distressed walls; and minimalist, utilitarian furnishings—but it's the music that matters here, and what better foil for the best of live blues and rock from a hometown legend. Expect a downtown crowd of music lovers and plenty of music-industry professionals. *Doors generally open at 8 p.m.; jazz Sat. 4–7 p.m.* $$$

Hot Tip: Jeff himself takes to the stage Thursday nights for his special brand of blues, and on Saturdays plays with his own Jazz Kings in a free matinee.

Mod Club Theatre
722 College St. W., Little Italy, 416-588-4663 • Hipster

The Draw: Owned by former glam-rocker Mark Holmes, this club is where the hottest new bands and DJs perform.

The Scene: A full-service entertainment complex and bar, including a state-of-the-art sound and light system, a full wall-size screen for video and film screenings, and enough cred and cool to bring the hipsters out in droves. The "Mod Club" movement began as a series of parties with Brit-pop overtones hosted at other city clubs, before it found this home on College. *Open daily 9 p.m.–3 a.m.* $$

Hot Tip: Saturday nights you'll find most of the crowd dressed up in Brit-pop cool of go-go boots and minis and long fake eyelashes, so come prepared.

Phoenix Concert Theatre
410 Sherbourne St., St. Lawrence, 416-323-1251 • Hipster

The Draw: A legend in the Toronto entertainment scene, the Phoenix delivers 18,000 square feet of funky and original spaces devoted to music and much more.

The Scene: The Stones and Metallica have played on the main stage here, where the main floor features a 50-foot marble bar and a huge dance floor outfitted with the latest in sound and light. Le Loft overlooks the scene below with its own bar. The Parlour has pool tables to test your mettle. Look for fashion shows, arts events, and more, along with live concerts and the hottest DJs in town. *Opening hours change depending on who's playing. Check the website for current listings.* $$$

Hot Tip: There's sure to be a hot crowd Saturday nights, when famed alternative-rock radio station 102.1 FM broadcasts live on air.

Best: Cool Art Spaces

Toronto is Canada's epicenter for the fine arts, with a loyal local following for galleries and shows. Many of the city's arts institutions are undergoing, or have recently undergone major renovations and additions to make them even more inviting.

Art Gallery of Ontario
317 Dundas St. W., Chinatown, 416-979-6648 • Arts & Entertainment

The Draw: One of North America's premier art museums, with a vast in-house collection and the clout to pull in international blockbuster shows.

The Scene: The tenth-largest art museum in North America, the AGO houses a permanent collection of over 36,000 works representing 1,000 years of European, Canadian, and Inuit art. Shows often feature luminaries of the Canadian and international art scene. It's the hub of the fine arts in Toronto and intersects with the international arts scene. *Open Tues. 11 a.m.–6 p.m.; Wed. 11 a.m.–8:30 p.m.; Thurs. & Fri. 11 a.m.–6 p.m.; Sat. & Sun. 10 a.m.–5:30 p.m.* $$

Hot Tip: The AGO is currently undergoing a renovation designed by famed architect Frank Gehry, so watch for developments. Work began in spring 2005, with projected completion in spring 2008. In the meantime, it's open for business as usual.

401 Richmond
401 Richmond St. W., Entertainment District, 416-595-5900 • Hipster

The Draw: Old industrial building gets makeover as hip center for art galleries, studios, and arts organizations.

The Scene: The building itself is a rabbit warren of hallways and doors, but pick up a guide and you'll do just fine finding 401's many tenants. They include Gallery 44, devoted to contemporary photography; the collective YYZ Artists' Outlet Studio, the Dub Poets' Collective; film festival offices; among others. Add a hip cafe, and the atmosphere is all about cutting-edge creativity. *Hours vary according to tenants, and special events occur in evenings, but galleries are typically open Tues.–Sat. noon–5 p.m.*

Hot Tip: Make your way to the rooftop patio in good weather for a laid-back place to kick back and watch the bustle of the Entertainment District.

Power Plant Gallery
231 Queen's Quay W., Harbourfront, 416-973-4949 • Hipster

The Draw: Three cool art spaces in a contemporary and newly refurbished arts complex on the Harbourfront.

The Scene: The goal of the exhibits here is to challenge and excite in the name of contemporary art in flexible indoor spaces. In addition to a smaller indoor gallery space, outdoor venues are used extensively whenever possible to showcase installations or film screenings. *Open Tues.–Sun. noon–6 p.m.; Wed. noon–8 p.m.* $

Hot Tip: The Power Plant runs an ambitious program of lectures, talks, and other special events—check the website (www.thepowerplant.org) for what you might run into.

Best Dance Clubs

Toronto's clubs are red-hot these days and highly competitive. You'll have to pass muster with door staff, but once inside, you can expect fab décor, long drink lists, and scads of well-dressed partiers grooving to the beats.

Afterlife Nightclub
250 Adelaide St. W., Entertainment District, 416-593-6126 • Hot & Cool

The Draw: Three floors and four levels of over-the-top style and cutting-edge sound systems have made this a perennial favorite of twenty- and thirty-somethings.

The Scene: On the lower-level dance floor, splashes of colored lighting illuminate gyrating and scantily clad dancers and all the reflective surfaces of the bar in a darkened room, while the music throbs from a high-tech sound system. You can take a break from dancing in a quieter lounge upstairs, which overlooks the downstairs action. Then higher still, it's pale beauty in stark white with blue lights for intimate conversations in sexy and more upscale surroundings. The crowd is young and fun-loving, and heats up the dance floor all night long. *Open Fri.–Sat. 10 p.m.–3 a.m.* $$

Hot Tip: The roof has one of the best patios in Clubland, and if hunger strikes, the BBQ is fired up all night long.

BaBaLu's
136 Yorkville Ave., Bloor/Yorkville, 416-515-0587 • Hot & Cool

The Draw: This hot Latin dance club with a high-fashion, celeb-studded crowd is a place to see and be seen.

The Scene: Mirrored walls and bright Latin-flavored colors dominate the room, where everyone, male and female, is dressed to kill and grooving to hot Latin beats. Expect a VIP scene of Hollywood stars and pro-sports icons on the other side of the velvet rope, and a hot and sweaty dance floor. The dim lighting adds to the exclusive, urban ambience. *Open Wed.–Sun. 9 p.m.–3 a.m.* $$$

Hot Tip: Thursdays are especially hot with a regular crowd of stylin' Latin-dance aficionados who get there before 9 to heat up the dance floor in advance of the crowds.

Sugar Club
57 Duncan St., Entertainment District, 416-597-0202
• Arts & Entertainment

The Draw: You'll find cool grooves and no attitude in this swank and fashionable spot in Clubland.

The Scene: The lighting glows, friendly and flattering; the room is fashionably minimalist with a silvery waterfall. The vibe is upscale and welcoming and the beats are made for dancing. Crowds of stylish clubbers come to sip well-mixed martinis while the DJ spins R&B and house. *Open Thurs.–Sat. 9 p.m.–3 a.m.* $$

Hot Tip: Thursday nights media types come out for after-work drinks and networking.

Best | # Ethnic Dining

This city has over 80 ethnicities who speak more than 100 languages, so it's no surprise that the dining scene has international flair. From new arrivals to old favorites, there's a taste for every palate and a palate for every taste.

Babur
273 Queen St. W., Entertainment District, 416-599-7720 • Hipster

The Draw: Superb Northern Indian cuisine with a hip ambience on a busy corner.

The Scene: From a simple dining room, sitar music plays as you watch the chefs energetically assemble your choices. The long menu of Northern Indian classics includes meat and fish as well as vegetarian dishes. From foodies who've read the rave reviews to hip creative professionals who live and work in the area, people come from all over town to sample the cuisine. *Open daily for lunch and dinner 11 a.m.–11:30 p.m.* $$

Hot Tip: Don't hesitate to try this place, even if your knowledge of Indian cuisine is limited, as staff here are friendly and very knowledgeable.

Caju
922 Queen St. W., Parkdale, 416-532-2550 • Hipster

The Draw: A sunny slice of Brazil in Toronto in a cool contemporary setting.

The Scene: The crowd is Queen West hipsters and foodies who've come to check out the buzz on this new twist to the Toronto dining scene. *Caju* comes from the Brazilian word for cashew nut—only a hint of the exotic names and flavors you'll enjoy, like sirloin grilled with garlic butter served with crispy cassava chips. Join the crowds in the vibrant dining room for a Brazilian-flavored cocktail, and enjoy the sophisticated, loungey aura of the place. *Open for dinner Tues.–Sat. 5–11 p.m.; Sun. 5–10 p.m.* $$$

Hot Tip: Try the signature drink, a cocktail called the Caipirinha, made with lime and cachaca, a Brazilian liqueur.

Ouzeri
500A Danforth Ave., Greektown, 416-778-0500 • Classic

The Draw: Upscale Greek-Mediterranean ambience in good old Greektown, complete with a busy streetside patio.

The Scene: A lively European cafe ambience is set by blue awnings and a wrought-iron railing, dotted with potted greenery in the summer. Ouzeri has been packing in the crowds for years, and the mixed crowd looking for fun stays for drinks after dinner. The menu features an extensive list of Greek classics with starters like tzatziki and marinated olives, proceeding to prawns, octopus, and specialties like dolmades. The ambience is warm and bustling, big on food and friendly service. It's a boisterous and festive place to kick back and pretend you're on the sunny Mediterranean, with the most coveted seats on the patio. *Open for lunch and dinner Mon.–Thurs. 11:30 a.m.–midnight; Fri.–Sat. 1:30 p.m.–2 a.m.; Sun. 11:30 a.m.–midnight.* $$$

Hot Tip: Try a platter for two with a selection of seafood, quail, and other delicacies.

Best | ## Fine Dining

Torontonians love to dine on the town, and a dizzying array of enticing choices is available these days. At these establishments, your hosts' attention to detail encompasses the entire dining experience, extending from mood and décor to service and, of course, cuisine.

Auberge du Pommier
4150 Yonge St., Uptown, 416-222-2220 • Arts & Entertainment

The Draw: Old-school French classics served in a rustic former woodcutter's cottage for extra atmosphere.

The Scene: The Auberge has long been synonymous with high-end French dining in Toronto. The mood here is refined, the crowd dressed to the nines. Seamless French country elegance is done here with panache: cut stone walls, huge barn beams, wood-burning fireplaces, and in the summer, a garden terrace. This romantic French restaurant in the very best tradition is sure to impress. *Open for lunch Mon.–Fri. 11:30 a.m.–2:30 p.m.; for dinner Mon.–Sat. from 5 p.m.* $$$$

Hot Tip: Extend your appreciation for French flavors to the cocktail list, and try the enticing Auberge Cosmopolitan of berry-and-citrus-infused vodka, cranberry juice, and Grand Marnier.

Opus
37 Prince Arthur Ave., Bloor/Yorkville, 416-921-3105 • Hot & Cool

The Draw: Glamorous dining for a posh crowd just steps from fashionable Yorkville.

The Scene: Located in a restored Victorian townhouse, this eatery caters to an upper-class clientele with restrained elegance. In the dining room, the sexy spot lighting and grand columns, white linens, and leather seating create a sober, Manhattan-style effect. The fare is high-end French-continental and the friendly owners are the hosts. *Open daily for dinner 5:30–11:30 p.m.* $$$$

Hot Tip: The homemade ice cream provides a rich end to your meal.

Pangaea
1221 Bay St. N., Bloor/Yorkville, 416-920-2323 • Hot & Cool

The Draw: Warm and sexy Mediterranean ambience, a gourmet menu, and a savvy wine list.

The Scene: Gold-colored walls accented in aqua blue rise high above the wood plank floors to create a warm backdrop for the crowds of fashionable uptown and Yorkville types who flock here. Tucked in a nondescript office complex, Pangaea has become a popular oasis of light and fine food, with an inventive Mediterranean–Pan-Asian menu. A friendly, festive atmosphere and a selection of vintage wines round out the experience. *Open for lunch and dinner Mon.–Sat. 11:30 a.m.–11:30 p.m.* $$$$

Hot Tip: The congenial owners often staff the small but chic bar above the dining room in the afternoons, and are happy to chat or share their wine expertise.

Best Gay Bars

With the continent's second-largest gay population, Toronto's Gay Village has always had a host of bars and clubs. But along with the old favorites, in recent years a growing demand for more stylish venues has resulted in a newly revamped scene.

Byzantium
499 Church St., Gay Village, 416-922-3859 • Hipster

The Draw: A sophisticated restaurant with a busy bar-lounge and lengthy, inventive cocktail list.

The Scene: The crowd is mixed gays and hip straights, with an overall sheen of fashionable downtowners, and the bar, separated from the dining room, is seldom empty. The playful Gay Village mood comes in sophisticated tones here, still friendly but not so raucous as some places. A richly colored dining room with lush florals and formal seating offers a menu of globally inspired and often exotically flavored dishes. After the dinner hour, the action at the bar really heats up. *Open daily for dinner 5:30–11 p.m.; bar open Sun.–Wed. 5:30 p.m.–1 a.m., Thurs.–Sat. 5:30 p.m.–2 a.m.*

Hot Tip: Check out the long martini list carefully—the Byzantium original Sonomatini (vodka, cabernet sauvignon, and sweet vermouth) comes highly recommended.

Hair of the Dog
425 Church St., Gay Village, 416-964-2708 • Classic

The Draw: Upscale pubbing on Church Street with close ties to the gay community.

The Scene: Think pub but bright and spotless, the woods polished and gleaming. The owners double as publishers of *Fab*, a high-end gay lifestyle magazine, and their connections to the gay community make for large and diverse crowds. A perennial favorite in the Gay Village, Hair has a bustling and friendly ambience, just as a pub should. The menu is casual, including pizza and light fare, but along with the brews comes an extensive selection of specialty wines and a long martini menu. *Open for lunch and dinner Mon.–Fri. 11:30 a.m.–2 a.m.; Sat.–Sun. 10 a.m.–2 a.m.*

Hot Tip: The kitchen's open until 1 a.m. for between-martini casual snacks.

Inspire
491 Church St., Gay Village, 416-963-0044 • Arts & Entertainment

The Draw: Glass-fronted restaurant-lounge for the style-conscious Boys' Town scene.

The Scene: The contemporary décor is minimalist and refined with plain white walls and glass-and-chrome furnishings custom-made in Bangkok. The menu also takes its cue from the Far East with Pan-Asian fusion whose invention results in a menu of dizzying length. But Inspire aspires to more than good food, attracting a mixed scene of downtown hipsters, gay and straight. The bar stools are made for perching and posing while you take in the stylish crowd. *Open daily 5 p.m.–2 a.m.*

Hot Tip: The wine list has a nice selection of vintage white burgundies if you're a fan.

THE PERFECT TORONTO

Best — Gay Dance Clubs

The competition's fierce in Toronto's gay dance-club scene. The result is a slew of fabulous dance emporiums, both strictly gay and straight-friendly, where the beats are fast and the crowds huge.

5ive Nightclub
5 St. Joseph St., Downtown/Yonge, 416-964-8685 • Hot & Cool

The Draw: Dance club with a scene of good-looking partiers here for the DJs and live shows for every taste.

The Scene: The room is huge, with splashes of colored lighting and nooks and corners in addition to the main attraction—the big dance floor. The beats are furious, and the crowd gets wilder as the night goes on. The minimalist design is reinvented weekly to go along with the shows. 5ive plays host to performances by the hottest DJs, fashion shows, and the original Northbound Leather fetish night. This is a happening dance club with ambitious events programming. *Open Wed.–Sat. 10 p.m.–3 a.m.* $$$

Hot Tip: Check listings for nights when you can feast your eyes on professional dancers.

Fly Nightclub
8 Gloucester St., Gay Village, 416-410-5426 • Hot & Cool

The Draw: Hot gay-male dance club with multiple floors of style and flash.

The Scene: About 1,000 revelers pass through the doors of Fly on any given Saturday night, when the Canada's best DJs pump out the beats till 7 a.m. If you've seen *Queer as Folk*, this is the series' original Babylon Club, and that's the celeb-studded scene of wild partying you'll find here, with the latest in sound and light systems cranking it out to the huge dance floor. The monster facility—10,000 square feet—also includes quieter lounge areas where you can take a break from the dancing. Fly is consistently voted best dance club by locals. *Open Fri. 10 p.m.–3 a.m.; Sat. 10 p.m.–7 a.m.* $$

Hot Tip: There's a bistro downstairs where you can fuel up before hitting the dance floor.

Lüb Lounge
487 Church St., Gay Village, 416-323-1489 • Hot & Cool

The Draw: Space-age sleek restaurant-lounge that draws style-conscious crowds.

The Scene: The sign glows blue on the glassy front of Lüb, giving a hint of its modern approach to Gay Village style inside. There's a laid-back, relaxed vibe here during the week, but on weekends DJs get the youngish crowds off the cushioned seating and onto the dance floor. This is a dance club with great style and panache, and the crowds dress for it. The club's design was featured in *Canadian Interiors* magazine. *Open Mon.–Wed. 4 p.m.–midnight; Thurs.–Fri. 4 p.m.–2 a.m.; Sat. noon–2 a.m.; Sun. noon–1 a.m.* $$

Hot Tip: Take your choice from a long list of martinis and cocktails—the Cucumber Classic (Hendrick's gin and vermouth) is very popular.

Best | # Guided Tours

Forget about boring bus tours. In Toronto, even hepcats will find tours of facilities that will amuse, entertain, and enlighten with little-known insights.

Artinsite

416-979-5704, www.artinsite.com • Arts & Entertainment

The Draw: The real scoop on Toronto's art scene through a guided tour of art galleries, studios, and architectural sites given by a local art expert.

The Scene: See Toronto with an artist's eye. Longtime arts journalist Betty Ann Jordan is also a columnist with stylish *Toronto Life* magazine, and she leads tours of art galleries and studios in Toronto. Scheduled tours can include art instruction or theory and history, even a tour of impressive private collections. Call ahead and book for the tour in the area of your choice based on your own interests. *Tours available afternoons and evenings. Call in advance to make arrangements.* $$

Hot Tip: Jordan leads a free tour of Yorkville galleries the first Thursday evening of every month starting at 6:30 p.m.

CHUM/Citytv Building

299 Queen St. W., Entertainment District, 416-591-5757 • Hot & Cool

The Draw: Hub of the most recognized media empire in town.

The Scene: The CHUM/City empire and its historic downtown location are home to the coolest Canadian broadcasters, including music video station Much Music. Your tour of this innovative broadcaster includes the open-studio concept newsrooms, as well as a view of cable specialties like Much. You'll get an entertaining inside view of how television is made. Bumping into local celebs is a given, and you may just run into an international superstar. *Tours offered afternoons Mon.–Fri. Call ahead for details.* $

Hot Tip: Check out Speakers' Corner, a self-operated video booth where Torontonians tell the audience how they see the world, with the results broadcast later. In the warm months, check to see what movies are playing outdoors in the huge parking lot.

Steam Whistle Brewing Company

The Roundhouse, 255 Bremner Blvd., Harbourfront, 416-362-2337, ext. 246 • Hipster

The Draw: Boutique brewery becomes one of the coolest spots in town.

The Scene: When upstart microbrewery Steam Whistle took over the historic John Street Roundhouse in the shadow of the CN Tower in 1998, the owners set out not only to produce a fine beer, but to be the hottest brew in town. They succeeded, and are now a mainstay in virtually every hot nightclub and bar in Toronto. Take a walk along the catwalks for a look at how it all gets put together, and enjoy a tasting of their signature pilsner afterward. *Tours offered Mon.–Sat. every hour 1–5 p.m.* $

Hot Tip: Steam Whistle's become a popular venue for corporate and other events, so call ahead in case it's closing for a private party.

THE PERFECT TORONTO

Best Historic Buildings

While it's a thoroughly modern city, Toronto wears its history with pride. You can get a glimpse of the city's grand past in carefully restored locales.

Casa Loma
1 Austin Terr., Uptown, 416-923-1171 • Classic

The Draw: An imposing medieval castle overlooking modern-day Toronto on a manicured six-acre estate.

The Scene: It took prominent early twentieth-century Toronto businessman and industrialist Sir Henry Pellatt nearly three years and 300 men to build his dream home, a re-created medieval castle with Norman, Gothic, and Romanesque influences. Six acres of manicured gardens surround the building, with its towers and turrets, richly decorated suites with original antiques, a vast Great Hall with huge oak beams, secret passages, and an 800-foot tunnel connecting the main building with the stables and carriage house. *Open daily 9:30 a.m.–5 p.m. (last entry at 4 p.m.) The Casa Loma Gardens are open daily 9:30 a.m.–4 p.m. May–Oct. and are included with your admission to Casa Loma.* $

Hot Tip: Climb to the top of a turret for a breathtaking view of the modern city below.

St. Lawrence Market
92 Front St. E., St. Lawrence, 416-392-7219 • Hipster

The Draw: Come for the food, or just to check out the crowds at this food mecca that bustles on Saturday mornings.

The Scene: The St. Lawrence Market bustles with a cross-section of Toronto. And the Market delivers something for everyone in clean, bright efficiency, with the traditional array of meats, cheeses, and produce, as well as specialties like caviar and smoked salmon, organic coffees and teas, prepared foods, and baked goods. The first floor also houses jewelry, clothing, and gift retailers. *Open Tues.–Thurs. 8 a.m.–6 p.m.; Fri. 8 a.m.–7 p.m.; Sat. 5 a.m.–5 p.m.*

Hot Tip: Check the Market Gallery for exhibits, open most days until 4 p.m.

Spadina House
285 Spadina Rd., Uptown, 416-392-6910 • Arts & Entertainment

The Draw: A beautifully restored Edwardian charmer on well-tended grounds.

The Scene: The house began its life as a country estate in Victorian times, evolving into a townhouse in the Edwardian era as the city began to grow around it. Begun in 1866, the house retains its original furnishings and artwork and chronicles the lives of the Austin family (and upper-class Torontonians in general) throughout the twentieth century. In particular, the Austins were great patrons of the arts, and made their home a showcase for their favorite pieces. *Open Sept. 4 to Dec. 31, Tues.–Fri. noon–4 p.m.; Sat.–Sun. and holidays noon–5 p.m.; May 1 to Labor Day, Tues.–Sun. noon–5 p.m.* $

Hot Tip: Wander the six-acre gardens, home to some 300 varieties of plants and flowers.

Best | # Jazz Clubs

Jazz has never gone out of style in Toronto. Fueled by the hugely successful Downtown Jazz Festival, the world's greats have made this city a home away from home, and a superb place to catch great music.

Montreal Bistro & Jazz Club
65 Sherbourne St., St. Lawrence, 416-363-0179 • Arts & Entertainment

The Draw: This club is dedicated exclusively to world-class live jazz and its fans.

The Scene: Since 1979, countless jazz greats and stars from Van Morrison to Diana Krall have passed through these hallowed doors. The Montreal has taken its well-deserved place in the jazz scene, and serious jazz lovers come to hear the music. *Open Mon.–Fri. 11:30 a.m.–closing; Sat. 5:30 p.m.–closing.* $$

Hot Tip: Check listings for CD launch parties, where you can mingle with the musicians.

Rex Hotel Jazz & Blues Bar
194 Queen St. W., Entertainment District, 416-598-2475 • Classic

The Draw: This downtown beer parlor has become a venerable home of jazz and blues with an honest musician-friendly feel.

The Scene: The audience will be thick with musicians and art-school types, and music lovers dressed in anything from Prada to Levis who come first and foremost for the great music—12 different acts per week—and casual, relaxed vibe. Canada's finest musicians play here against a post-modern retro tavern-chic backdrop. The Rex is an industry and a local jazz community mainstay. *The hotel is open 24 hours; restaurant daily 11 a.m.–midnight; Live music Mon.–Tues. 9:30 p.m.–1 a.m.; Wed.–Fri. 6:30–8:30 p.m., 9:30 p.m.–1:00 a.m.; Sat. 3:30–6:30 p.m., 7–9 p.m., 9:30 p.m.–1 a.m.; Sun. 3:30–6:30 p.m., 9:00 p.m.–midnight.* $$$

Hot Tip: Be prepared for anything—as one of the central venues during the annual Downtown Jazz Festival, the Rex hosts the likes of Harry Connick Jr. and Ani DiFranco, who show up from time to time for an impromptu jam.

Top o' the Senator
253 Victoria St., St. Lawrence, 416-364-7517 • Arts & Entertainment

The Draw: Manhattan-style retro-swank setting and live tunes with fine dining thrown into the mix.

The Scene: The digs are posh and the acoustics just about perfect in this jazz boîte reminiscent of hedonistic pre-WWII clubs. The emphasis here is on contemporary music, heavy on the bebop and livelier versions of jazz, just right for the martinis-and-cosmopolitans ambience. The menu doesn't suffer from attention to the music, and includes house-aged beef in a classic steakhouse menu. This is upscale jazz for the swing set, catering to an over-thirty crowd. *Open Tues.–Sat. 8:30 p.m.–1 a.m. (first set starts at 9:30 p.m.); Sun. 8 p.m.–midnight (first set starts at 8:30 p.m.)* $$$

Hot Tip: A dinner and live-music package guarantees your seating at the first show.

Best Late-Night Eats

As Toronto's club scene has grown, so has the city's appetite for good eats at any hour of the day or night. From high-end to cafe-style, there's something to please every palate after the rigors of clubbing.

Bistro 333
333 King St. W., Entertainment District, 416-971-3336 • Classic

The Draw: Mediterranean bistro goes Clubland-slick with club-friendly hours.

The Scene: The sexy lighting against the polished woods and the curving chair backs of a classic bistro interior draws hordes of hungry clubbers. They feast on a menu of creative pastas and risottos, along with steak and seafood, in an intimate setting. Just downstairs from a club, this is a space made for partiers in search of elegant and satisfying sustenance. *Open for lunch and dinner Sun.–Wed. 11:30 a.m.–11:30 p.m.; Thurs. 11:30 a.m.–1 a.m.; Fri.–Sat. 11:30 a.m.–4 a.m.* $$$

Hot Tip: The nightclub upstairs is open until 3 a.m. if you feel the need to work off some of those carbs.

Room Service/Room 471
471 Richmond St. W., Entertainment District, 416-703-6239 • Hot & Cool

The Draw: Upscale Italian eatery designed especially for the clubbing classes.

The Scene: Most restaurant-lounges begin as a dining room and end the evening as a martini lounge, but at this address, dinner and clubbing go hand in hand. At 10 p.m. the kitchen opens, and the aroma of fine authentic Italian cuisine spreads through the chic dining room. Meanwhile, the DJ spins until closing and the cocktails flow until last call at 2 a.m. The menu changes seasonally, but typically features gourmet pastas, among other delicacies. *Open Thurs.–Sun. 10 p.m.–5 a.m.* $$$

Hot Tip: Try the antipasto plate for a wealth of Mediterranean-flavored bites.

7 West Cafe
7 Charles St. W., Bloor/Yorkville, 416-928-9041 • Classic

The Draw: Charming artsy and romantic cafe in a restored semi-detached Victorian.

The Scene: A kitchen open 24/7 can attract all sorts. Here you can expect a hip crowd with a solid quotient of club refugees in the wee hours. Twinkling lights and antique mirrors accent bare brick walls and wood furnishings, which are all the right ingredients for inspired late-night feasts from a casual menu of pasta, pizza, and panini. Add a patio deck in the summer, and it's the perfect solution to hunger pangs with an uptown gloss. *Open daily 24 hours.* $$

Hot Tip: The panini are both quickly served and superb no matter what the hour.

Best

Late-Night Hangouts

With a lively club scene, Toronto's got something for everyone. When it comes to partying after midnight, though, these clubs offer an experience that you can be sure you won't find anywhere else.

El Convento Rico
750 College St. W., Little Italy, 416-588-7800 • Hipster

The Draw: Throbbing Latin rhythms, an eccentric décor, and a wild crowd of partiers both gay and straight.

The Scene: Mixing glitzy retro-glam décor with sublime Latin-flavor music, live or via the city's hottest DJs, this is Toronto's much vaunted multiculturalism at its most mischievous and sexy. Add an enthusiastic staff, floor shows, and free salsa lessons for the uninitiated, and it adds up to the ultimate hip dance party. *Open Thurs.–Sun. 9 p.m.–3 a.m.* $$

Hot Tip: The over-the-top Latina Drag Queen Shows start at 1 a.m. on Saturdays.

Shanghai Cowgirl
538 Queen St. W., Entertainment District, 416-203-6623 • Hipster

The Draw: Themed retro diner for scenesters.

The Scene: This 1950s retro diner has its post-modern tongue firmly planted in its cheek. After a full night of clubbing, revelers congregate here to chow down on traditional diner fare like hamburgers, french fries, and grilled cheese, along with quirky menu offerings like drunken mussels and ghetto chicken that you can watch being prepared in the open kitchen. This haunt attracts hipsters at any time of day, but come late to watch the parade of club kids young and old. *Open Sun.–Thurs. 10:30 a.m.–midnight; Fri.–Sat. 10:30 a.m.–4 a.m.*

Hot Tip: Check out the new patio for late-night al fresco fun.

Ultra Supper Club
314 Queen St. W., Entertainment District, 416-263-0330 • Hot & Cool

The Draw: Chic supper club and lounge that becomes a late-night dance hot spot.

The Scene: Early in the evening, Ultra is a posh dining room and lounge with booths perfectly set up to allow the crowds to see and be seen. Dig into opulent contemporary cuisine served up elegantly by expert staff. Then, after the kitchen closes on the weekends, they move the tables out of the way, and it morphs into a hot dance club for the fashionable crowd. *Open Mon.–Wed. 5:30 p.m.–midnight; Thurs.–Sat. 5:30 p.m.–2 a.m.* $$

Hot Tip: Thursdays, check out the "Beauty Bar" for on-site consultations with a beautician, gift bags, and other goodies—and be sure to try out the Makeover Martini.

Best Martinis

At one time, "going out for drinks" meant a bland standard menu of wine, beer, or shots. No longer. These days, Toronto nightclubs compete to outdo each other in the area of creative mixology.

Flow Restaurant + Lounge
133 Yorkville Ave., Bloor/Yorkville, 416-925-2143 • Hot & Cool

The Draw: Sleek and stylish lounge for an upscale clientele.

The Scene: You'll know why it's called Flow from the moment you walk in—the water flows everywhere here, beginning in the bubbly glass railings as you descend the stairs from the lounge to the restaurant area. The scene is typical Yorkville, upscale and fashionable, and the over-thirty crowd certainly enjoys kicking back the cocktails. The exotic drink list designed for high-end tippling is matched by an exotic menu of fusion cuisine. *Open Mon. 11:30 a.m.–10:30 p.m.; Tues.–Wed. 11:30 a.m.–11 p.m.; Thurs.–Fri. 11:30 a.m.–2 a.m.; Sat. 5 p.m.–2 a.m.*

Hot Tip: Even if martinis are your main goal, the decadent dessert list is definitely worth a look.

La Rouge Executive Club
257 Adelaide St. W., Entertainment District, 416-260-5551 • Classic

The Draw: Two stylish and contemporary floors of cool club beats.

The Scene: This stylish retreat for the beautiful people sports an elegant bar in a sweeping curve at one end of the dance floor that serves a mean martini to a discerning crowd. In the lounge, the execs let down their hair on the extravagantly comfortable couches. *Open Thurs.–Sun. 9 p.m.–3 a.m.* $$

Hot Tip: For high-end clubbing that includes valet parking, private entrance, and access to a private lounge, go for the Platinum package.

Rain
19 Mercer St., Entertainment District, 416-599-7246 • Hot & Cool

The Draw: A stunning Toronto Asian-fusion restaurant-lounge with a seductive décor, including waterfall walls, and a distinctly A-list clientele.

The Scene: One of Toronto's perennial hot spots, Rain consistently draws crowds to its austere, water-themed space. Rain is a feast for the senses, complete with 15-foot waterfalls, a backlit frosted-glass bar, and bamboo elements to divide the space. Although the drink list is Asian-flavored, the martini is the drink of choice. The mood and setting are just right for lounging and sipping with the beautiful people. The equally inventive menu of Asian fare is served on slate, river rocks, and Japanese pottery. *Open Tues.–Sat. 5:30–11 p.m.*

Hot Tip: If you want to combine dinner with your drinks, make your reservation well in advance—waiting lists of up to a month aren't uncommon here.

Best

Meet Markets

Downtown Toronto has a healthy population of single professionals, both young and old. The club scene responds in kind with venues that let the beautiful people find each other.

C-Lounge
456 Wellington St. W., Entertainment District, 416-260-9393 • Hot & Cool

The Draw: The C-Lounge is a pure contemporary fashion statement in warm neutrals and dark leathers, with a stylish crowd to match.

The Scene: The leather couches are separated by airy drapes, and the sexy staff are dressed to kill. A fab ladies' room and two Aveda stylists in a spa area accessible to both the ladies and the guys prove this is clubbing gone ultra-posh. The scene is young, fashionable, and looking to hook up, with the odd celeb and pro-sports figure adding to the glam mood. Low lights and intimate seating make it the perfect place for serious flirting. Two large windows look out at the patio, complete with a wading pool; in good weather, you can lounge in comfort by the candlelit water. *Open Wed. 10 p.m.–1 a.m.; Thurs. 9 p.m.–2 a.m.; Fri.–Sat. 10 p.m.–2 a.m.* $$$

Hot Tip: For extra exclusivity, get on the VIP list for a private outdoor cabana poolside.

Crocodile Rock
240 Adelaide St. W., Entertainment District, 416-599-9751 • Classic

The Draw: The partying downtowners who keep it hopping every night of the week.

The Scene: It's noisy and yes, all green, but you'll find a relaxed, good-time ambience in this crocodile-themed bar. Join the mixed crowd of fun-loving professionals for a guaranteed night of good old-fashioned partying to a classic-rock soundtrack. You'll meet all types at this jovial spot. If you need to refuel, try the tasty wood-oven pizza and Cajun offerings. *Open Wed.–Fri. 4 p.m.–2 a.m.; Sat. 7 p.m.–2 a.m.*

Hot Tip: Check out Thursdays, when appetizers are half-price and the pool tables are free all night long.

West Lounge
511 King St. W., Entertainment District, 416-361-9004 • Hot & Cool

The Draw: A high-style club with an exclusive atmosphere that draws hordes of beautiful people on the make.

The Scene: An address that doesn't actually exist leads to a sign and a doorway leading downstairs, where you have to pass inspection before you're allowed into one of the city's most stylish clubs. This is the perfect place to find others as beautiful as you, with a crowd of supermodel types and men on the prowl. The below–street-level space is nonetheless warm and inviting, with pale couches, drapery, and rich artwork on the walls—just the right backdrop for posing. *Open daily 5 p.m.–2 a.m.* $$

Hot Tip: Thursdays, dance to retro and old-school rock and nibble on free hors d'oeuvres.

THE PERFECT TORONTO

Best — Only-in-Toronto Attractions

Check out these sights that only Canada's largest city, with its British-Empire origins overlaid by waves of multiculturalism and a dynamic population, could produce.

Distillery District
55 Mill St., Distillery District • Arts & Entertainment

The Draw: Meticulously authentic restoration of a historic industrial neighborhood that's since become an arts and music center and a favorite Hollywood film spot.

The Scene: Cut-stone walls and rough-hewn beams, original signs and iron fixtures set the tone for a handsome restoration of what was once the largest distillery in the British Empire. Now home to dozens of art galleries, arts organizations, and studios, along with restaurants and other retailers, it also hosts monthly outdoor art exhibitions, the Jazz Festival, and the Blues Festival, along with weekly arts and musical events.

Hot Tip: Watch out for the presence of trailers, which should alert you if a shoot is in progress. Over 800 productions have used it as a backdrop over the last decade.

Kensington Market
West of Spadina Road between College & Dundas Streets, Chinatown • Classic

The Draw: Colorful multi-ethnic area with shops and curiosities to boggle the mind.

The Scene: The fruit and vegetable stands spill onto the sidewalk, the air is fragrant with pastries and coffee, curries and Ethiopian spices. Amid a cacophony of languages, you pass storefronts offering fine Italian linens and Pakistani embroidery, exotic teas, and intriguing designer second-hand and vintage clothing. Toronto's international character can really be felt here, as all the flavors of the world converge in a lively spectacle. Even if you don't buy, you will have loads of fun looking.

Hot Tip: Linger over coffee in the Moonbean Cafe and watch the haggling in the stalls.

Yorkville Shopping District
Around Bloor Street & Avenue Road, Bloor/Yorkville • Hot & Cool

The Draw: Canada's most expensive shopping district, home of designer boutiques and chic restaurants.

The Scene: In the 1970s, Yorkville was known for hippies, the unwashed, and the rebellious—my, how times have changed. These days, Yorkville is Toronto's most chic shopping address, haunt of the international jet set. From Bloor just west of Yonge Street, chic retailer Holt Renfrew announces the beginning of the shopping district with a dazzling array of designer inventory. Chanel, Gucci—the boutiques follow one after the other down Bloor to Avenue Road and Hazelton Lanes, a mall for the rich and fabulous. Yorkville also boasts many hotels, nightclubs, and restaurants.

Hot Tip: Local media use the term "Four Seasons crowd" to describe a celeb-studded group, with good reason, so hang at the Four Seasons for the best chance of spotting any stars in town.

Best Romantic Rendezvous

Décor that seduces, intimate seating, attentive service, and a meal that befits a special occasion—these are the ingredients for a romantic evening. And these Toronto restaurants really go out of their way to set the right mood for you and your loved one.

Rosewater Supper Club
19 Toronto St., St. Lawrence, 416-214-5888 • Arts & Entertainment

The Draw: Flawless historic renovation that offers fine dining in grand style.

The Scene: Boasting dining rooms with 22-foot ceilings, sumptuous upholstery, and hand-painted cornice moldings, the Rosewater is a step back into Victorian-era romance and glamour. There are lounges at different levels, and live jazz plays in the Front Lounge. With a menu that has been awarded the Distinguished Restaurants of North America Award two years in a row, the feast here is not only for the eyes. *Open for lunch Mon.–Fri. 11:30 a.m.–2:30 p.m.; dinner Mon.–Sat. 5:30–10 p.m.* $$$

Hot Tip: Linger after the main course and choose from a selection of over a dozen artisan cheeses to savor with your date over dessert wine.

Sen5es Restaurant & Lounge
The SoHo Metropolitan, 318 Wellington St. W., Entertainment District, 416-935-0400 • Hot & Cool

The Draw: A mood of contemporary opulence with a warm and intimate ambience.

The Scene: Sen5es aims to please all the senses—and it largely succeeds with its muted, textured, dimly lit bar, gorgeous food, and fantastic wine list. Just off the entrance to the SoHo Met, the glass wall divides the area into a lounge that glows in shades of gold accented with jewel tones. Brazilian-born and much-celebrated executive chef Claudio Aprile inspects every dish before it leaves his open kitchen. *Restaurant open Wed.–Sun. 6–10 p.m.; bar and bistro open daily 4 p.m.–1 a.m.* $$$$

Hot Tip: Both the lounge and dining room have plenty of quiet corners for a tête-à-tête, so be sure to let your preferences be known when you make your reservation.

Truffles
Four Seasons Hotel Toronto, 21 Avenue Rd., Bloor/Yorkville, 416-928-7331 • Classic

The Draw: The only restaurant in Canada to earn the CAA/AAA five-diamond award 11 years in a row.

The Scene: Wrought-iron gates usher you into a rarefied atmosphere of seriously over-the-top pampering. Truffles is Toronto's favorite spot for special occasions, and you'll find your fellow diners as impeccably turned out as the highly acclaimed continental cuisine. With service that's attentive to a fault, this is truly the perfect spot to impress. *Open for dinner Mon.–Sat. 6–10 p.m.* $$$$

Hot Tip: Splurge on a special occasion and order the four- or five-course tasting menu.

THE PERFECT TORONTO

Best | Scene Bars

Where a stylish bar opens, the beautiful people follow. Toronto's thriving nightlife scene continually ups the ante to offer scenesters the most bang for their bucks. Though crowds can be fickle, these venues have the official scenesters' stamp of approval.

Crystal Room
567 Queen St. W., Entertainment District, 416-504-1626 • Hipster

The Draw: Artsy Parisian-flavored bar and lounge with a Queen West spin.

The Scene: The look is Belle Epoque Paris with a modern sheen. West End hipsters perch artfully at the ornate whitewashed bar, and sheer drapes separate the über-cool who sit on beds in the VIP area. A shimmering tiled bar on the second floor is the perfect spot to watch the beautiful crowd gyrate on the dance floor. Downstairs, the denizens of Queen Street order cocktails from yet another carved and decorative bar and play pool. Best of all, the friendly staff are cool and lacking in attitude. *Open Fri.–Sat. 9 p.m.–2 a.m.* $$

Hot Tip: The downstairs fireplace is a welcome spot to escape from inclement weather.

Lobby
192 Bloor St. W., Bloor/Yorkville, 416-929-7169 • Hot & Cool

The Draw: At this chic Yorkville address, a doorman with a discerning eye means that you'll be sure to find a chic and fabulous crowd here.

The Scene: A glass front looks onto the street, and behind the velvet ropes await discerning door staff—if you make it past them, there's a lounge of white cushions that highlights the beautiful people ensconced in them. A long bar and dazzling crystal chandelier dominate the dining room in the back. A cute menu offers trendy items, but the real draw is the long martini list and the chance to mingle with a designer crowd. *Open for lunch Tues.–Sat. noon–2:30 p.m.; for dinner 6–11 p.m.; bar open Tues.–Sat. 11 a.m.–2 a.m.* $$

Hot Tip: Ask about the VIP area, where you'll get table-side bottle service for your vodka.

YYZ Restaurant & Wine Bar
345 Adelaide St. W., Entertainment District, 416-599-3399 • Hot & Cool

The Draw: Subterranean lounge that has become one of Toronto's premier spots to see and be seen.

The Scene: Modular chrome tables with lots of stainless steel, silver vinyl, white arborite, and absinthe-colored glass louvers make this stylish hot spot gleam, but it's only a backdrop for the fashionistas who flock here, along with a liberal sprinkling of celebrity stardust. YYZ are the call letters for Pearson Airport, and this started the airport-style lounge trend. *Open for dinner Mon.–Wed. 5–10 p.m.; Thurs.–Sun. 5–11 p.m.; open for cocktails Mon.–Wed. 4:30–11:30 p.m.; Thurs.–Sun. 4:30 p.m.–1 a.m.*

Hot Tip: YYZ's wine list netted it a *Wine Spectator* magazine award, so sample from the over 20 vintages available by the glass.

Seafood Restaurants

Best

No matter how far inland they live, Canadians have a great love of seafood. In Toronto, it results in a wealth of restaurants that specialize in the bounty of the ocean, with delectable seafood flown in daily from both coasts.

Joso's
202 Davenport Rd., Bloor/Yorkville, 416-925-1903 • Classic

The Draw: Fresh seafood presented with flair for a designer crowd.

The Scene: It may have been the bustling see-and-be-seen patio looking out at the chic boutiques of Yorkville that first drew the Hollywood stars, wealthy locals, and savvy travelers, but it's the mouth-watering seafood and stunning presentation that keep the place humming year after year. Friendly and knowledgeable servers bring fresh seafood table-side, and choices include a whole fish grilled over a wood fire. Seafood is king here, and dinner is part spectacle and part performance art. *Open for lunch Mon.–Fri. 11:30 a.m.–2:30 p.m.; for dinner Mon.–Sat. 5:30–10:30 p.m.* $$$$

Hot Tip: Reservations are a must—the place is tiny, and the patio seats only 14.

Pure Spirits Oyster House & Grill
55 Mill St., Distillery District, 416-361-5859 • Arts & Entertainment

The Draw: Toronto's latest oyster bar and fresh seafood joint, with a jazzed-up Distillery District vibe.

The Scene: The historical Distillery District is enjoying a renaissance, and Pure Spirits is right at the heart of it. Crowds flock here for the lively atmosphere, fine seafood, and great outdoor patio. Funky light fixtures and big windows let in lots of natural light—the look is contemporary and draws a mixed crowd of upscale locals and travelers. Menu choices include non-seafood and even vegetarian options. *Open for lunch and dinner Sun.–Thurs. 11:30 a.m.–10 p.m.; Fri.–Sat. 11:30 a.m.–11 p.m.* $$$

Hot Tip: During the summer months, Pure Spirits' hot outdoor patio enjoys a virtually constant stream of live jazz and other events hosted at the District.

Starfish Oyster Bed & Grill
100 Adelaide St. E., St. Lawrence, 416-366-7827 • Classic

The Draw: Bright New York–style bistro ambience and seafood that's fresh daily in charming surroundings overlooking St. James Cathedral.

The Scene: A smart black sign over the shiny glass front of this restored historic building announces this gourmet seafood eatery. The professional downtowners who have transformed this neighborhood from a once shabby area into condo heaven love this intimate bistro. Oysters come in several varieties, as do other delicacies of the sea. For landlubbers, there are non-seafood options as well. *Open for lunch Mon.–Fri. noon–3 p.m.; for dinner Mon.–Sat. 5–11 p.m.* $$$

Hot Tip: For an all-out mollusk orgy, try the 100 Malpeque small choice oysters with a magnum of Heidseick champagne.

Best — Sexy Lounges

Toronto's club scene has grown up in the past decade. Nowadays, the discerning reveler has a wide variety of fabulous choices for the ultimate lounge experience.

Budo Liquid Theatre
137 Peter St., Entertainment District, 416-593-1550 • Hot & Cool

The Draw: Arguably the best name ever for a lounge, featuring three floors of Asian-inspired style and beautiful people to provide the theater.

The Scene: The contemporary zen lounge has a minimalist feel, highlighted by Japanese poetry and art, and a 35-foot waterfall. Grab one of the signature fruit martinis and sink into a white chair on the rooftop patio for a leisurely evening amid a handsome crowd. This is one of Clubland's hot spots for the upscale thirty-and-up crowd looking for an over-the-top good time. *Open Thurs.–Sat 9:30 p.m.–3 a.m.* $$

Hot Tip: Dress to impress—this see-and-be-seen spot is quite the singles magnet.

Habitat Lounge
735 Queen St. W., Parkdale, 416-860-1551 • Hipster

The Draw: Contemporary high-style restaurant-lounge with Queen West cred.

The Scene: A small bar glows to one side, as a crowd of creative professionals—Toronto parlance for the designers, ad people, and film and television types who've taken over the city's West End—lounge artfully on the white couches. Farther back, creative fusion cuisine is served on leather banquettes to still more beautiful people, and at the back, another small bar glows red over the chic cocktail crowd. This is designer lounging at its very best. *Open Tues.–Sat. from 6 p.m.* $$

Hot Tip: Thursday nights, the DJ takes over the sound system for an evening of serious electronic grooves.

Therapy Ultra Lounge
203 Richmond St. W., Entertainment District, 416-977-3089 • Hot & Cool

The Draw: All the right ingredients for a hot club experience—stylish décor, inventive cocktails, and a scene of fashionable clubbers who love it.

The Scene: The room is dark and throbs with the beats from a state-of-the-art sound system while the lights glow, warmly enhancing the sultry mood. The cocktail list plays tongue-in-cheek homage to therapeutic greats, with drinks like the Dr. Phil, featuring Finlandia cranberry vodka, melon liqueur, amaretto, and cranberry juice. There's a menu of Asian fusion, but the super-fashionable over-thirty crowd comes here mainly to see and be seen on the overstuffed couches. *Open Wed.–Sun. 9 p.m.–3 a.m.; Thurs.–Fri. open from 4:30 p.m. for after-work drinks.* $$

Hot Tip: Come Friday nights to start the weekend with the fashionable downtowners who come ready to party.

Best Spas

Male or female, everyone is indulging in the spa experience these days. Toronto's burgeoning spa scene offers a wide selection of treatments and options, with more establishments springing up all the time.

Elizabeth Milan Day Spa

Fairmont Royal York, 100 Front St. W., Entertainment District, 416-350-7500 • Arts & Entertainment

The Draw: Celebrity-level spa services with hints of exotic self-indulgence.

The Scene: Just off the lobby of the Royal York Hotel, a bubble of over-the-top pampering awaits amid lush greenery and flowers. Treatment rooms have a neoclassical theme, with candlelight glowing softly and more fresh flowers to please the senses. Signature services include the seductive Chocolate Body Indulgence, grape, and mud treatments. Expect to feel like an A-lister while you're here. *Open Mon.–Wed. 9 a.m.–7 p.m.; Thurs.–Fri. 8:30 a.m.–8 p.m.; Sat. 8:30 a.m.–7 p.m.* $$$$

Hot Tip: Feel like a princess and treat yourself to a Balinese Beauty Ritual, developed to cater to royal princesses on their wedding day.

Pantages Anti-Aging & Longevity Spa

Pantages Hotel Suites, 200 Victoria St., Downtown, 416-367-1888 • Hot & Cool

The Draw: Rejuvenating treatments based on the ancient Ayurvedic system of health.

The Scene: The Pantages' treatments take into account a person's entire personality—mind, body, and spirit. Signature treatments feature hydrotherapy, including a full-body Vichy shower, and couples facilities. This chic new spa will pamper you with its wide range of services—from traditional Swedish and hot-stone massages to the exotic Deep Sea Body Cleanse and the Emerald Green Clay detoxifying body toner. Be sure to sample a drink from the aqua bar. *Open daily 9 a.m.–10 p.m.* $$$$

Hot Tip: Ask about Botox and other medical services provided on site by staff doctors.

Stillwater Spa

Park Hyatt Toronto, 4 Avenue Rd., Bloor/Yorkville, 416-926-2389 • Classic

The Draw: Elegant and established spa for the well-heeled and in the know, located conveniently in Yorkville. A perfect way to relieve the stress of a full day of shopping.

The Scene: You'll find an air of pedigreed refinement here amid the pale fixtures and soft sounds of naturally running water. Seasoned attendants make your experience one of renewal. Aqua therapies are their specialty, and warm water can be incorporated into massage and other treatments. A longtime favorite of wealthy Torontonians. *Open Mon.–Fri. 9 a.m.–10 p.m.; Sat. 8 a.m.–10 p.m.; Sun. 10 a.m.–5:30 p.m.* $$$$

Hot Tip: Contact the spa concierge to ask about a spa-inspired lunch menu created by the Park Hyatt's executive chef, then relax by the fireplace and enjoy.

THE PERFECT TORONTO

Best — Summer Patios

They say that there are two seasons in Toronto—winter and patio season. You'll find hardy Torontonians out on the patio somewhere even when temperatures hover around the freezing mark.

Lago
207 Queen's Quay W., Harbourfront, 416-848-0005 • Classic

The Draw: A 120-seat patio beside the sparkling blue waters of Lake Ontario, and a lively crowd of locals and out-of-towners kicking back in the summertime.

The Scene: Located in the historic Queen's Quay Terminal, this is lakeside-patio living gone high style. Mixed crowds enjoy the great outdoors with marble tables, high-backed booths, and even candlelight on the upper level. The menu is light and fresh and hits the spot when you're dining al fresco. *Open May–Sept. Mon.–Fri. 11 a.m.– 11 p.m.; Sat.–Sun. 11 a.m.–midnight.*

Hot Tip: Try one of the luscious martinis specially designed for Lago by the Martini Club.

Roof Lounge
Park Hyatt Toronto, 4 Avenue Rd., 18th Fl., Bloor/Yorkville, 416-924-5471 • Classic

The Draw: A friendly hotel lounge with a terrific view of the city from the rooftop patio.

The Scene: Expert mixologist Joe Gomes has been dancing his way around the bar at this swanky watering hole for the last 45 years. Well-heeled travelers and generations of locals have come for the refined yet congenial ambience, the fab cocktails, and the view over the city. This perennial favorite is a true Toronto institution. *Open daily 11 a.m.–2 a.m.*

Hot Tip: With a wood-burning fireplace, this rooftop patio and lounge doubles as a refuge from bad weather.

Sky Bar
132 Queen's Quay E., Harbourfront, 416-869-0045 • Hot & Cool

The Draw: The summer patio scene for an exclusively high-end clientele, where al fresco is strictly upmarket.

The Scene: Torontonians get relatively few warm summer nights, so they must make the most of them. Sky Bar has all you could ever want on a balmy evening. A distinctly upscale crowd congregates here during the summer months to sip fabulous cocktails and admire the gorgeous view—and each other. A beefy bouncer guards the stairs to the view you won't be able to get enough of, especially after dark when the lights make even the traffic look pretty. On weekends, the DJs and dancing crowd show up dressed to the nines and looking to make the most of a summer's evening. *Open seasonally May–Oct., Thurs.–Sat. 10 p.m.–3 a.m.* $$

Hot Tip: Thursdays are fashion-industry nights when the girls strut the catwalk.

Best | # Swanky Hotel Bars

Over the last five years or so, many of Toronto's biggest hotels have undergone a wave of renovations. What resulted was a kind of competition for stunning design, extending to that staple of all travelers, the hotel bar.

Avenue

Four Seasons Hotel Toronto, 21 Avenue Rd., Bloor/Yorkville, 416-964-0411 • Classic

The Draw: One of the most fashionable restaurant-lounges in town, with a plum location in the Four Seasons.

The Scene: There may be no better place to catch up with the A-listers who frequent the hotel than in these sophisticated surroundings. Chic and sleek, this highly polished spot draws an upper-crust crowd of handsome business types, stylish shoppers, and the odd celeb. The 20-foot yellow onyx bar shines like glass. *Open for lunch Mon.–Sat. 11:45 a.m.–3 p.m.; for dinner Mon.–Sat. 3 p.m.–1 a.m.; Sun. 4 p.m.–midnight; Sun. brunch 10:30 a.m.–2:30 p.m.*

Hot Tip: Order from the posh snack menu, which includes mini Kobe beef, foie gras burgers, and other gourmet delights.

Azure Restaurant & Bar

InterContinental Toronto Centre, 225 Front St. W., Entertainment District, 416-597-8142 • Arts & Entertainment

The Draw: A fashionable restaurant-lounge dominated by a shimmering art installation.

The Scene: *Liquid Veil*, the mesmerizing azure-blue glass art installation by Stuart Reid, sets a mood of contemporary elegance that's matched by the scene of well-dressed visitors and downtowners. A soaring wall of windows provides natural light even in bad weather. The extensive martini list and fairly lengthy list of wines are complemented by a continental-based menu. *Open daily 6 a.m.–11 p.m.*

Hot Tip: Join downtowners Thursdays for happy-hour cocktails, and check for wine-tasting specials.

Library Bar

Fairmont Royal York, 100 Front St. W., Downtown, 416-368-2511 • Classic

The Draw: Old-school elegance with overtones of a gentleman's club in a posh hotel.

The Scene: Heavy wood furniture and a carved, polished bar, leather upholstery, and richly colored drapes are the backdrop to a scene of high-powered businesspeople, politicians, and visiting VIPs, as well as upscale travelers looking for a refined place to relax. The well-suited and well-coiffed sip well-mixed drinks and nibble from a casual lounge menu. *Open Mon.–Fri. noon–1 a.m.; Sat. 5:30 p.m.–1 a.m.*

Hot Tip: Ask for the latest in an ever-changing menu of cocktail creations.

THE PERFECT TORONTO

Best Trendy Restaurants

Whether you're looking for small plates or fusion, tasting menus or open kitchens, Toronto's dining scene always has more than its fair share of trendsetting dining rooms—which draw fashionable crowds looking for the newest and the best.

Lee
603 King St. W., Entertainment District, 416-504-7867 • Hot & Cool

The Draw: Fusion masterpieces for diners in the know on a hip stretch of King Street.

The Scene: Foodies and fashionistas alike have been making Lee the talk of the town. The crowds come to Lee, funky spiritual sister to super-refined Susur, just next door, to sample the fusion creations of star chef Susur Lee. Sit at a pink Lucite table on a purple upholstered banquette and let your fashionable server guide you through a menu of over 30 tapas-size small-plate selections. *Open for lunch Mon.–Sat. noon–2:30 p.m.; dinner Mon.–Sat. 6 p.m.–10 p.m.* $$

Hot Tip: A plate-glass wall faces the street—ask for a table near it for a prime see-and-be-seen spot.

Monsoon
100 Simcoe St., Entertainment District, 416-979-7172 • Hot & Cool

The Draw: Starkly handsome Asian-inspired décor and fusion masterpieces for the chic downtown set.

The Scene: The décor makes a dramatic statement in glowing red and gold, black and wood, and the downtown crowds love to sink into the black leather couches in the warmly lit lounge. The scene is young and stylish, the crowd sophisticated urbanites. White linens and glowing wall treatments set an elegant mood in the dining room where exotic Japanese fusion is served on gorgeous plates of colored glass, accompanied by an extensive wine list. *Open for lunch Mon.–Fri. 11:30 a.m.–2:30 p.m.; for dinner Mon.–Sat. from 5 p.m.* $$$$

Hot Tip: For a busy late-afternoon to evening scene, join the lively after-work crowd that flocks here Thursdays and Fridays.

Perigee
55 Mill St., Distillery District, 416-364-1397 • Arts & Entertainment

The Draw: Four chefs prepare your meal in *Food Network* style right in the dining room.

The Scene: Dinner is theater at Perigee, created as you watch in the dramatically lit sunken kitchen where creativity rules and the meal is ordered not by dish or type of food, but by the number of courses. Well-heeled foodies and diners in the know will share in the experience as you check out one of the trendiest concepts in fine dining in Toronto. The historic District ambience of bare brick walls and wooden beams is given minimalist treatment here. *Open for dinner Tues.–Sat. 5:30–9 p.m.* $$$

Hot Tip: A tasting menu that changes daily is available, but for a real treat, put yourself in the chef's hands and ask for the five-, six-, or seven-course blind tasting menu.

Best Views

Toronto's natural setting on the shores of Lake Ontario is truly beautiful, though you'd be hard-pressed to see the lake from street level. Here are some of the best places to get access to that million-dollar view—including two restaurants with top-notch cuisine that would be worth going out of your way for even if they were at ground level.

CN Tower
301 Front St. W., Harbourfront, 416-868-6937 • Classic

The Draw: The world's tallest freestanding structure, isn't that enough?

The Scene: In a mere 58 seconds you've traveled in a glass elevator at a speed of 15 mph straight up to a look-out level at 1,136 feet. Could there be a better view not only of metropolitan Toronto but of the countryside beyond, and out onto Lake Ontario? Only from the Sky Pod, farther up at 1,465 feet and offering views 100 miles out, or looking straight down through the Glass Floor at a mere 1,122 feet. The mind-boggling visuals are enhanced by both casual and fine dining (at 360, the world's highest revolving restaurant). *Open daily 10 a.m.–10 p.m.* $$

Hot Tip: Even if you have other plans for dinner, stop by 360 to savor a bottle from the vast 10,000-bottle wine cellar.

Panorama
55 Bloor St. W., 51st Fl., Bloor/Yorkville, 416-967-0000 • Hot & Cool

The Draw: Consistently voted most romantic date spot—and best martinis—by locals.

The Scene: This restaurant-lounge has lots of eye appeal with its stunning view of Toronto and well beyond. In the summer, upscale locals flock to the popular rooftop patio, all decked out with teak seating, to sip from a long list of martinis and cocktails and enjoy casual nibbles. The décor is minimalist and sleek, a fine backdrop for the mesmerizing view. Yes, you'll find tourists here, but the more, the merrier! *Open daily 5 p.m.–2 a.m.* $$$$

Hot Tip: Panorama hosts over 150 special events a year, so there's something new happening every week.

Scaramouche
1 Benvenuto Pl., Uptown, 416-961-8011 • Arts & Entertainment

The Draw: Glassed-in elegance and high style atop a tower lays the city at your feet.

The Scene: For more than two decades, Scaramouche has maintained an irreproachable reputation for fine dining. But it really sets itself apart from the competition with its stellar location perched high above the city with a sparkling view of the urban skyline and the lake beyond. The banks of windows make the most of it, and you're certain to enjoy one of the finer meals in the city in this chic setting. *Open for dinner Mon.–Sat. from 5 p.m.* $$$$

Hot Tip: Ask for a window table. And save room for the desserts, made in-house and a local legend. For a leisurely meal, avoid the frenetically busy Saturday nights.

THE PERFECT TORONTO

Best — Ways to Enjoy a Sunny Day

Toronto has a relatively short summer. So when the weather's favorable, Torontonians go outside in droves. These are the places locals flock to when they want to make the most of the glorious sunshine.

The Beaches
The Beaches • Classic

The Draw: Pebbly beaches on the blue waters of Lake Ontario.

The Scene: Torontonians have saved some shoreline for urban beaches where locals can go in the summer. Beginning at the lakeside bistro near Lakeshore and Coxwell, you can explore the pebbly beaches and blue waters of the lake heading east. Past the water treatment plant, the bluffs begin; at their base are beaches that extend a mile or two along the lakeshore to Scarborough Bluffs Park.

Hot Tip: If hunger or restlessness strikes, slip up to Queen Street East to explore eclectic shops and restaurants.

High Park
1873 Bloor St. W., Parkdale • Hipster

The Draw: Stroll or take in the arts at Toronto's biggest inner-city park, covering nearly 400 acres on the city's western waterfront.

The Scene: At the western edge of the city, High Park is an urban retreat of tended greenery and trees, complete with a lake and swans. You can stroll for hours along the trails, and casual refreshments are available at a kiosk. In the summer, Torontonians even take the arts outdoors. From late June until Labor Day, you can catch Shakespeare performances. Performed in a charming pastoral amphitheatre, the productions by CanStage (www.canstage.com) are consistently well reviewed and well attended. The same venue also hosts the annual Scream in High Park, a literary reading series that runs from late June until early July (www.thescream.ca).

Hot Tip: The wealthy Toronto couple who founded High Park lived at Colborne Lodge, and today the Regency-era villa is open for viewing. (Call 416-392-6916 for times.)

Toronto Islands
Bay St. & Queen's Quay, Harbourfront, 416-392-8193 • Classic

The Draw: Beaches and a laid-back island experience in sight of the CN Tower.

The Scene: Hop aboard a ferry and switch gears. Toronto Islanders have always had a distinctly counterculture reputation. These days the Islands are home to natural and amusement parks, mellow beaches (including a clothing-optional stretch at Hanlan's Point), B&Bs, art galleries, restaurants, and curio shops, and the Islanders take pride in their lush gardens. The pace is slower here, and you can spend the day strolling, sunning, or simply admiring the Toronto skyline. $

Hot Tip: Feeling energetic? Take the ferry to Ward's Island and rent a bike or a boat at the dock. If you're feeling mellow, the Rectory Cafe is a short stroll from the pier.

Best Ways to Escape a Rainy Day

Torontonians are a hardy lot, and they love to go out no matter what the weather. But when Mother Nature's less than welcoming, the city offers myriad ways to escape.

Allan Gardens Conservatory
19 Horticultural Ave., St. Lawrence, 416-392-1111 • Hot & Cool

The Draw: When you need a touch of greenery on a gray winter's day, these classy indoor gardens will do the trick.

The Scene: Of the greenhouses, surely the most beautiful is the central one, with a high-domed cathedral roof, to showcase a vast collection of tropical and other plants. Savor what's said to be the city's best collection of amaryllis, along with gorgeous and impressive plantings of flowering hibiscus, cacti, and delicate orchids. The greenhouses are set up to mimic several different environments (from tropical to arid) to add to the variety. *Open Mon.–Fri. 9 a.m.–4 p.m.; Sat.–Sun. 10 a.m.–5 p.m.*

Hot Tip: Make for the dome for Toronto's largest collection of Madagascar pines.

Royal Ontario Museum
100 Queen's Park, Bloor/Yorkville, 416-586-5549 • Classic

The Draw: Canada's largest museum, with an enormous collection of artifacts, housed in neo-gothic splendor.

The Scene: A captivating retreat from the cold, the ROM hosts shows that are certain to entertain, surprise, and impress with stunning visuals. A rich collection of tens of thousands of artifacts make the permanent collection a feast for the senses, and world-class traveling international shows make it a museum experience like no other. *Open Mon.–Thurs. 10 a.m.–6 p.m.; Fri. 10 a.m.–9 p.m.; Sat.–Sun. 10 a.m.–6 p.m.* $$

Hot Tip: Every Friday from 4:30 p.m. to 9:30 p.m., admission to the permanent collections is free, and includes event programming such as lectures, music, dance, and films. Check the website for listings.

Tea Room
Windsor Arms Hotel, 18 St. Thomas St., Bloor/Yorkville, 416-971-9666
• Classic

The Draw: The ultimate in old-world refinement and a fashionable ode to a quite civilized tradition.

The Scene: Join the fashionable, as well as neighborhood regulars who've been coming forever to enjoy this ritual. Perch on the overstuffed upholstery as you sample a traditional afternoon tea that features a selection of loose-leaf teas, fresh scones with preserves and Devon cream, sandwiches, and petits fours. Built in 1927, the Tea Room is an officially designated historic property, and has always projected a certain upper-class charm. *High tea is served 1:30 p.m. & 3:30 p.m. daily.* $$$$

Hot Tip: Ask to be seated in one of the velvet loveseats by the fireplace for an especially cozy experience.

The Toronto Experience

Dive into the Toronto of your choice with one of four themed itineraries: *Hot & Cool* (p.70), *Arts & Entertainment* (p.98), *Hipster* (p.124), and *Classic* (p.152). Each is designed to heighten your fun-seeking experience by putting you in the right place at the right time—the best restaurants, nightlife, and attractions, and even the best days to go there. While the itineraries, each followed by detailed descriptions of our top choices, reflect our very top picks, a few additional noteworthy options are included in the listings.

Hot & Cool Toronto

Toronto's got a sleek and stylish side that's ready to show you a sizzling good time from morning till night and morning again. You'll find a wide array of buzzing A-list hot spots to choose from. Chic restaurants, exclusive nightclubs, posh hotels, and top-tier attractions are all packed into this three-day itinerary. So throw on your dancing shoes, order a martini or two, and get ready to lounge, drink, dance, and party late, late into the night!

Hot & Cool Toronto: The Itinerary

Our Hotel Choice: The internationally acclaimed **Hotel Le Germain**, because it is the very pinnacle of style and impeccable service.

Prime Time: Thurs.–Sat.

Day 1

Morning: Start your exploration of the city by hopping in a cab to Bloor Street and enjoy a light breakfast at **Futures Bakery & Cafe**, where you can sit on the heated patio year-round. If you're off to a late start and are in the mood for French crepes, head to **Crepes à Go Go** for sweet treats served with Gallic charm. Once you've fueled up, it's a short stroll west along Bloor to the chic **Bata Shoe Museum**, where you can spend the morning being educated on the history of this *all-important fashion accessory*.

Lunch: Head south to King Street near Spadina, where you can choose between the inventive small plates menu at **Lee**, the newly opened more casual venue of world-renowned chef Susur Lee, or stylish comfort food at **Brassaii**, one of Toronto's most popular destinations. Note that in good weather, Brassaii's *buzzing courtyard patio* draws crowds.

Afternoon: Head a few blocks east to the Entertainment District, to scope out Toronto's most original media empire with an afternoon tour of the **CHUM/Citytv Building** and the **Museum of Television** just next door. Watch out for big crowds of squealing teenagers if they're interviewing rock stars at CHUM's MuchMusic video station. For *libations* this afternoon, hook up with stylish downtowners at the equally stylish **Monsoon**. Or, for a lively summer patio scene, and since you'll be spending the evening in chic Yorkville, head uptown to catch the after-work crowd at the buzzing **Prego Della Piazza** on Bloor.

Dinner: It's dinner in Yorkville, so dress to the nines for an elegant meal at the warm, Mediterranean-style **Pangaea**, on Bay Street just north of Bloor. For a cozier, more romantic setting, classic Italian cuisine, and the odd celebrity sighting, the sophisticated Euro-chic **Sotto Sotto Trattoria** on Avenue Road always draws crowds. If you're more in the mood for *champagne and caviar*, enjoy an over-the-top evening at the ultra-posh **Opus**, just a few blocks west of Avenue Road.

Nighttime: Yorkville is lined with stylish nightclubs these days, and those listed here are among the most glittering. **Club 22** in the historic Windsor Arms Hotel has live music starting at 9 p.m. and its own private cigar lounge. You'll find lots of flashy Latin-style dancing on offer at **BaBaLu's**, or for a really immaculate lounge experience, head to **Flow Restaurant + Lounge**, known for drawing a polished and festive crowd of New Yorkville types looking for late-night fun. To check out the hot gay (but hetero-friendly) club scene, hop in a cab to the stylish **Lüb Lounge**. Still looking to party after midnight? The sparkling **Lobby** is just getting started. Or, if hunger strikes, join the other *late-night revelers* for elegant French tapas-style small bites at **Michelle's Brasserie**.

Day 2

Morning: Everyone who comes to Toronto must stroll up Yonge Street—the longest street in the world—at least once, so make your way toward Bloor and settle in at the **Casa Cafe**. Have a light breakfast and *leisurely coffee* as you contemplate the morning's options. Walk to Chinatown to visit the colorful **Textile Museum of Canada**—and don't forget to hit the gift shop on the way out. If the weather's fine and you're up for a challenging round of golf, it's about a half hour's drive north to Maple, where the **Eagles Nest Golf Club** is located.

Lunch: Stay downtown and have lunch in the Financial District. **Bistro 990** draws an attractive crowd of Bay Street financial types (and occasionally a celeb or two) who come for the fine *French cuisine*. If that doesn't tempt you, **Oro**, a gorgeous restaurant in the same neighborhood, serves inventive continental-based fusion cuisine.

Afternoon: Stroll back east along King toward Bay Street to check out the **Toronto Stock Exchange Media Centre** (it's the continent's third-largest stock exchange) and take in the fast pace of the Financial District. A little farther east in the **King Street East Furniture District**, you'll find more shopping opps, specializing in *designer furniture stores*—you'll come upon no less than a dozen along the way. By late afternoon, it's high time you relax with a drink in hand. Retrace your steps on King to the area dubbed Clubland, and join the fashionable downtowners at the sleek **Indian Motorcycle Cafe & Lounge**. If a contemporary, yet more sumptuous, experience strikes your fancy, it's only a few blocks further to the aptly named **Sen5es Restaurant & Lounge**.

Dinner: It's your choice of deluxe ethnic fare this evening. **Xacutti**, one of the city's most talked-about *hot spots*, offers a unique and inventive menu of Indian fusion in a minimalist setting in the newly chic Little Italy. Featuring elegant Pan-Asian food from a top chef, **Susur** is highly rated and internationally recognized, though you'd better reserve well in advance. Back in Clubland, **Banzai Sushi** is a slick treat for fans of both Japanese cuisine and culture.

Nighttime: Pick your flavor, or if you're feeling especially hardy, sample them all. In Clubland, **Budo Liquid Theatre**'s rooftop patio is always hopping when the weather's good. A little farther west, the **C-Lounge** offers posh lounging and a poolside deck. For energetic twenty- and thirty-somethings, the **Afterlife Nightclub** has the hottest Friday night in town. **5ive Nightclub** is a *hot dance emporium*, gay but straight-friendly, if you're up for a wild and late night of partying. After midnight, join the other trendsetters for martinis that change monthly at **2 Cats Cocktail Lounge**, or join the fashionable scene at **West Lounge**.

Day 3

Morning: After a late night of clubbing, recover in gracious comfort at **Sen5es Bakery & Cafe** with a selection of divine baked goods and a cappuccino. Then head off for a stroll in climate-controlled comfort and take in the lush greenery at the serene **Allan Gardens Conservatory**, a few blocks east of Yonge on Jarvis. If some over-the-top *pampering* sounds more like your cup of tea, the **Pantages Anti-Aging & Longevity Spa** is just a walk away on Victoria Street. If gardens or spa pampering don't tempt you, take a **SkyDome Tour** of the huge sports and entertainment complex with the world's first fully retractable roof (currently called the Rogers Centre).

Lunch: For lunch, head back north to Bloor, then up a short block north on Avenue Road to Yorkville for *gourmet sushi* at the popular **Sushi Inn**. Or, to prepare for the afternoon's spending spree, make your way a little farther east on Bloor to high-end retailer Holt Renfrew. Once inside this posh department store, try not to be distracted by the gorgeous designer wares on display, and take the elevator to the second floor to the bright white **Holt's Cafe** for lunch with a very fashionable crowd.

Afternoon: Take that disposable income and spread it over the **Yorkville Shopping District**. You'll find countless shopping opportunities awaiting you, from Holt Renfrew to the designer boutiques that line both sides of Bloor from Yonge Street to Avenue Road. A block north, Hazelton Lanes offers a wide range of upscale wares. Take the time to stroll the cobbled streets of Yorkville, where you'll find art galleries and antique shops. You'll likely be in need of a refreshing pause before dinner. Sample the superb martinis and savor *the stunning view* at **Panorama**, located on the 51st floor of the Manulife Centre. Alternatively, you'll be downtown for the evening, so for a perfect spot to have a drink and to get the evening started, **Rain** offers minimalist style in a restaurant with a lounge feel and has a fine people-watching bar that's lit from within.

Dinner: Three stylish restaurants await you this evening, depending on your mood. Head to the *perennially buzzing* **Coco Lezzone Grill and Porto Bar** in Little Italy if you feel like enjoying Mediterranean cuisine among fashionistas. The quite new and instantly popular **Crush Wine Bar** offers refined French dining in an elegant room with soaring ceilings. Or make your way to the sleek and sultry **Luce** for Italian creations in a refined atmosphere among the beautiful people.

Nighttime: Tonight offers a variety of clubbing options in the aptly named Entertainment District. **YYZ Restaurant & Wine Bar** is a *super-sleek haunt* for the stylish cocktail set. Or join the crowds at **Therapy Ultra Lounge** and order a Dr. Phil martini. If the weather's fine, you'll want to make haste and head to the lake for a stunning view from close up: dress up and get thee to the patio at the see-and-be-seen **Sky Bar**.

After midnight, the **Ultra Supper Club** turns into *a swank dance party*, and if you're hungry after that, **Room Service/Room 471** caters to posh late-night clubbers with an upscale Italian menu. For the boys, **Fly Nightclub** pumps out the beats until breakfast time.

> **Morning After:** Head to the sunny celeb-magnet **Sassafraz Cafe** in Yorkville, where a gourmet brunch is served up with live jazz—but book ahead or come early to get a table.

Hot & Cool Toronto: The Hotels

Four Seasons Hotel Toronto
21 Avenue Rd. (Cumberland St.), Bloor/Yorkville,
416-964-0411 / 800-819-5053, www.fourseasons.com/toronto

From the outside, it looks like just another concrete downtown high-rise, but within, it's a world of posh pampering with a staff renowned for setting new standards in service. Everyone in town knows that the concierge at the Four Seasons can get you whatever you need, accustomed as they are to catering to a well-heeled clientele heavy on rock stars and Hollywood royalty. Expect no less than the best—the finest linens, most sumptuous furnishings, exquisite attention to detail. Spacious suites cocoon guests in old-world luxury, while the Yorkville Suites, with lake or city views, are individually furnished and include original works of art. Superior rooms are located on the corners of the building and offer a walk-out balcony and panoramic city views. Amenities include a heated indoor-outdoor pool with a sun deck and 24-hour fitness facilities with state-of-the-art equipment and spa services. The highly rated Truffles, one of Toronto's top destination restaurants, and the fashionable restaurant Avenue, are both here. Conveniently located in the heart of Yorkville, this is the perfect place to stay if you're in town for the many shopping opportunities. $$$$

Hotel Le Germain
30 Mercer St. (Blue Jays Way), Entertainment District,
416-345-4500 / 866-345-9500, www.germaintoronto.com

Hotel Le Germain opened to much fanfare in 2003, and has largely lived up to its stellar reputation. High-end design and an equally high standard of service characterize Toronto's first boutique hotel. The feel is contemporary but warm, with lots of wood accents and textural features, like thick sculptural drapery. All of it serves as a perfect backdrop for the impeccably dressed guests, composed of supermodels, celebrities, and other chic, discerning travelers. Standard rooms come with down-filled duvets, Frette linens, and Aveda toiletries. Ask for a spacious deluxe king room with a lake view. The library just off the lobby boasts a cozy open-hearth fire, a cappuccino bar, and high-speed Internet access, and there are state-of-the-art fitness facilities and a massage room on site. Reserve well in advance for the two-story apartment suite with dining area, fireplace, and terrace. One of Toronto's best Italian restaurants, Luce, adjoins the lobby. $$$$

Pantages Hotel Suites
200 Victoria St. (Shuter St.), Downtown/Yonge,
416-362-1777 / 866-852-1777, www.pantageshotel.com

The latest addition to Toronto's new but increasingly competitive boutique hotel market, the Pantages has its own unique approach to contemporary luxury. Every one of the 111 rooms here is a suite, and each features Egyptian linens, a rain forest showerhead and flat-screen television, and an attractive European kitchen, complete with a wide range of gourmet snacks. Deluxe suites are all different, and some are up to 530 square feet in area, and are decorated in contemporary style with warm neutral colors and dark woods. The guiding principle of design here is to ensure the traveler's well being and to promote a healthy lifestyle. Quartz crystals are left on the pillow in lieu of chocolate. The Serenity floor offers a completely unique experience with floors scented to release the fresh aroma of the ocean. Inspired by a zen lifestyle, the 14 rooms on this floor feature Jacuzzi tubs, air purifiers, water fountains, yoga mats, and a 24-hour in-room meditation channel. There are top-notch fitness facilities, and a 9,000-square-foot spa complete with water bar. This is an impressive contemporary renovation of what was formerly a historic theater, where the refined upscale traveler can enjoy an astonishingly serene hotel experience in the heart of the city. $$$$

Windsor Arms Hotel
18 St. Thomas St. (Bloor St.), Bloor/Yorkville, 416-971-9666,
www.windsorarmshotel.com

From the moment it threw open its doors a century ago, this classy haunt for the rich and famous has never been just a place to sleep, but also a chic spot to see and be seen. Sweeping grandeur greets you at the entrance—from the lobby to the gallery level, all done in neutrals and dark wood trim. You may share your stay with the stars, who love the Old World elegance that is matched with modern standards of excellence (it boasts the highest staff-to-guest ratio in Canada). Twenty-four luxury suites and two luxury rooms are available, tastefully furnished and outfitted with fine Frette linens, state-of-the-art sound systems, Jacuzzi tubs, and high-speed Internet access. The 1,500-square-foot Sultan Suites feature a king-size bed, two bathrooms, and a fireplace in the den, but ask for the one with a second fireplace in the bathroom for the ultimate in luxury. Expect celebrity-level pampering, including 24-hour butler service and room service—even a Bentley at your disposal as a limousine. Amenities include a fine spa featuring a wide range of services and a pool, as well as stylish dining and lounging options in the Courtyard Cafe, Club 22, and the Tea Room. $$$$

Hot & Cool Toronto: The Restaurants

Banzai Sushi
134 Peter St. (Richmond St.), Entertainment District, 416-341-0404, www.banzaisushi.ca
Best Asian Restaurants

Newly opened in late 2004 in the Entertainment District, Banzai aims to bring a combination of high-end Japanese cuisine and equally high style to the club-restaurant mix. Despite the fierce competition in the neighborhood, Banzai does manage to offer something fresh. The dining area in the back offers comfortable seating for a menu of Japanese fare that looks as good as it tastes. After dining, the club crowd retires to the shiny Lucite bar that heats up toward the end of the evening with its own scene of fashionable tipplers. Cocktails, which you can select from a drink list that features a nice selection of sake, are mixed up by servers as well turned-out as the clientele. *Open daily for dinner 5 p.m.–2 a.m. $$$*

Bistro 990
990 Bay St. (St. Joseph St.), Financial District, 416-921-9990

With impeccable style and service, the perennially popular Bistro 990 serves up Provençal-style bistro cuisine to hungry Hollywood types, savvy Financial District denizens, and others in the know. A big striped awning lends a continental flavor to this bustling celebrity-studded bistro, and low ceilings and yellow stucco contribute to the upscale European feel of the place. Offerings include succulent grilled flank steak in bordelaise sauce, corn-crusted sea bass, and desserts baked on the premises. *Open for lunch Mon.–Fri. noon 3 p.m.; dinner daily 5:30–11 p.m.; bar open daily until 1 a.m. $$$$*

Brassaii
461 King St. W. (Spadina Ave.), Entertainment District, 416-598-4730, www.brassaii.com

Brassaii is all about style, delivered with an artistic twist. You enter through a wrought-iron gate into a courtyard patio that's a summer favorite and where you'll share your meal with life-sized metal sculptures of hounds. Set back from the street, the dining rooms beyond are handsome and modern, filled with natural light from large black-framed windows that look out to the courtyard. The young and fashionable love the dining room's long leather banquettes, filling them from breakfast through dinner. After supper, the lounge area, appointed with blue carpets, brick walls painted white, and black leather couches, heats up with an attractive crowd. Add a brushed-stainless bar, and the corner of King and Spadina is suddenly a mecca of cool for any meal of the day. Breakfast features fresh fare like lemon blueberry pancakes, while dinner is French bistro meets comfort food with classics like roast chicken and mashed potatoes. *Open for breakfast, lunch, and dinner Mon.–Fri. 7 a.m.–midnight; open for dinner Sat. 5 p.m.–midnight.* $$$

Casa Cafe
828 Yonge St. (Bloor St.), Bloor/Yorkville, 416-923-3810

Casa Cafe is a welcome bubble of calm. Brick walls punctuated with the work of local artists and a relaxed cafe ambience are complemented by gourmet coffees and a light menu of baked goods, salads, sandwiches, and other treats made on the premises. This is simply the perfect oasis in which to grab a bite, linger over latte, or just regroup after a busy morning shopping in Yorkville. *Open for breakfast, lunch, and dinner Mon.–Fri. 8 a.m.–9 p.m.; Sat. 10 a.m.–10 p.m.; Sun. 10 a.m.–5 p.m.* $$

Coco Lezzone Grill and Porto Bar
602 College St. W. (Clinton St.), Little Italy, 416-535-1489, www.cocolezzone.ca
Best Always-Hot Restaurants

It's always Fashion Week at Coco, favorite haunt of celebs like Teri Hatcher and U2's Edge, as well as Prada-clad locals and a few tourists too. The style is grand—columns and arches, and majestic hanging light fixtures contrasted by dark woods and rich red drapes. A menu of Italian classics, heavy on pasta and risotto, with mains of lamb, veal, Black Angus strip loin, and a good quotient of fresh seafood, is prepared with a level of artistry that fits the surroundings. The dinner rush is busy, with the noise levels growing as the night goes on. This is Toronto's high-end scene at its best, so come early for a drink at the bar to check out the stylish crowd, and wear your best so you can feel like a star yourself. *Open daily for dinner 4 p.m.–2 a.m.* $$$

Crepes à Go Go
244 Bloor St. W. (Admiral St.), Bloor/Yorkville, 416-922-6765

If hunger pangs can wait till mid-morning, Crepes à Go Go will satisfy with baguettes, patisseries, and, of course, delectable crepes offered both in the form of sweet desserts and heartier savory meals. Take-out is extremely popular, and there are only four tables from which to savor the French cafe atmosphere, purportedly so authentic it's a favorite with displaced Montrealers. At least one visit is a must for francophiles and anyone with a hankering for tantalizing patisserie treats. *Open for brunch, lunch, and dinner Tues.–Sat. 10:30 a.m.–8 p.m.; Sun. 9:30 a.m.–5 p.m.* $$

Crush Wine Bar

455 King St. W. (Spadina Ave.), Entertainment District, 416-977-1234, www.crushwinebar.com

A big, airy dining room awash in natural light gives this popular wine bar a sophisticated look. Crush attracts a well-groomed and well-heeled crowd of locals and visiting celebs in the know, and is said to be a favorite haunt of internationally acclaimed author Margaret Atwood. High-backed chairs, exposed brick, and lots of wooden accents warm the room. An upscale French bistro menu offers the likes of vichyssoise and poached salmon—all beautifully presented. Of course the wine list is extensive, and the staff both attentive and knowledgeable. Reservations are always recommended, and you may want to come early to sip a glass or two at the room-length bar before settling in for your meal. *Open for lunch and dinner Mon.–Fri. 11:30 a.m.–10:30 p.m.; dinner Sat. 5 p.m.–10:30 p.m.* $$$

Futures Bakery & Cafe

483 Bloor St. W. (Bathurst St.), Bloor/Yorkville, 416-922-5875

Located right in the heart of Yorkville, this is the place to gear up for some serious shopping. Open 24 hours a day and featuring a protected all-season patio, Futures Bakery & Cafe on Bloor is a trendy and popular spot at any hour of the day. Its divine breads are served at many of Toronto's best restaurants, and here in a standard breakfast and light cafe menu. Genuinely friendly service, the leisurely pace, and patio seating make it the perfect place for people-watching, very-late-night snacking, or getting a fresh and flavorful start to the day. *Open daily 24 hrs.* $

Holt's Cafe

50 Bloor St. W. (Bay St.), Bloor/Yorkville, 416-922-2223, www.holtrenfrew.com

After you've waded through several million dollars worth of designer clothing in Holt Renfrew, Holt's Cafe provides a welcome respite from the excesses of fashion. All dressed up in whites with shiny surfaces and bright lights with a wide bank of windows overlooking Yorkville, the Cafe sports a starkly minimalist look. A dauntingly fashionable set lunches on soup and salad, and Holt's specialty, tartines. These open-faced sandwiches are made with bread imported from the Poilâne bakery in Paris three times weekly. Perfect for an elegant bite between shopping sprees, Holt's is a favorite with fashionistas of all ages. *Open for lunch and dinner Mon.–Wed. 10 a.m.–6 p.m.; Thurs.–Sat. 10 a.m.–8 p.m.; Sun. noon–6 p.m.* $$$$

Indian Motorcycle Cafe & Lounge
355 King St. W. (John St.), Entertainment District, 416-593-6996

See Hot & Cool Nightlife, p. 88 for description.
Open daily for lunch, dinner, and cocktails 11:30 a.m.–2 a.m. $$

Lee
603 King St. W. (Bathurst St.), Entertainment District, 416-504-7867
Best Trendy Restaurants

Lee is the other brainchild of superstar chef Susur Lee, located next door to his ultra–high-end restaurant, Susur. With Lee, the master lets down his hair just a little; the ambience is still upscale, but it's a bit funkier and decorated in warmer colors. Pink Lucite tables contrast-copper screens and warm orange walls, all of it visible from the street through a plate-glass window. Lee's reputation in Toronto is stellar, and his fans and trendsetters have followed him to the once-dreary stretch of King Street that now houses this almost constantly buzzing dining room. The fusion menu takes inspiration from the continental side and is priced to bring his creations to the masses. A menu based around small plates includes sensations such as caramelized cod and rich coconut soup with lime and mint. *Open for lunch Mon.–Sat. noon–2:30 p.m.; dinner Mon.–Sat. 6–10 p.m.* $$

Luce
Hotel Le Germain, 30 Mercer St. (Blue Jays Way), Entertainment District, 416-599-5823, www.germaintoronto.com

Housed in the chic Hotel Le Germain, Luce offers style and substance to the VIP clientele that flocks here. You'll find old-school regional Italian cooking gone high concept, served artfully in appropriately cosmopolitan surroundings. The mood is quiet in an exquisitely refined way. Luce opened with little fanfare, gradually building a solid clientele of foodies and upscale locals, and often-glamorous hotel guests. Small plates might feature inventions like sautéed ravioli with espresso chestnut, and mains include crunchy glazed quail, guinea fowl, and cod three ways, all complemented by an almost exclusively Italian wine list. *Open daily for dinner 5:30–10:30 p.m.* $$$$

Michelle's Brasserie
162 Cumberland Ave. (Yorkville Ave.), Bloor/Yorkville, 416-944-1504, www.labrasserie.ca

French cuisine goes country at Michelle's, which serves hungry shoppers and upscale trendsetters French classics with a twist. Art Nouveau wrought ironwork adds to the brasserie charm. At the handsome marble bar is an extensive beer list with brews from Germany, Belgium, and France, as well as various Canadian provinces. With the kitchen open until closing at 2 a.m., you'll find late-night Yorkville clubbers snacking on lobster and mussels, steak, prime rib, sandwiches, and tapas-style small plates. The heated garden patio is open year-round. *Open for lunch and dinner Tues.–Sat. 11:30 a.m.–11 p.m.; bar (late-night menu available Thurs.–Sat.) open until 2 a.m.* $$

Monsoon
100 Simcoe St. (Peter St.), Entertainment District, 416-979-7172, www.monsoonrestaurant.ca
Best Trendy Restaurants

Monsoon glows with a hot tropical feel. Join the fashionable downtown crowds with a drink in the cozy lounge area, which is dominated by a long wooden bar lined with glasses and gleaming bottles. Sink into the black leather upholstery and enjoy the busy happy-hour ambience of this popular hot spot before heading in for dinner. The dining room is elegantly understated in white linens and black lacquer chairs and features a Pan-Asian menu that sparkles with flavorful creativity as evidenced by offerings like crab cakes with cucumber namasa and coconut aioli. *Open for lunch Mon.–Fri. 11:30 a.m.–2:30 p.m.; for dinner Mon.–Sat. from 5 p.m.* $$$$

Opus
37 Prince Arthur Ave. (St. George St.), Bloor/Yorkville, 416-921-3105, www.opusrestaurant.com
Best Fine Dining

A small, sleek, curved bar greets you upon entering Opus off a leafy Yorkville street. It's charming, but a mere prelude to the main attraction here—a seriously sexy dining room. It's all about understated Manhattan-style glamour. Taupe walls contrast with black leather seating and white linens, and the most distinctive feature is the large columns covered over in gleaming wood. Fellow diners are equal parts discerning, fashionable, and well heeled, and the ambience is all grown-up sophistication. The menu features fine French-based fusion cuisine that changes regularly and includes high-end delicacies. Splurge and order the caviar and champagne—this is definitely the best place to do it. *Open daily for dinner 5:30–11:30 p.m.* $$$$

Oro
45 Elm St. (Bay St.), Financial District, 416-597-0155, www.ororestaurant.com

A happy marriage of style and substance, Oro takes classical cooking to new heights with a contemporary approach and a flair for visuals both on and off the plate. Stylish downtowners and Bay Street heavies alike flock to this local favorite for the ever-changing cuisine, with influences ranging from hearty Italian to exotic Moroccan, complemented by a serious wine list. In addition to the warm, spacious main dining room, Oro offers a number of private rooms for parties or meetings. *Open for lunch Mon.–Fri. noon–2:30 p.m.; dinner Mon.–Sat. 5:30–10:30 p.m.* $$$

Pangaea

1221 Bay St. N. (Bloor St.), Bloor/Yorkville, 416-920-2323, www.pangaearestaurant.com
Best Fine Dining

A sophisticated crowd regularly turns out to enjoy the stylish, civilized experience at this popular spot. Steps from the frantic bustle of Bay and Bloor, Pangaea is an airy space in warm Mediterranean hues of gold and blue, where tiny lights twinkle from a high ceiling of distressed white metal onto light wood floors. While the décor is all about inviting warmth, it's the excellence of the food that keeps this upscale eatery buzzing with stylish Yorkville shoppers in the afternoon and an uptown crowd at the dinner hour. Well reviewed in local and national media, the Mediterranean-inspired menu is heavy on seafood and pastas, along with regional exotica like caribou. *Open for lunch and dinner Mon.–Sat. 11:30 a.m.–11:30 p.m.* $$$$

Panorama

55 Bloor St. W., 51st Fl. (Bay St.), Bloor/Yorkville, 416-967-0000, www.panoramalounge.com
Best Views

See Hot & Cool Nightlife, p. 90 for description.
Open daily 5 p.m.–2 a.m. $$$$

Prego Della Piazza

150 Bloor St. W. (Avenue Rd.), Bloor/Yorkville, 416-920-9900

See Hot & Cool Nightlife, p. 90 for description.
Open daily for lunch noon–3 p.m.; dinner 5–11 p.m. $$$$

Rain

19 Mercer St. (Blue Jays Way), Entertainment District, 416-599-7246
Best Martinis

See Hot & Cool Nightlife, p. 91, for description.
Open Tues.–Sat. 5:30–11 p.m. $$$$

Room Service/Room 471
471 Richmond St. W. (McDougall St.), Entertainment District, 416-703-6239, www.room471.com
Best Late-Night Eats

Room 471's raison d'être is to serve as a late-night supper club for the hungry denizens of Clubland and beyond. The kitchen opens at 10 p.m. to serve up Italian classics from the people who've been dishing them up at Sotto Sotto Trattoria for decades. The elaborate menu of salads and antipasti includes delicacies like carpaccio beef and salmone affumicat. The place to see and be seen after a full night of partying, it's packed after midnight with stylish revelers looking for a sophisticated late-night bite. *Open Thurs.–Sun. 10 p.m.–5 a.m.* $$$

Sassafraz Cafe
100 Cumberland St. (Bellair St.), Bloor/Yorkville, 416-964-2222, www.sassafraz.ca
Best Brunches

Busy day and night, Sassafraz has long seduced local and international fans with its sunny décor and menu. Photos of the many celebs who've been here line the bright dining room. For Canadiana, try the game duo of roasted double venison chops and grilled bison tenderloin. Brunch comes with live jazz, and crowds flock here for gourmet offerings like huevos rancheros and vodka-smoked salmon. Nestled in an old-fashioned home, it becomes a VIP mecca during the Toronto Film Festival. *Open for lunch Mon.–Fri. 11:30 a.m.–2 a.m.; Sat. & Sun. brunch 11 a.m.–4 p.m., dinner 5 p.m.–2 a.m.* $$$$

Sen5es Bakery & Cafe
The SoHo Metropolitan, 318 Wellington St. W. (Blue Jays Way), Entertainment District, 416-935-0400, www.senses.ca

Exquisite pastries, sublime chocolates, and an original lunch menu replete with fresh and delicate flavors all served in an elegant room at a chic downtown location make Sen5es a popular destination. Stylish downtowners welcomed the move of Sen5es from its longtime location on Bloor to the busy Entertainment District in the ultra-luxe SoHo Metropolitan condo and boutique hotel complex, and fill it from morning until just before the supper hour. Along with the sweets, the menu features quiche with a feather-light pastry, seared tuna, greens, decoratively plated and served by black-clad servers with a smile. *Open for breakfast and lunch daily 8 a.m.–4 p.m.* $$$

Sen5es Restaurant & Lounge
The SoHo Metropolitan, 318 Wellington St. W. (Blue Jays Way), Entertainment District, 416-935-0400, www.senses.ca
Best Romantic Rendezvous

Sen5es is certainly an apt name for this handsome establishment, where all of your senses are sure to be engaged before the evening is over. The dining room is elegant and muted, and retains the warm glow of the adjoining lounge area. South American–born executive chef Claudio Aprile inspects every dish before it leaves the open kitchen that allows anticipating diners and foodie fans to watch his sous chefs at work. The menu of continental fusion changes based on seasonally fresh ingredients, and is complemented by an extensive wine list. With the inviting lounge just steps away, consider extending your experience with an aperitif or a nightcap. *Restaurant open for dinner Wed.–Sun. 6–10 p.m.; bar and bistro open daily 4 p.m.–1 a.m.* $$$$

Sotto Sotto Trattoria
116A Avenue Rd. (Tranby St.), Bloor/Yorkville, 416-962-0011, www.sottosotto.ca

This romantic subterranean hideaway is a slice of authentic Italy in Yorkville. As well known to the celebrity circuit as to discerning locals, Sotto is located steps below street level, in a warm labyrinthine dining room of ochres accented by wood, stone walls balanced by crisp white linens. Though its reputation makes Sotto Sotto a perennial hot spot for a well-dressed Euro-chic crowd, plenty of quiet nooks and intimate lighting make this the perfect retreat for a romantic tête à tête as well. The menu includes no fewer than 15 pasta entrées, including spaghetti al cartocio with shrimp, king crab, scallops, calamari, and mussels. Other options include risotto, seafood, meats, and a sumptuous dessert menu. The staff are as authentically Italian as the food here, and obviously used to catering to their famous clientele—they're warm, friendly, and efficient. *Open for dinner Sun.–Thurs. 5:30–11 p.m.; Fri.–Sat. 5 p.m.–midnight.* $$$$

Sushi Inn
120 Cumberland St. (Hazelton Ave.), Bloor/Yorkville, 416-923-9992

One of many glass-fronted boutiques and restaurants on this block of Cumberland Avenue, the Sushi Inn can be distinguished from the rest by the long lines of stylish clientele waiting for take-out at this Japanese boîte. The dizzying variety of sushi and sashimi makes it hard to choose from the vast menu, but your friendly and efficient servers can make the experience a pleasure. Despite the relatively unassuming décor, you'll find the place packed through the lunch hour and well into dinner on both floors. Superlative dining and upscale people-watching set a nice Yorkville tone and keep the crowds coming. *Open for lunch and dinner Sun.–Thurs. 11:30 a.m.–11:30 p.m.; Fri.–Sat. 11:30 a.m.–midnight.* $$$

Susur
601 King St. W. (Bathurst St.), Entertainment District, 416-603-2205, www.susur.com
Best Always-Hot Restaurants

Susur Lee, a true fusion superstar, is one of the world's premier chefs today. A visit to Susur is sure to convince you that the master is at the top of his game. The neutral setting is a calming backdrop for a meal that is high drama from start to finish. The dining room is consistently packed with disciples waiting for his exquisite and elaborate culinary and visual creations, like habanero-stuffed polenta croquette and fava beans in Thai bisque, or rib-eye of bison in black truffle sauce. It's so decadently flavorful, so artistically presented, it can almost create sensory overload. For a complete experience, place yourself in the chef's hands and order a tasting menu you'll never forget. Susur is one of the city's most talked-about restaurants, so reserve as soon as you know you're coming to town. *Open Mon.–Sat. 6–10 p.m.* $$$$

Ultra Supper Club
314 Queen St. W. (Soho St.), Entertainment District, 416-263-0330
Best Late-Night Hangouts

See Hot & Cool Nightlife, p. 92 for description.
Open Mon.–Wed. 5:30 p.m.–midnight; Thurs.–Sat. 5:30 p.m.–2 a.m. $$$

Xacutti
503 College St. W. (Palmerston St.), Little Italy, 416-323-3957
Best Always-Hot Restaurants

One of the city's hottest restaurants, Xacutti made a name for itself from the moment it opened even in the intensely competitive dining scene of Little Italy. With an innovative menu of Indian fusion delicacies, served in a minimalist, almost stark setting, it has set a new standard for excellence that keeps A-listers coming in droves. In taking classical Indian cooking and adapting it to local and seasonal ingredients, chef Brad Moore opens a world of possibilities, with menu offerings like rabbit on chilied missi roti (a flatbread) or lamb rack with spiced masala potatoes. The entire experience is flawlessly polished. *Open for dinner Mon.–Fri. 6:30 p.m.–1 a.m.; for lunch and dinner Sat. 10:30 a.m.–2 a.m.; Sun. brunch 10:30 a.m.–3 p.m.* $$$$

Hot & Cool Toronto: The Nightlife

Afterlife Nightclub
250 Adelaide St. W. (Duncan St.), Entertainment District, 416-593-6126, www.afterlifenightclub.com
Best Dance Clubs

This is one of Toronto's perennial Friday-night hot spots, where the club kids in their twenties come for loud, crowded, raucous fun. The Afterlife has three stylish floors to offer its crowd of partiers, all here to dance the night away and lounge on the fashionable couches. Pale neon-blue lighting glows in the dimly lit danceteria as the dance floor heats up to house, R&B, and electronica, and bartenders mix up their potions. This is a guaranteed party atmosphere, and quite a happening meet market. There's no dress code, but call ahead to get on the guest list and escape those long lines. *Open Fri.–Sat. 10 p.m.–3 a.m.* $$

BaBaLu's
136 Yorkville Ave. (Hazelton Ave.), Bloor/Yorkville, 416-515-0587
Best Dance Clubs

Dress to impress, and you'll have a better chance of getting into this hot Latin dance club. Beyond the velvet rope, a high-fashion crowd of VIPs, including visiting Hollywood royalty, order bottles of expensive champagne. Mirrored walls, dim lighting, and throbbing Latin rhythms make for a very sexy dance floor. BaBaLu's really heats up after 11 p.m., so come early or be prepared to wait in line to mingle with that sexy urban crowd. *Open Wed.–Sun. 9 p.m.–3 a.m.* $$$

Budo Liquid Theatre
137 Peter St. (Queen St. W.), Entertainment District, 416-593-1550, www.budolt.com
Best Sexy Lounges

Amid the frenetic pace of Clubland at night, Budo Liquid Theatre offers a more calming, zen-inspired lounge vibe. Ultra-fashionable clubbers pack the place, perching on the comfy couches. A waterfall soothes with its trickling sounds and sparkling visuals, and warm spotlighting glows against the wooden fixtures. There are more private VIP areas on each of the two floors inside, so be sure to ask about bottle service and the fine champagnes on offer. It's the ultimate in see-and-be-seen lounging, and known as a place to meet like-minded, equally fabulous folk. Summers, the rooftop patio, boasting a large Buddha head and candlelight, opens up and comes alive with an elegant crowd. People come primarily for the fabulous drinks and the sexy ambience, but note that there is a dining area serving Pan-Asian cuisine. *Open Thurs.–Sat. 9:30 p.m.–3 a.m.* $$

C-Lounge
456 Wellington St. W. (Draper St.), Entertainment District, 416-260-9393, www.libertygroup.com
Best Meet Markets

For swank clubbing at its finest, the C-Lounge is a hot spot for the 25-and-over club crowd. From the valet parking to Aveda hair and makeup artists on call in the ladies' room, C-Lounge sweats the details, and the good-looking and well-dressed crowd laps it up. Sheer curtains divide a room that glows with warm lighting. A polished crowd reclines on leather couches. Summer brings a courtyard patio with a pool, drapery, and potted trees on the deck, and Lounge Thursdays feature complementary hors d'oeuvres and a DJ from 5 to 9 p.m. On Fridays and Saturdays, the place really heats up after 10 p.m. There's a dress code, so come prepared to pass the door staff's inspection. Call ahead to ask about a VIP wristband for access to all areas. *Open Wed. 10 p.m.–1 a.m.; Thurs. 9 p.m.–2 a.m.; Fri.–Sat. 10 p.m.–2 a.m.* $$$

Club 22
Windsor Arms Hotel, 18 St. Thomas St. (Bloor St.), Bloor/Yorkville, 416-971-9666, www.windsorarmshotel.com
Best Cigar Lounges

Tucked away in the Windsor Arms Hotel, this gem provides a sophisticated respite from the hustle and bustle of Yorkville. Supermodel types perch on the white leather stools at the polished bar, and well-heeled loungers groove to live piano through the cocktail hour. Then it's on to live bands or DJs in the evening. This is chic clubbing at its best—not for those looking for a raucous party. Posh patrons enjoy private humidor lockers in the Cigar Lounge, along with a fine selection of cognacs, ports, and scotches. *Open as club and lounge Wed.–Sat. 5 p.m.–2 a.m.* $$

5ive Nightclub
5 St. Joseph St. (Yonge St.), Downtown/Yonge, 416-964-8685, www.5ivenightclub.com
Best Gay Dance Clubs

With throbbing music and a sexy staff, this is Gay Village clubbing at its best. But in a very Toronto twist, you don't have to be one of the boys to enjoy this straight-friendly club. 5ive aims to give you the ultimate dance-club experience, so expect an event every night of the week, including DJs, hunky dancers, fashion shows, and more, along with the best sound systems, light shows, and a massive crowd of revelers ready to dance until the wee hours. On Saturday nights, it's quite the scene, so be sure to come early or be prepared to wait in line. *Open Wed.–Sat. 10 p.m.–3 a.m.* $$$

Flow Restaurant + Lounge
133 Yorkville Ave. (Hazelton Ave.), Bloor/Yorkville, 416-925-2143, www.flowrestaurant.com
Best Martinis

A restaurant-lounge oozing high style and good taste, Flow is the ultimate Yorkville haunt. The design is set by clean lines and warm earth tones of brown and taupe, spiced up with colored murals and striped upholstery. The sophisticated lounge is a perennial hot spot teeming with a young but polished A-list crowd. Flow is equally popular as a restaurant with a menu featuring an eclectic range of dishes, from pasta to Pan-Asian fusion to an excellent osso bucco. *Open Mon. 11:30 a.m.–10:30 p.m.; Tues.–Wed. 11:30 a.m.–11 p.m.; Thurs.–Fri. 11:30 a.m.–2 a.m.; Sat. 5 p.m.–2 a.m.*

Fly Nightclub
8 Gloucester St. (Yonge St.), Gay Village, 416-410-5426, www.flynightclub.com
Best Gay Dance Clubs

Fly is arguably Toronto's premier gay-male dance cub, where the beats are fast and furious and the staff is super hot. It's a hot spot for visiting Hollywood royalty, and the place where the dance club scenes in *Queer as Folk* are filmed. Three floors of style await your pleasure, with quieter conversation-friendly alcoves tucked around the dance floors that vibrate with good-looking revelers. The crowd is mixed but welcoming and straight-friendly. Open Saturday nights until 7 a.m. the following morning, it's the place to go when you literally want to dance the night away. *Open Fri. 10 p.m.–3 a.m.; Sat. 10 p.m.–7 a.m.* $$

Indian Motorcycle Cafe & Lounge
355 King St. W. (John St.), Entertainment District, 416-593-6996

Forget any notions of hard-rock motorcycle hangouts—this one's slick, modern, and strictly upscale. A small shop with Indian Motorcycle memorabilia and machines opens into a vast room of polished blond-wood floors accented with black leather furniture, flickering candles, chrome fixtures, and soaring windows. A small sparkling bar gives way to a dining room on the first floor, then it's up the central see-and-be-seen staircase to the lounge. A casual menu of pasta, pizza, meat, and fish staples is surprisingly well done, all the ingredients fresh and flavorful and served piping hot by attractive staff dressed in black. This is one of the "it" places to play for fashionable downtown crowds who come for the buzzing after-work scene and then stay into the evening, when the action in the upstairs lounge heats up. Call to check for DJs and other nightly entertainment. *Open daily for lunch, dinner, and cocktails 11:30 a.m.–2 a.m.*

Lobby
192 Bloor St. W. (Avenue Rd.), Bloor/Yorkville, 416-929-7169
Best Scene Bars

If you're looking for Toronto's "in" spot, look no further. White couches and white drapes are a perfect foil for the chic and well-heeled crowd. Riding the city's craze for clubs disguised as the lobby of a boutique hotel, Lobby does it with Yorkville style. Come early to enjoy champagne in the lounge, later in the evening to enjoy the music and the buzzing bar scene. There is an amusing menu of "urban comfort food" in the back-of-the-room dining area, featuring items like mac 'n' cheese with foie gras. Be prepared to pass a test of careful scrutiny by the door staff, but once inside, groove on the deluxe vibe and perfectly concocted martinis. *Open for lunch Tues.–Sat. noon–2:30 p.m., for dinner 6–11 p.m.; bar open Tues.–Sat. 11 a.m.–2 a.m.* $$

Lüb Lounge
487 Church St. (Wellesley St.), Gay Village, 416-323-1489, www.lub.ca
Best Gay Dance Clubs

Upstairs, the lounge is cozy and quiet during the week, but it's absolutely hopping on weekends with a nightly change of DJs creating a groovy and happening musical mix. The crowds are young, fashionable, and mostly boys looking to party. All clean lines in white, dark red, and black, the whole is anchored by a cool swirl of a bar. The menu is a casual mix of pizza, panini, and quesadillas prepared fresh and flavorfully, but the real star here is a lengthy cocktail list, including the Will and Grace Martini (a luscious concoction of raspberry vodka, Grand Marnier, champagne, cranberry, and lime) and the myriad champagne cocktails. *Open Mon.–Wed. 4 p.m.–midnight; Thurs.–Fri. 4 p.m.–2 a.m.; Sat. noon–2 a.m.; Sun. noon–1 a.m.* $$

Monsoon
100 Simcoe St. (Peter St.), Entertainment District, 416-979-7172,
www.monsoonrestaurant.ca
Best Trendy Restaurants

See Hot & Cool Restaurants, p. 81 for description.
Open for lunch Mon.–Fri. 11:30 a.m.–2:30 p.m.; for dinner Mon.–Sat. from 5 p.m.

Panorama
55 Bloor St. W., 51st Fl. (Bay St.), Bloor/Yorkville, 416-967-0000,
www.panoramalounge.com
Best Views

Of course you'll come first for the unparalleled view. The city spreads out around you from the corner of Yonge and Bloor, and is intriguing by day and sparkling with city lights after dark. But the real reason to come here is for the cocktails—voted the best in town by the readers of a Toronto daily newspaper, and proving an appeal that's more than skin deep. The city's highest summer patio is softly lit and romantic, and furnished in plantation teak. The main room inside has floor-to-ceiling windows and minimalist but comfortable contemporary furniture. You'll find an eclectic menu of favorites like cheese fondue, pizzas, and rich desserts to complement those fabulous drinks. With such a sexy ambience, it's no surprise that Panorama is a favorite romantic date spot. The summer patio scene is lively but not raucous. Panorama draws a sophisticated clientele year-round. *Open daily 5 p.m.–2 a.m.*

Prego Della Piazza
150 Bloor St. W. (Avenue Rd.), Bloor/Yorkville, 416-920-9900

Prego is a handsome restaurant decorated in a masculine, Italianate style with a celebrity-rich summer patio that overlooks busy Bloor at Avenue Road. Current legislation allows for smoking areas in restaurants until 2007, provided those areas are separately ventilated, and Prego has accommodated the rules with two separate dining rooms. You'll find the same streamlined menu of steaks and seafood, done efficiently and with some imagination, on both sides, but take note—the smoking side has the bar and the piano, and is most reliably full of well-dressed crowds looking to let down their hair most days of the week from late afternoon well into the evening. *Open daily for lunch noon–3 p.m.; dinner 5–11 p.m.*

Rain
19 Mercer St. (Blue Jays Way), Entertainment District, 416-599-7246
Best Martinis

You may have to wait a month for reservations, but it's worth the trouble. While it's no longer at the very top of the "it" list of Toronto restaurants, Rain still packs in a crowd of celebs and stylish locals who come to drink, dine, and see and be seen among the other trendy elite. The room, located in what was formerly a women's prison, is stunning, with a design inspired by Southeast Asia and dominated by two 15-foot waterfalls. Come for cocktails at the glowing bar that's lit from within, or make an evening of it and enjoy a Pan-Asian fusion meal among the beautiful people. *Open Tues.–Sat. 5:30–11 p.m.*

Sen5es Restaurant & Lounge
The SoHo Metropolitan, 318 Wellington St. W. (Blue Jays Way), Entertainment District, 416-935-0400, www.senses.ca
Best Romantic Rendezvous

All done up in gold accents, highlighted by glowing spotlights and a bright sparkling bar, wide overstuffed couches, and intriguing contemporary art, Sen5es' lounge makes for a decidedly chic and sexy spot for a drink. There are plenty of romantic, shadowy corners for hushed, private conversation, or you can sit at the bar if you're in the mood to see and be seen among the other stylish clientele. Whether you're here just for drinks or settling in for a leisurely dinner, a sophisticated and polished experience awaits. *Restaurant open for dinner Wed.–Sun. 6–10 p.m.; bar and bistro open daily 4 p.m.–1 a.m.*

Sky Bar
132 Queen's Quay E. (Lower Jarvis St.), Harbourfront, 416-869-0045, www.theguvernment.com
Best Summer Patios

Prada meets Gucci at Toronto's swankiest roof patio, which is part of the huge Guvernment entertainment complex on the Harbourfront, and which stays open from spring until late fall. With the lake twinkling flirtatiously under the stars and chic patrons sipping designer martinis amid the slick white furnishings, this is the place where upscale revelers make the most of the good weather. Thursdays, when a DJ comes to play groovy tunes, are very popular. A door staff guards the entrance to this rooftop paradise, so dress to fit in with a designer crowd. *Open seasonally May–Oct., Thurs.–Sat. 10 p.m.–3 a.m.* $$

Therapy Ultra Lounge

203 Richmond St. W. (Bedford St.), Entertainment District, 416-977-3089, www.therapylounge.com
Best Sexy Lounges

Stylish singles come here to meet the same, making the scene while sipping on creatively mixed cocktails. A mix of corporate downtowners and glamorous types, Therapy's crowd is all grown up, but still young enough to let loose. Tiled columns, glowing red lights, and stainless-steel fixtures punctuate the darkened room of the lounge, and upstairs there's a dance floor. A bar glows invitingly, attracting designer-clad patrons to sample from the tongue-in-cheek drink list that includes the Dr. Phil Martini. Therapy is known for some of the friendliest staff in Clubland. Fridays and Saturdays, the place is packed with beautiful people from 10 p.m. on, so call at least 48 hours ahead to get on the guest list. There's a style code, so be sure to dress your best. *Open Wed.–Sun. 9 p.m.–3 a.m.; Thurs.–Fri. open from 4:30 p.m. for after-work drinks.* $$

2 Cats Cocktail Lounge

569 King St. W. (Portland St.), Entertainment District, 416-204-6261, www.2cats.ca
Best Cigar Lounges

2 Cats is swanky and stylish, just like the upscale crowds who love to sink into the low leather couches or perch at the long bar. This is a perfect spot to order a swishy cosmopolitan, where you can check out the other well-dressed patrons in their natural habitat. Or join the cool crowd in the separately ventilated cigar lounge. The design is contemporary, with clean lines and polished wood floors, and the spotlighting makes for a warm and sexy ambience. The extensive cocktail menu changes on a regular basis, so be sure to ask what's new. The fabulous thirtyish crowd has made this one of their favorite after-midnight haunts on the weekends. *Open Tues.–Fri. 5 p.m.–2 a.m.; Sat. 8 p.m.–2 a.m.* $$

Ultra Supper Club

314 Queen St. W. (Soho St.), Entertainment District, 416-263-0330
Best Late-Night Hangouts

As the name suggests, this is a club that has gone all out to win the fickle hearts of Toronto diners and clubbers, and it's paid off in spades with the crowds of beautiful people in velvet-rope lineups. Gold sheers separate the space, which is punctuated by shiny white tables and black chairs, enhanced by glowing mood lighting. Sink back into the overstuffed booths, elevated on a platform for maximum see-and-be-seen status. An artful menu of fusion is characterized by pure flavors and fresh ingredients. After midnight, they move the tables out of the way, and the place morphs into a hot dance club for a well-dressed crowd ranging from black-clad twenty-somethings to the well-preserved and young at heart. DJs play old-school to electronica, although word is that the scenesters only flock to the dance floor for vintage Prince. Make reservations for a late dinner to avoid the lines. *Open Mon.–Wed. 5:30 p.m.–midnight; Thurs.–Sat. 5:30 p.m.–2 a.m.* $$

West Lounge
510 King St. W. (Bathurst St.), Entertainment District, 416-361-9004, www.westlounge.com
Best Meet Markets

From the moment you reach the spot where 510 King St. W. should be—if in fact it did exist—getting inside the West Lounge is half the adventure. Follow the sign and go down a back alley, and if you've dressed up and made nice with the door staff, there's a chance you'll get past the velvet rope to this über-cool underground three-room nightspot. This is where the beautiful people come to play mating games; models, other fashionistas, and men in Armani mingle and mix in high style. This is a club where a classy vibe mixes with that famous center-of-the-universe attitude for a totally Toronto club experience. The décor is offbeat, featuring richly colored faux-marble walls and glass panes that drip with translucent optical film. Ask about the exclusive VIP area for bottle service, and come late for the hot after-midnight scene. *Open daily 5 p.m.–2 a.m.* $$

YYZ Restaurant & Wine Bar
345 Adelaide St. W. (Charlotte St.), Entertainment District, 416-599-3399, www.yyzrestaurant.com
Best Scene Bars

Sleek, shiny, and subterranean, YYZ—the code for Toronto's Pearson International Airport—beckons from the sidewalks of Adelaide West deep in Clubland. Fashionable crowds flock to the lounge soon after dark on weekends, and the noise levels rise as the hours tick by. Pan-Asian fusion cuisine is on offer in the dining area, but the real draw here is the sexy see-and-be-seen party crowd, who sip creatively mixed cocktails at shiny modular tables, checking out the competition. *Open for dinner Mon.–Wed. 5–10 p.m.; Thurs.–Sun. 5–11 p.m.; open for cocktails Mon.–Wed. 4:30–11:30 p.m.; Thurs.–Sun. 4:30 p.m.–1 a.m.*

Hot & Cool Toronto: The Attractions

Allan Gardens Conservatory
19 Horticultural Ave. (Jarvis St.), St. Lawrence, 416-392-1111, www.collections.ic.gc.ca/gardens/opening.html
Best Ways to Escape a Rainy Day

A jewel in an urban setting, the Allan offers spacious indoor and outdoor gardens for your enjoyment, making it both the perfect cure for nasty weather and a way to make the most of a sunny day. Grand indoor conservatories feature domed cathedral ceilings, and plantings of flowers both domestic and exotic in various environments—tropical house, arid house, and palm house, among others. Outdoor gardens lend themselves to leisurely exploration, with fountains and architectural features that add to Mother Nature's beauty. The facilities are wheelchair accessible and, best of all, free. *Open Mon.–Fri. 9 a.m.–4 p.m.; Sat.–Sun. 10 a.m.–5 p.m.*

Bata Shoe Museum
327 Bloor St. W. (St. George St.), Bloor/Yorkville, 416-979-7799, www.batashoemuseum.ca
Best Chic Museums

If you've always associated the word museum with stuffy educational exhibits, let the Bata change your mind. Asked to come up with a jewel to showcase Toronto socialite Sonja Bata's huge collection of shoes, architect Raymond Moriyama created a five-story structure inspired by the idea of a shoebox. Permanent and changing exhibitions include shoes of the stars and elements of pure design, as well as collections that highlight the fascinating social history of shoes. You don't have to be a fashionista to appreciate the design, nor do you need to be curious about Shaq's shoe size to enjoy what this chic little museum has to offer. Attention to detail and helpful staff make for an interesting experience in very attractive surroundings. *Open Tues.–Wed. 10 a.m.–5 p.m.; Thurs. 10 a.m.–8 p.m.; Fri.–Sat. 10 a.m.–5 p.m.; Sun. noon–5 p.m.* $

CHUM/Citytv Building
299 Queen St. W. (John St.), Entertainment District, 416-591-5757
Best Guided Tours

With unique open-concept studios, the CHUM/Citytv building is one of the most identifiable media centers in Canada. The CHUM/Citytv empire is home

HOT & COOL • ATTRACTIONS

to an independent media network of local and cable specialty channels. The open-concept studio design means that newscasts offer a view of all the technical and other staff that keep the station humming. Music video station MuchMusic interviews the stars at street level while crowds of squealing fans congregate on the sidewalk. Tours of the studios and other facilities are gratis and offered throughout the afternoons—call ahead for times and details. *Tours offered afternoons Mon.–Fri. Call ahead for details.* $

Eagles Nest Golf Club
10000 Dufferin St., Maple, Ontario, 905-417-2300, www.eaglesnestgolf.com

Newly opened in 2004, this challenging 18-hole golf course about a half hour's drive north of the city was designed by renowned architect Doug Carrick. Featuring rugged sand dunes and sod-wall bunkers and grasses, this highly rated public course has a par of 72 and is known for tough greens. Set in green rolling hills just north of the city, Eagles Nest is popular with the new, modern golfer. And after a stimulating round of links-style golf, head to the 36,000-square-foot waterside clubhouse facilities to rehash the game over drinks or dinner. $$$$

King Street East Furniture District
King Street East between Jarvis and Parliament, St. Lawrence

In recent years, this area of King Street East has become a mecca for furniture and home accessory showrooms, but you won't find any tacky flowered upholstery or DIY cheapies here. No fewer than a dozen major retailers showcase high-end designer furniture on this strip of King, making it worth a trip for window-shopping and browsing for new ideas. Furniture is elevated to the level of pure design at Up Country (214 King St. E., www.upcountry.ca), and check out the ultra-mod Zanzibar bar stools at Abitare Design (234 King St. E., www.abitaredesign.com), which are pretty unusual, but quite comfortable and available in a range of glowing colors. Whether you use it as a shopping opp or gallery experience, it's a fine way to spend an afternoon.

Museum of Television
277 Queen St. W. (McCaul St.), Entertainment District, 416-599-7339, www.mztv.com

Next door to the historic flagship digs of the CHUM media empire, and above the CHUM/Citytv Store, is an ode to the television, not as a cultural institution, but as a physical object with its own kind of beauty. While its impact on our lives has been huge and much discussed, the television receiver as furniture, with a history of its own, has never received this kind of studied treatment before. Permanent and changing exhibits look not only at the history of the television set, but at other twentieth-century cultural curiosities such as vintage cars in Latin America. Tours of the Museum are included when visiting the CHUM/Citytv facilities. These quirky and eye-opening displays will ensure that you'll never take your television set for granted again. *Tours are offered afternoons Mon.–Fri. as part of the CHUM/Citytv tours. Call ahead for details.* $

Pantages Anti-Aging & Longevity Spa

Pantages Hotel Suites, 200 Victoria St. (Shuter St.), Downtown/Yonge, 416-367-1888, www.pantagesspa.com
Best Spas

For an over-the-top spa experience, a full 9,000 square feet of tranquil and stylish pampering await at the Pantages. Twelve treatment rooms offer a place to refresh and revitalize, catering to both male and female clientele, with facilities and special packages for couples. Treatments follow Ayurveda, a 5,000-year-old system of health management developed in India. Have a full-body Vichy shower or massage, or have the aqua sommelier help you choose from over 100 varieties of bottled water. Many exclusive products and services are available, including hot-stone massage and Kona-coffee-and-vanilla body treatments. *Open daily 9 a.m.–10 p.m.* $$$$

SkyDome Tour

1 Blue Jays Way (Front St.), Entertainment District, 416-341-2770, www.rogerscentre.com

It's billed as "The World's Greatest Entertainment Centre." Take the tour and judge for yourself. The 11.5-acre facility has an interior volume, with the roof shut, of 56.5 million cubic feet, and is home field to MLB's Toronto Blue Jays and the Canadian Football League's Toronto Argonauts. It's also a 50,000-plus–seat venue for acts like U2 and Britney Spears. The roof separates into four sections that open in a circular motion, raising the height of the roof to 282 feet, or 31 stories. The tour takes approximately one hour, and allows an insider's look at this massive facility, including a museum area with memorabilia from past shows, a video about its construction, and access to areas typically off limits to the public, such as the playing field, private boxes, and team dressing rooms. Call well in advance to book your tour, since availability will depend on the facility's busy schedule. $

Textile Museum of Canada

55 Centre Ave. (Dundas St.), Chinatown, 416-599-5321, www.textilemuseum.ca

In a nondescript high-rise in an out-of-the-way corner just off Chinatown, the Textile Museum is announced by a garage door painted as a jewel-toned tapestry. Once inside, you'll follow a charmingly quirky staircase, painted at ground level in a melon color that brightens to golden yellow as you go up the stairs. Four levels of temporary and permanent displays feature textile-based creations as well as their history and cultural context—sumptuous hand-knotted carpets in rich and brilliant colors, intricate laces and linens, tapestries and quilts. The permanent collection includes more than 10,000 textile pieces than span almost 2,000 years of history and 190 regions across the globe. A gift shop offers exquisite silk and handwoven scarves and purses, books, and other items. You can wander through on your own, or join a guided tour on Sundays. *Open Tues. 11 a.m.–5 p.m.; Wed. 11 a.m.–8 p.m.; Thurs.–Fri. 11 a.m.–5 p.m.; Sat.–Sun. noon–5 p.m.* $

Toronto Stock Exchange Media Centre
130 King St. W. (York St.), Financial District, 416-947-4676, www.tse.com/en/mediacentre

The Toronto Stock Exchange is North America's third largest, and is currently housed in suitably flashy and imposing digs in the TSX Tower on King Street near Yonge. While visitors have not been allowed on the trading floor for some years due to security concerns, the TSX Broadcast Centre, on the ground floor, was developed to fill the gap. Mod and glitzy, the high-tech and camera-ready Centre houses a small self-directed museum display, and several interactive terminals where you can check out stocks. Up the stairs, a gallery overlooks the media center where five national media companies tape live news feeds and interviews. The slick design and the buzz of the financial types checking their portfolios all add to the frenzied atmosphere. *The gallery is accessible to visitors Mon. and Fri. and most days throughout the summer (call ahead for current schedule).*

Yorkville Shopping District
Around Bloor & Avenue Rd., Bloor/Yorkville
Best Only-in-Toronto Attractions

In the 1970s, Yorkville was the favorite haunt of hippies and anti-establishment types. Like the hippies who grew up and cleaned up their act, the neighborhood's done the same. Popular with visitors and native Torontonians alike, the Bloor/Yorkville area is now home to Canada's most expensive shopping district. Hazelton Lanes offers a range of designer boutiques, and the flagship Holt Renfrew department store hearkens from Bloor with a selection of designer wares said to be unrivaled in North America. Come ready to shop until you drop—you'll find everything from the standard upscale brands like Chanel and Gucci to smaller independent boutiques, art galleries, and antique shops.

Arts & Entertainment Toronto

Decades ago, a few theatrical visionaries began putting world-class productions in front of Toronto audiences, and the response was both immediate and dramatic. Today, Toronto is the continent's third-largest center for theater and live stage shows. The fine arts flourish in the city's many galleries and respected arts institutions. If you add a thriving live-music scene, where both local and international greats come to play, you'll discover that Toronto delivers a show-stopping good time.

Arts & Entertainment Toronto: The Itinerary

Our Hotel Choice: **Le Meridien King Edward Hotel**, because this sumptuously appointed and luxurious classic has long been a favorite with VIPs and heads of state, and today still evokes a theatrical grandeur.

Prime Time: Thurs.–Sat.

Day 1

Morning: Start your day of exploration with a bang at **Nanoo Cafe** on Front Street, where you can enjoy *a leisurely cappuccino* as you watch the locals rush off to the office. Once you're suitably fueled up, it's a few blocks to the **Art Gallery of Ontario** on Dundas. Check out the neighborhood along the way—the AGO sits right on the edges of Toronto's busiest downtown, Chinatown. Once you're inside, invest in a catalog and take your time.

Lunch: After contemplating art all morning, it's time for *a theme lunch* at **Agora**, the AGO's cafe; the menu here complements major shows with thematically appropriate dishes. Or, if you're ready for a change of scene, stroll north to the hallowed halls of the University of Toronto to lunch among academic types at a beloved local gem, the **Gallery Grill**. (But be sure to make a reservation ahead of time at this popular spot.)

Afternoon: Take a walk south to the **Harbourfront Centre**, right at the foot of York Street. From gallery shows to literary readings and dance performances, there's always something of interest happening here. In good weather, a walk down the Harbourfront makes for *a sparkling interlude* in your afternoon. If the stress of travel and gallery-hopping have left you drained, make a reservation for celebrity-level pampering at **Elizabeth Milan Day Spa** in the Royal York Hotel. As the afternoon winds to a close, return to your hotel, throw on your dress-up clothes, and join the spiffy after-work crowds in the mahogany-paneled lounge of the **Rosewater Supper Club**.

Dinner: After easing your way into the evening with a drink, it's time to select a restaurant that will satisfy all your senses. Consider staying at Rosewater, where you're guaranteed to spend a splendid evening. But if you're looking for a change of scene, here are some of the finest restaurants to choose from. **Scaramouche** is a cab ride from the downtown area, but it's well worth the trip to this destination restaurant with *a glittering view*

ARTS & ENTERTAINMENT

of the city from atop the Avenue Road hill. You'll have to dress the part for your other dining options, located in two of the city's most style-conscious neighborhoods. **Mistura** awaits in Yorkville and offers a contemporary spin on Italian cuisine. In Little Italy, make your way to the beloved **Trattoria Giancarlo** for a more classical approach to Mediterranean fare.

Nighttime: After dinner, let the music be your guide. If a leisurely evening of sipping wine to a background of French cabaret sounds appealing, head straight over to **Le Saint Tropez** in the Entertainment District. Or maybe you'd rather dance than just listen—if so, the **Sugar Club** offers an upscale club ambience without the Clubland attitude. For jumping swing jazz, walk to Wellington Street and join the crowds at the **Reservoir Lounge**, where you might just see Nick Nolte if he's in town. For the boys, check out stylish **Inspire** in the Gay Village. After midnight, gather with the beautiful people at Toronto's only *Russian vodka bar*, **Pravda Vodka Bar**, where you can choose among 50 varieties and order caviar to accompany it, for a luxurious end to the evening's festivities.

Day 2

Morning: A morning stroll to Kensington Market makes for a pleasant start to the day if the weather's nice. At **Moonbean Coffee Company**, a flavorful fair-trade brew and a slice of nana (banana) bread will help you prepare for the busy day ahead. *Antiques* are this morning's theme. Take a cab north to **Spadina House**, where you can stroll the manicured grounds and check out an Edwardian townhouse whose original decorations reflect the art scene in Toronto throughout the twentieth century. Or, if you're in need of a little retail therapy at this point, head a few blocks back south to the **Toronto Antique Centre**, in the Entertainment District. In a spacious and airy building, you'll find over 30 dealers who have a wide and eclectic range of antiques and collectibles on offer.

Lunch: Head just east of downtown to one of two elegant restaurants located in the charming surroundings of St. James Cathedral and the Toronto Sculpture Garden Park. **La Maquette** offers Mediterranean-French cuisine in a romantic glassed-in conservatory-like room with a soaring cathedral ceiling and a view overlooking the Sculpture Garden. **Biagio Ristorante** features *Northern Italian classics*, which you can savor on the flagstone patio tucked away at the back of the building.

ARTS & ENTERTAINMENT • ITINERARY

Afternoon: After lunch, continue east down King Street, to Parliament and then Mill Street to the historic **Distillery District**. This fascinating area contains the world's largest collection of restored Victorian industrial architecture, and is now home to more than 20 art galleries, studios, and other shops. In the summer, you'll also catch *outdoor jazz* and temporary exhibits. Don't forget to make a stop at **Balzac's Cafe** for a relaxed beverage among the gallery owners.

Dinner: Stay in the District for dinner at the über-trendy **Perigee**. Chefs prepare your multicourse selections in a kitchen right in the middle of the dining room as you watch—a must for foodies! If seafood tempts you, **Pure Spirits Oyster House & Grill** is just around the corner, also in the Distillery District, with a *hot summer patio* for your pleasure. Just a few blocks north of the District, French cuisine served with real Gallic charm beckons at **Provence Delices**.

Nighttime: The flavor of the evening is jazz. Stay in the District for the tunes at the **Boiler House**. On Sherbourne, the legendary **Montreal Bistro & Jazz Club** is for the *serious jazz listener*. Back downtown, the **Top o' the Senator** puts the emphasis on modern and global beats in a swanky room. To dance until 3 a.m. in a posh club that was once a real courthouse, head to the **Courthouse Chamber Lounge**.

Day 3

Morning: Have a look before you make your breakfast selections at **Marché**, as there's plenty to choose from. Whether you're preparing to enjoy a challenging 18 holes of golf at **Lionhead Golf & Country Club**, or stay in town to continue your *arts exploration*, this is an excellent way to start your day. If you're staying in town, check out the show at the **Gardiner Museum of Ceramic Art**, the continent's only venue devoted exclusively to this beautiful art form. Or, for an inside look at Toronto's most well-known and gorgeous historic theater, join the tour of the **Elgin/Winter Garden Theatre** on Yonge Street.

Lunch: If gourmet dim sum served with *fine dining flair* sounds like your cup of tea, try highly acclaimed **Lai Wah Heen**, located on the second floor of the Metropolitan in Chinatown. Otherwise, you can enjoy inventive continental fusion in a beautiful room among stylish folk at **Azure Restaurant & Bar** in the InterContinental Hotel.

Afternoon: Book a tour well in advance with **Artinsite**, a tour company which allows you to get an insider glimpse of the city's galleries and neighborhoods with a guide—and a local's expertise. Or head back to the AGO and **Cinematheque Ontario** for an afternoon screening of foreign and art films with a well-informed crowd. For libations in the late afternoon, think ahead to dinner. If you're staying downtown, you'll want to sip *martinis* among the movers and shakers at **Jump Cafe & Bar** in the Financial District. Heading uptown to Yonge and Eglinton? Then sample a glass of wine from the huge cellar at **Centro Grill & Wine Bar**.

Dinner: After Centro, stay in the 'hood and enjoy a romantic evening of *fabulous French cuisine* in a rustic setting at the **Auberge du Pommier**. This is where Toronto locals go for a special night out. Closer to downtown, intimate and charming little **Gamelle** offers more low-key French fare in Little Italy. If you're hankering for something a little splashier, **Biff's** serves up continental cuisine in a gleaming Art Nouveau room right across the street from the Hummingbird Centre.

Nighttime: Tonight's the night to check out Toronto's live theater offerings, but be sure to check the listings and call ahead to reserve tickets. After the show, head to **My Apartment** in Clubland, where the over-thirty set go to *dance* and play mating games. Or, if serious music's what you're after, the blues play until 1 a.m. at **N'awlins**. If hunger strikes again, you'll be happy to know that the kitchen at the nearby **KitKat2/Club Lucky** serves up Italian classics till 2 a.m.

Morning After: Join the throngs of Torontonians for a stylish brunch in gorgeous surroundings at the **Cafe Victoria**, housed in the King Eddy (Le Meridien King Edward). This Toronto institution and perennial Sunday-morning favorite is a fitting setting for a final outing on the town.

Arts & Entertainment Toronto: The Hotels

InterContinental Toronto Centre
225 Front St. W. (Simcoe St.), Entertainment District,
416-597-1400 / 800-422-7969, www.torontocentre.intercontinental.com

One of a wave of hotel renovations completed in the last few years, this $30-million retrofit got it right—it was an investment in pure style that sets the InterContinental distinctly apart from the rest. All the downtown hotels have their share of business-class clientele, but the InterContinental's high-end design and ideal location in the Entertainment District make it just as appealing to upscale vacationers. The vast lobby is contemporary and minimalist, with a bank of windows splashing natural light onto the marble floors. All 280 deluxe rooms and 11 suites have a view of either the lake or downtown Toronto, along with high-speed Internet access, an oversize marble bathroom, opening bay windows, and twice-daily housekeeping. For all-out luxury furnished in modern, sophisticated style, and your very own sunny lakeside patio, ask for the two-bedroom Waterview Suite. Located in the lobby, Azure Restaurant & Bar is a sophisticated and stylish bar and lounge, a favorite of local downtown professionals as well as out-of-towners. The InterContinental is also home to the Victoria Spa, where you can splurge on an herbal body-glow polish or go for a traditional Ayurvedic massage. $$$

Le Meridien King Edward Hotel
37 King St. E. (Victoria St.), St. Lawrence,
416-863-9700 / 800-543-4300, www.toronto.lemeridien.com

This Toronto landmark has been pleasing clientele from Margaret Thatcher to Britney Spears for over a century. Le Royal Meridien King Edward Hotel celebrated its 100th anniversary in 2004 and wears its age gracefully. You'll be swept away by the grandeur of what the locals affectionately call the King Eddy. From the moment you enter the foyer with its soaring ceilings, you'll understand its appeal to the international jet set. Rooms are artfully furnished in reproduction Edwardian style, complete with dark cherrywood and mahogany furniture, fine linens, and marble bathrooms. Note that the Crown Club rooms offer 355 square feet of luxury, including a king-size bed and a variety of city views. For the most posh rooms, ask for one of the Royal Suites, 1,800 square feet of luxury that includes a spacious living area. Some have a skylight or second bathroom. Amenities include a well-equipped 1,500-square-foot fitness room and the European-style Nouvelle

Marie Health Spa. The Cafe Victoria boasts a sumptuous dining room. This is an opulent home away from home for the discerning traveler who likes comfort and is looking to avoid the generic and tour-isty—and perhaps rub shoulders with the entertainment world's elite. $$$$

Metropolitan Hotel
108 Chestnut St. (University Ave.), Chinatown,
416-977-5000 / 800-668-6600, www.metropolitan.com/toronto

Located at the intersection of the Financial District and Chinatown, the Met is a classy alternative to the downtown hotels. The Met's low-key elegance and ideal location close to financial markets, theaters, museums, and all the downtown attractions have made it popular with a wide range of upscale travelers. The Metropolitan's owners are committed to delivering an exceptional experience, and they've succeeded by paying attention to the details. Standard features include Italian linens on European natural-down duvets, and high-speed Internet access. Executive suites include an oversize marble bathroom with a whirlpool tub and walk-in closet. The furnishings and décor in richly textured neutrals add to the tastefully understated luxury of the place. You can swim year-round in a heated indoor pool, or stay in shape at the health club. The Met's reputation for excellence extends to its restaurants. Lai Wah Heen has won international recognition for gourmet Cantonese cuisine, and Hemispheres Lounge & Bistro offers beautifully plated Asian fusion in a more casual atmosphere. $$$

Sutton Place
955 Bay St. (Gerrard St.), Financial District,
416-924-2221 / 866-378-8866, www.toronto.suttonplace.com

The chairs and couches of the Sutton Place's elegant lobby are often occupied by upscale travelers who've been making this hotel a special-occasion venue for decades. Marble floors are covered with sumptuous rugs and ersatz Victorian furniture that give the room an understated European elegance. Sutton Place offers low-key luxury that has attracted all kinds of guests—from business types to vacationers, celebrities to heads of state. Original art and antiques grace all the rooms, which include 64 luxury suites that measure 540 square feet and provide a living room. Ask for a corner King Room, which comes with an oversize bed and two huge windows that allow you to scope out downtown. La Grande Residence, a hotel within a hotel, is geared toward extended stays. Special amenities include 24-hour room service and twice-daily maid service, gourmet continental cuisine at Accents Restaurant & Bar, and a spacious health club. Grande Residence suites include a living room, a full kitchen, and heated marble floors. $$$$

Arts & Entertainment Toronto: The Restaurants

Agora
Art Gallery of Ontario, 317 Dundas St. W. (McCaul St.), Chinatown, 416-979-6612, www.ago.net

Have your lunch in grand style, on white linens beneath cathedral ceilings at Agora in the Art Gallery of Ontario. Refined patrons of the arts sample from a menu by chef Anne Yarymovich that is ingeniously tied thematically to the gallery's major shows. Modigliani, for example, was naturally paired with Italianate inventions like monkfish, osso bucco, smoked tuna and warm roasted figs. Agora is only open for lunch (brunch on Saturday and Sunday), and you'll find that discerning downtowners flock here for the inventive cuisine, as do a good number of ladies who lunch. You don't need to appreciate the paintings to love the fresh cuisine or the elegant and airy dining room. *Open for lunch Mon.–Fri. noon–2:30 p.m.; brunch Sat.–Sun. 11 a.m.–2:30 p.m.* $$$

Auberge du Pommier
4150 Yonge St. (York Mills St.), Uptown, 416-222-2220, www.oliverbonacini.com
Best Fine Dining

Located in a historic building built from two stonecutters' cottages, the Auberge is one of Toronto's premier special-occasion dinner destinations. A whitewashed building with a black roof and French doors set a romantic tone, and the warmly lit interior is classic white with ornate moldings and arches. Pale linens offset comfortable seating to create an overall impression of classic elegance. In the summer months, be sure to ask for seating on the garden terrace. An extensive wine list complements the French-Mediterranean cuisine, beautifully prepared with the finest ingredients. Savory choices include crispy seared tuna with spiced tartare, peppered pineapple, and petit pois salad. If you're in need of a memorably refined evening of pampered service and fine dining, Auberge is certain to deliver. *Open for lunch Mon.–Fri. 11:30 a.m.–2:30 p.m.; for dinner Mon.–Sat. from 5 p.m.* $$$$

Azure Restaurant & Bar

InterContinental Toronto Centre, 225 Front St. W. (Simcoe St.), Entertainment District, 416-597-8142, www.torontocentre.intercontinental.com
Best Swanky Hotel Bars

Part of the multimillion-dollar renovation of the InterContinental Hotel, Azure is a handsome hotel lounge with a solidly polished and fashionable clientele. While drawing its fair share of traveling business accounts, Azure has also won the hearts of locals. Downtown professionals make it a regular stop for happy hour on Thursdays and Fridays. Soaring banks of windows brighten the room with natural light, making it a great cure for bad-weather blues. White linen tablecloths and chandeliers in the dining area add to the bright and open feel. But the scene-stealer without question is the inviting lounge area, dominated by the art installation that anchors the bar. The glassy creation, called *Liquid Veil*, was commissioned from local artist Stuart Reid, and provides an elegant and artistic foil for the martini-loving crowds. *Open daily 6 a.m.–11 p.m. $$$$*

Balzac's Cafe

55 Mill St. (Parliament St.), Distillery District, 416-207-1709, www.balzacscoffee.com

Canadians are seldom far from a good cup of coffee, but Balzac's has done a particularly outstanding job of perfecting the cafe experience. Part of the historic Distillery District complex, Balzac's is housed in an airy, high-ceilinged space with exposed wooden beams and a gorgeous antique mirror behind the coffee bar. Bright young things expertly serve up your brew of choice (including fair-trade coffees) while you take in the spectacular antique chandelier. Then head up the stairs to sip in relaxed comfort along with the gallery owners and artists who occupy the studios nearby. This is the perfect place to take a break after browsing the shops and galleries of the District. *Open Mon.–Fri. 7 a.m.–8 p.m.; Sat.–Sun. 9 a.m.–8 p.m. $*

Biagio Ristorante

155 King St. E. (Jarvis St.), St. Lawrence, 416-366-4040

Biagio aims to impress from the moment you enter. An attractive crowd of downtowners and foodies love the Old Town elegance of this historic dining room located in St. Lawrence House. Soaring ceilings and gracious moldings are balanced by simple white linens to create a sophisticated look. Tucked in the back of the historic building and away from the street, a beautiful wrought-iron fence makes the flagstone patio one of the city's most refined spots for al fresco dining. It's a popular spot to lunch on a summer's day, hidden away from the bustle of downtown. An extensive menu of Northern

Italian classics has earned it a Distinguished Restaurants of North America award. Order a glass of wine from the vintage cellar to accompany your leisurely meal. *Open for lunch Mon.–Fri. noon–2:30 p.m.; dinner Mon.–Sat. 6–10 p.m.* $$$$

Biff's
4 Front St. E. (Yonge St.), St. Lawrence, 416-860-0086, www.oliverbonacini.com

Directly across the street from the Hummingbird Centre, the refined and classy Biff's buzzes with well-dressed pre- and post-theater crowds. Floor-to-ceiling windows face busy Front Street, and that glossy veneer of sophistication continues inside with a long gleaming bar, white linens, and Art Nouveau light fixtures. The cuisine is upscale French done with imagination and artistry, the wine list is long, the service is impeccable, and the martinis are well reviewed. For a quiet drink—very quiet!—come during showtimes and have that long bar mostly to yourself, or come early and join the theatergoers for the pre-show buzz. *Open daily for lunch noon–3 p.m.; dinner 5–11 p.m.* $$$$

Cafe Victoria
Le Meridien King Edward Hotel, 37 King St. E. (Victoria St.), St. Lawrence, 416-863-4125, www.toronto.lemeridien.com
Best Brunches

Dine in a gorgeous designated historic site. Floor-to-ceiling windows, elaborate plasterwork, and high ceilings create an expansive and airy dining room. The Cafe Victoria has played host to celebrities and international dignitaries from Mick Jagger to the royal family, and has been a hometown favorite for generations. Cafe Victoria hums with a crowd of locals and upscale hotel guests. All meals are sumptuous, but brunch is a sublime and perennial Toronto Sunday favorite. Reservations are essential. *Open for breakfast, lunch, and dinner Mon.–Fri. 6:30 a.m.–11 p.m.; Fri.–Sat. 11 a.m.–1 a.m.; Sun. 9:30 a.m.–11 p.m.; Sun. brunch 10 a.m.–3 p.m.* $$$$

Centro Grill & Wine Bar
2472 Yonge St., upper level (Eglinton Ave.), Uptown, 416-483-2211, www.centrorestaurant.com

See Arts & Entertainment Nightlife, p. 115, for description. *Open for dinner Mon.–Sat. 5–11 p.m.* $$$$

Gallery Grill
7 Hart House Circle, 2nd Fl. (Queen's Park), University of Toronto, 416-978-2445

Housed in a venerable building on the University of Toronto campus, with tall neo-Gothic windows and soaring ceilings, this is surely one of the loveliest dining rooms in the city. Reservations are a must at this hideaway of fine dining, open only for lunch and known to academics and savvy Torontonians for its leisurely Old World atmosphere. The menu consists of fresh updates on traditional classics like warm spinach salad and eggs-in-the-hole. The service is attentive and efficient. If you pay attention, you may even catch some juicy academic gossip from the next table over. *Open for lunch Mon.–Fri. noon–2:30 p.m.; brunch Sun. noon–3 p.m.* $$$

Gamelle
468 College St. W. (Markham St.), Little Italy, 416-923-6254, www.gamelle.com

Gamelle is as beautiful as its name, with a romantic aura that invites intimate tête-à-têtes. From the rough wood floors to the open kitchen, Gamelle provides a perfect setting for couples who want to imagine that they're dining somewhere in the French countryside. This rustic bistro is a neighborhood favorite, popular with a young professional crowd as well as foodies who've read the rave reviews. To the intimate French mood, add a delectable menu that mixes tradition with innovation. *Open for lunch Tues.–Fri. noon–2:30 p.m.; dinner Mon.–Wed. 6–10 p.m.; Thurs.–Sat. 6–11 p.m.* $$$

Inspire
491 Church St. (Wellesley St.), Gay Village, 416-963-0044
Best Gay Bars

See Arts & Entertainment Nightlife, p. 116 for description. Open daily 5 p.m.–2 a.m. $$$

Jump Cafe & Bar
1 Wellington St. W. (Yonge St.), Financial District, 416-363-3400, www.oliverbonancini.com

The movers and shakers of Bay Street know a good thing when it comes along, and they've flocked to Jump since its opening. Palm trees and lots of natural light characterize the understated décor. What you'll love is the bustling Financial District vibe—even on a Saturday—and the stellar offerings of continental cuisine with mixed influences. Fish dishes, especially salmon, come highly recommended. Jump can be very busy and the noise levels do rise, but there are more-secluded corners for private conversations, or to seal that all-important deal. *Open for lunch and dinner Mon.–Fri. noon–midnight; dinner Sat. 5 p.m.–midnight.* $$$

KitKat2/Club Lucky
117 John St. (Pearl St.), Entertainment District, 416-977-8890, www.kitkattoronto.com

Don't get this one confused with the original KitKat on King, the popular casual eatery that's been packing them in for decades. With big windows and exposed brick, dark wood accents, and a gleaming, polished bar, this KitKat is more upscale, more polished, and has a separate and more casual whisky and cigar room downstairs. The dining room is busy with pre-theater crowds through the dinner hour, then bustles after midnight with hungry club refugees who come for southern Italian classics served by a friendly staff until 2 a.m. *Open for dinner Tues.–Sat. 4 p.m.–2 a.m.* $$$

Lai Wah Heen
Metropolitan Hotel, 108 Chestnut St., 2nd Fl. (University Ave.), Chinatown, 416-977-9899, www.metropolitan.com/lwh
Best Asian Restaurants

The entrepreneurs behind the Metropolitan Hotel chain have a simple philosophy—to deliver the best not only in accommodations, but to focus equal attention on the food and beverage side of the business. The result has been a number of award-winning restaurants. Lai Wah Heen starts with upscale continental service in posh surroundings and adds superb Cantonese cuisine. And it's clear they've got a successful concept at work—the Financial District types flock here for lunch. The dinner hour sees a handsomely dressed crowd of discerning locals, along with a smattering of expense-account types. Black ladder-back chairs, white linens, and a long elegant bar create a sophisticated and cosmopolitan dining room. Enjoy the latest in fine Cantonese, with its emphasis on tropical fruits and the exotic spices of the South Pacific, all of it served with continental flair. *Open for lunch daily 11:30 a.m.–2:30 p.m.; dinner from 5 p.m.* $$$$

La Maquette
111 King St. E. (Church St.), St. Lawrence, 416-366-8191, www.lamaquette.com

With the air of an estate conservatory, La Maquette is characterized by its sheer elegance. A well-dressed clientele comes here for the old-fashioned romance of this sparkling restaurant. La Maquette has often been voted the most romantic restaurant in town, and you'll easily see why. Marble-tiled floors highlight potted ferns and bouquets of lilies, and crystal chandeliers glitter overhead. You'll dine on a fine selection of Italian and French cuisine as you gaze through the huge banks of windows that illuminate the first floor. A grand staircase leads to a solarium beneath cathedral ceilings that overlooks St. James Cathedral and the Toronto Sculpture Garden. In the summer, a courtyard patio has the same view. *Open for lunch Mon.–Fri. noon–2:30 p.m.; dinner Mon.–Sat. 5–10:30 p.m.* $$$

Le Saint Tropez

315 King St. W. (John St.), Entertainment District, 416-591-3600, www.lesainttropez.com

See Arts & Entertainment Nightlife, p. 116 for description. Open daily 11:30 a.m.–midnight; cabaret from 8 p.m. daily. $$$

Marché

BCE Place, 42 Yonge St. (King St.), Downtown/Yonge, 416-366-8986

The Marché is a unique concept eatery, where fresh foods are laid out at various stations—bakery, sushi, grill, salads, and so on—and cooked to order on demand. On a busy downtown corner, the open and airy Marché bustles with before- and after-work crowds hooked on the delectable foods. The food stations are efficiently arranged, and the staff is friendly and attentive in preparing your individual selections. Don't expect ordinary cafeteria offerings—Marché uses only the finest ingredients, and you can see it all for yourself. Fresh fish and meats are cut to order, and a nice wine list and cocktails add to the experience. It's a colorful and flavorful option for breakfast, when the pastry chefs present their tantalizing pastries, and also ideal for a quick lunch in the heart of downtown. *Open daily for breakfast, lunch, dinner, and late night 9 a.m.–2 a.m.* $$$

Mistura

265 Davenport Rd. (Avenue Rd.), Bloor/Yorkville, 416-515-0009 www.mistura.ca

The Mediterranean flair of the exterior sets the tone for Mistura, which serves contemporary Italian fare to the stylish crowds of Yorkville. Inside, the dining room is candlelit and elegant, with spacious seating under glittering modern chandeliers. This is where the Yorkville crowds come to loosen up: the servers are friendly, and the chic, executive-laced crowds create a festive atmosphere. Feast on updated classics like veal scallopini and consider finishing off your meal with the molten dark-chocolate torte. *Open for dinner Mon.–Wed. 5:30–10 p.m.; Thurs.-Sat. 5:30–11 p.m.* $$$

Moonbean Coffee Company

30 St. Andrews St. (Kensington St.), Chinatown, 416-595-0327, www.moonbeancoffee.com

Enjoy a cup of java and a healthy start to the day in the midst of Kensington Market at the Moonbean. If the weather's good, take a seat on the front or back patio along with neighborhood regulars and downtowners. Here the java is of gourmet quality. Moonbean roasts its own beans, which makes for a deliciously flavorful cup. You can choose from over 50 varieties, many of them fair-trade and organic brews. Tea lovers will also find much to love here, with a wide selection to choose from. A light menu of baked goods beckons, including samosas and bagels. The nana (banana) bread comes highly recommended. For a heartier start to the day, try the fresh bagel with egg, cheese, and vegetables. *Open daily 7 a.m.–9 p.m.* $

Nanoo Cafe

57 Front St. E. (Church St.), St. Lawrence, 416-214-1852, www.nanoocafe.com

Locals always know where to find the best breakfast downtown, and at Nanoo you'll find a room that buzzes with white-collar types every weekday morning. Office denizens indulge in eggs and other standard but well-prepared offerings at white brushed-metal tables. The slick feel of the place comes from the wooden banquettes with black leather-cushioned backs and white space-age chairs. Efficiency is paramount—to get the worker bees to work on time—but the leisure traveler is welcome to stay and sip coffee refills while observing the downtown come to life. *Open for breakfast and lunch Mon.–Fri. 8 a.m.–3 p.m.* $$

Perigee

55 Mill St. (Parliament St.), Distillery District, 416-364-1397, www.perigeerestaurant.com

Best Trendy Restaurants

A media darling and crowd favorite from the moment it opened its doors in 2004, Perigee is one of Toronto's trendiest restaurants. But come prepared for a leisurely evening—dinner at Perigee is theater, and the results can take up to four hours. Four young chefs prepare your meal from a kitchen that dominates the dining room, to the delight of the upscale diners and Food Television Network junkies alike. Here you dine *omakase*. Originally a term used in Japanese cuisine, the omakase concept—meaning literally to put yourself in the chef's hands—is applied to classic continental fare at Perigee. Diners specify five, six, or seven courses, and identify whatever items the chef is to avoid, and sit back to see what surprises appear. Dinner becomes a relaxed, improvised experience as diners watch their courses take shape. Perigee's physical appeal is true to its Distillery District location and features exposed brick, wooden beams, and solid wood furnishings. Seating at Perigee is limited, so reservations are essential. Ask for a table by the window for the best views both inside and out. *Open for dinner Tues.–Sat. 5:30–9 p.m.* $$$$

Provence Delices
12 Amelia St. (Parliament St.), St. Lawrence, 416-924-9901, www.provencerestaurant.com

With a wine list that has earned it the Wine Spectator Award of Excellence since 1999, Provence has won its many fans with consistently high standards in both food and service. Discerning Torontonians and the odd traveler in the know flock to this warm Mediterranean dining room. White French doors lead to a summer patio, while inside crisp linens accent antique candelabras. Offerings are based on French classics and feature a sampling menu that includes baked stuffed mussels, tartine, and Malpeque oysters. Regular menu specialties include mustard flank steak, venison, and rabbit. A large selection of cheeses and wines by the glass complete your meal. Service is attentive and friendly, completing this enchanting experience in Gallic-flavored fine dining. *Open for lunch Tues.–Fri. noon–2 p.m.; dinner Tues.–Fri. 6–10 p.m., Sat.–Sun. 6–10:30 p.m.; brunch Sat.–Sun. noon–2:30 p.m.* $$$

Pure Spirits Oyster House & Grill
55 Mill St. (Parliament St.), Distillery District, 416-361-5859, www.purespirits.ca
Best Seafood Restaurants

Pure Spirits is a particularly handsome restoration of the original Gooderham Distillery's shipping room, with the exposed brick and dark wooden beams used to modern and glamorous effect against black leather and stainless steel. The crowd is handsomely dressed, a mixture of theatergoers, artsy locals, and a few tourists, and they keep things buzzing at the dinner hour on weekends. A long bar on one side flanks cozy tables and black leather booths, with windows that look out onto a cobblestone patio. In the summer the crowds come in droves to sit on the patio from the afternoon right into the evening, absorbing the District's historic appeal along with a full lineup of live jazz. The menu doesn't disappoint. Appetizer choices include a trio of seafood tartare and Irish Whisky–cured smoked salmon Napoleon, with main dishes like whole fish, ahi tuna, and salmon, along with pork tenderloin and strip loin. *Open for lunch and dinner Sun.–Thurs. 11:30 a.m.–10 p.m.; Fri.–Sat. 11:30 a.m.–11 p.m.* $$$

Rosewater Supper Club
19 Toronto St. (King St.), St. Lawrence, 416-214-5888, www.libertygroup.com
Best Romantic Rendezvous

In a city rife with historic renovations, this opulent retrofit of an 1852 landmark truly lives up to the superlatives—"stunning" hardly does it justice. Downtown crowds love the grand dining room with 22-foot ceilings and soaring windows. Columns and decorative moldings add to the sumptuous period design. The chefs work behind a transparent screen etched in roses, producing inventive dishes of French-global fusion. Join the chic after-work executive types in the elegant lounge for a stylish drink, especially on busy Thursdays when complimentary hors d'oeuvres draw crowds. *Open for lunch Mon.–Fri. 11:30 a.m.–2:30 p.m.; dinner Mon.–Sat. 5:30–10 p.m.* $$$$

Scaramouche
1 Benvenuto Pl. (Edmund St.), Uptown, 416-961-8011, www.scaramoucherestaurant.com
Best Views

Perched atop the Avenue Road hill and offering a fabulous view of the Toronto skyline, Scaramouche has long been synonymous with high-end dining. The contemporary décor belies its location in an unassuming high-rise. Toronto's well-to-do classes, along with movers and shakers looking to impress, have been making Scaramouche their restaurant of choice for years. Sophisticated, continental-inspired dishes please the equally sophisticated crowd. Reservations are essential, but be warned that regulars reserve the best tables weeks in advance. *Open for dinner Mon.–Sat. from 5 p.m.* $$$$

Top o' the Senator
249 Victoria St. (Dundas St.), St. Lawrence, 416-364-7517, www.thesenator.com
Best Jazz Clubs

See Arts & Entertainment Nightlife, p. 119 for description. *Open Tues.–Sat. 8:30 p.m.–1 a.m. (first set starts at 9:30 p.m.); Sun. 8 p.m.–midnight (first set starts at 8:30 p.m.)* $$$$

Trattoria Giancarlo
41 Clinton St. (College St.), Little Italy, 416-533-9619
Best Celeb Sightings

Sophia Loren came here for the intimate candlelit romance of the dining room and the authentic Italian cuisine. The Giancarlo was among the vanguard of swank upscale eateries that transformed the College Street area from quirky ethnic neighborhood to a stylish see-and-be-seen destination. The creative nouveau Italian cuisine features grilled meats and dishes, like swordfish with mint or jumbo quail spiced with sage. If you're here in the summer, you'll want to get a seat on one of Little Italy's busiest patios and settle in to check out the fashionable street scene. *Open for dinner Tues.–Sun. 6–10 p.m.* $$$

Arts & Entertainment Toronto: The Nightlife

Azure Restaurant & Bar
InterContinental Toronto Centre, 225 Front St. W. (Simcoe St.), Entertainment District, 416-597-8142, www.torontocentre.intercontinental.com
Best Swanky Hotel Bars

See Arts & Entertainment Restaurants, p. 106 for description.
Open daily 6 a.m.–11 p.m.

Boiler House
55 Mill St. (Parliament St.), Distillery District, 416-203-2121, www.boilerhouse.ca

In the short time since the Distillery District was transformed into a nouveau arts and entertainment complex, it's become synonymous with live jazz, and that's what keeps the Boiler House jammed with music lovers from all over Toronto and beyond. A long bar affords a great view of the stage, where musicians perform the standards along with more-modern selections. There's plenty of standing room for guests to enjoy a cocktail or sample a glass from the lengthy wine list. The large space is divided into a separate dining area, and there are cozy two-person booths that make the warehouse-type space feel more intimate. For the hungry, there's a menu of updated Creole cuisine. The music starts at 7 p.m. Wednesday through Saturday, and there's a jazz brunch on weekends starting at 11 a.m. *Open for dinner Wed. 5–10 p.m.; Thurs.–Sat. 5–11 p.m.; brunch Sat.–Sun. 11 a.m.–3 p.m.* $$

Centro Grill & Wine Bar
2472 Yonge St., upper level (Eglinton Ave.), Uptown, 416-483-2211, www.centrorestaurant.com

Young and Eligible is what locals call the uptown corner of Yonge and Eglinton, and even a casual observer is bound to notice the higher than average quotient of upscale young professionals here. What's also sprung up in the area is a collection of shops and restaurants that cater to this clientele. Centro pulls in not only these stylish locals, but Hollywood heavyweights like Kathleen Turner. The cool mod space features slick barstools around a polished wood bar and a two-level dining room. Dine on beautiful Italian cuisine at this glamorous spot, and select a bottle from an impressive wine list that has won it the Wine Spectator "Best of" Award of Excellence. *Open Mon.–Sat. 5–11 p.m.*

Courthouse Chamber Lounge
57 Adelaide St. E. (Yonge St.), St. Lawrence, 416-214-9379, www.libertygroup.com

The Courthouse was indeed a courthouse back in the day, a place where lawyers and judges presided over the fates of the unfortunate. Nowadays, the hallowed halls retain their judicial majesty and serve as a sober backdrop to an evening of posh lounging. A stylish over-thirty crowd has fallen hard for the luxe surroundings and packs the place after 11 p.m. The 25-foot ceilings soar over marble pillars and floors. Ornamental moldings, rich mahogany paneling, red velvet drapes, and four working fireplaces reinforce the sumptuous theme. The Courthouse Chamber Lounge is open Friday and Saturday only, and DJs play old-school and retro music for dancing or just listening. *Open Fri.–Sat. 8 p.m.–2 a.m.* $$

Inspire
491 Church St. (Wellesley St.), Gay Village, 416-963-0044
Best Gay Bars

One of the trendiest gay date spots in town, Inspire is part of the "new" Gay Village. Popular with the usual Church Street suspects as well as in-the-know downtowners, here you'll find b/g couples downing the martinis alongside the boys. Inspire's slick vibe beckons from the street with a glass front for maximum see-and-be-seen potential, and within, it's all about sleek minimalism with white walls and contemporary furnishings. There's also a handsome patio that's open in the summer months. A Pan-Asian menu does exist, but the spot lighting, white plastic bar, and shiny silver candles make for a more clubby ambience. Inspire exudes style, but is also known for a friendly and unpretentious atmosphere. *Open daily 5 p.m.–2 a.m.*

Le Saint Tropez
315 King St. W. (John St.), Entertainment District, 416-591-3600, www.lesainttropez.com

With walls in ochre washes accented with blue trim and a stylish courtyard that's heated year-round, Le Saint Tropez will make you feel as though you've arrived on the French Riviera. The bistro menu only enhances the illusion. The buzzing pre-theater crowds lap up Provençal-style dishes like steak frites and bouillabaisse, and are then replaced by those who've come to sip wine and watch the live French cabaret–style singers that play every night starting at 8 p.m. Well-dressed locals looking for a special evening on the town, and a smattering of visitors, love the warm, friendly mood. You'll be charmed by the personable service and French-flavored tunes. Dinner crowds may depend on theater offerings nearby, but you can count on a solid crowd of

ARTS & ENTERTAINMENT • NIGHTLIFE

music lovers on Thursdays and weekends. *Open daily 11:30 a.m.–midnight, cabaret from 8 p.m. daily.* $$

Montreal Bistro & Jazz Club
65 Sherbourne St. (Adelaide St.), St. Lawrence, 416-363-0179, www.montrealbistro.com
Best Jazz Clubs

Although a congenial menu of French bistro-style fare is served with efficiency, this club is for the serious jazzophile, and dinner here is only a prelude to an evening of legendary music. The Montreal is known worldwide as a home for live jazz. Wynton Marsalis makes this a stop when he's in town, as do other luminaries of the jazz world, like Kenny Barron and Oscar Peterson. Expect a mixed crowd of attentive listeners, ranging from the well dressed to more eccentric jazz fans. Note that this isn't a raucous party scene—here, it's all about the music. *Open Mon.–Fri. 11:30 a.m.–closing; Sat. 5:30 p.m.–closing.* $$

My Apartment
81 Peter St. (Adelaide St.), Entertainment District, 416-348-9884, www.myapartmentbar.com

My Apartment caters to fashionable downtown singles who love to check each other out in the unisex washrooms. Well-dressed professionals jam the bar and dance floor from 5 p.m. on Fridays, while Saturday nights heat up after 11 p.m. House DJs play a wide variety from salsa to retro as the crowd gyrates under flashing colored lights. A stainless-steel bar and wood floors give the newly refurbished club a sleek and modern look. A flashy dance bar without the pretensions of one, My Apartment is made for the mating games of the over-thirty professional set. *Open Thurs. & Sat. 9 p.m.–2 a.m.; Fri. 4 p.m.–2 a.m.* $$

N'awlins
299 King St. W. (John St.), Entertainment District, 416-595-1958, www.nawlins.ca

N'Awlins is an ornate, baroque boîte. Heavy dark carved wood furnishings, arches, and exposed brick conjure up the steamy South. Mixed crowds of music lovers come here for tunes with the same Mississippi Delta flavor. Oversize photographs of the jazz greats remind patrons why this veteran of King West exists as a seven-day-a-week venue for live jazz and blues. The music starts at 8 p.m. Thursday through Saturday and at 7 p.m. the rest of the week. Music lovers and pre-theater crowds come early to dine on spicy Cajun cuisine like Mississippi mussels. Saturday nights are busy after the dinner hour, and you can linger over the music until 1 a.m. *Open daily 5 p.m.–2 a.m.; live music Sun.–Wed. 7 p.m.–11 p.m.; Thurs. 8 p.m.–midnight; Fri.–Sat. 8 p.m.–1 a.m.* $$$

Pravda Vodka Bar
36 Wellington St. E. (Victoria St.), St. Lawrence, 416-306-2433, www.pravdavodkabar.ca

A glass front looks out on Wellington Street, and inside the sparkle continues with lacquered furnishings and a long gleaming bar. Vodka is indeed king at this chic downtown newcomer, with over 40 varieties on offer, including Siwucha, a Polish brand aged 50 years in oak barrels. The cocktail set are smitten with this upscale bar that looks to bring a little bit of Russia to Toronto. Alongside the vodka, naturally, comes caviar on blini or dark rye, along with other Russian specialties. The eccentric chandeliers and white furnishings set against black lacquer tables and chairs are a playfully posh take on Russian themes. It's the perfect setting for a late nightcap. There are drink specials on weeknights, and be sure to ask about special tastings. *Open Mon.–Wed. 5–10 p.m.; Thurs.–Sat. 5 p.m.–2 a.m.* $$

Reservoir Lounge
52 Wellington St. E. (Victoria St.), St. Lawrence, 416-955-0877, www.reservoirlounge.com

This legendary swing-jazz bar where live jazz plays seven nights a week is well known to an international audience of music lovers. Rub shoulders with musicians and visiting glitterati—Nick Nolte drops by when he's in town, as does Chazz Palminteri. Tom Jones has been known to take the stage. Bare brick walls contrasted with white linens and simple furnishings give the music center stage. For hungry listeners, a menu of light fusion cuisine features inventive tapas and reliably excellent thin-crust pizza. *Open Mon. 9 p.m.–2 a.m. (no cover); Tues.–Sat. 8 p.m.–2 a.m.; live music from 9:30 p.m.* $$

Rosewater Supper Club
19 Toronto St. (King St.), St. Lawrence, 416-214-5888, www.libertygroup.com
Best Romantic Rendezvous

See Arts & Entertainment Restaurants, p. 113 for description. *Open for lunch Mon.–Fri. 11:30 a.m.–2:30 p.m.; dinner Mon.–Sat. 5:30–10 p.m.*

Sugar Club
57 Duncan St. (Richmond St.), Entertainment District, 416-597-0202, www.sugarclub.ca
Best Dance Clubs

Dancing without the divas, a trendy club without the attitude, just cool music and drinks with a welcoming vibe—that's the Sugar Club for you. The DJs play house, disco, and '80s retro, and the dance floor really heats up after 10 p.m. Thursdays are known for an influx of fashion-industry regulars. Funky green lights set the mood, and a fun, friendly hip-hop crowd—together with expertly mixed martinis—makes for a smashing night on the town. The lounge area is quieter and more upscale. Here, even the doorman loses that Entertainment District 'tude. *Open Thurs.–Sat. 9 p.m.–3 a.m.* $$

Top o' the Senator
253 Victoria St. (Dundas St.), St. Lawrence, 416-364-7517, www.thesenator.com
Best Jazz Clubs

Heavy on the mahogany, linens, and sparkling glassware, Top o' the Senator is a high-end Manhattan-style steakhouse that doubles as a sophisticated jazz club. Complete with a fully stocked humidor, an extensive wine list, and prime U.S. beef dry-aged on the premises, the Senator aims to deliver an uncompromising quality of experience—and succeeds. But many come just to perch at the bar and soak up the swanky Sinatra-style vibe among well-dressed over-thirty types grooving to modern and global jazz over martinis. Take note that seating is limited, and on Friday and Saturday nights, your dinner reservation guarantees seating at the first set. *Open Tues.–Sat. 8:30 p.m.–1 a.m. (first set starts at 9:30 p.m.); Sun. 8 p.m.–midnight (first set starts at 8:30 p.m.)* $$$

Arts & Entertainment Toronto: The Attractions

Art Gallery of Ontario
317 Dundas St. W. (McCaul St.), Chinatown, 416-979-6648, www.ago.net
Best Cool Art Spaces

The eighth-largest art museum in North America, the AGO houses a renowned collection of over 36,000 pieces representing over 1,000 years of art history. As a well-respected world-class venue, it plays host to blockbuster traveling exhibitions of masters like Modigliani and the French Impressionists. True to its public mandate, the AGO includes a significant cross-section of Canadian art throughout history, along with collections of European art, prints, and drawings, and contemporary art. From the spring of 2005 until 2008, the AGO will continue to operate as usual as it goes through a significant retrofit, including a renovated exterior designed by famed architect Frank Gehry. *Open Tues. 11 a.m.–6 p.m.; Wed. 11 a.m. –8:30 p.m.; Thurs. & Fri. 11 a.m.–6 p.m.; Sat. & Sun. 10 a.m.–5:30 p.m.* $$

Artinsite
416-979-5704, www.artinsite.com
Best Guided Tours

For a real taste of the Toronto arts community, take a tour with the experts. Tours designed and led by Betty Ann Jordan, arts writer and columnist with chic *Toronto Life* magazine, take you right inside the studios and galleries that make the local arts scene hum. Neighborhood walks open your eyes to hidden treasures like all the funky new galleries on Queen Street West, or the private art collection at the Ydessa Hendeles Art Foundation. In addition, Jordan will introduce you to some of the city's top artists and art dealers. Check the website for scheduled tours, and ask about custom and special-interest walks. $$

Cinematheque Ontario
Jackman Hall, Art Gallery of Ontario, 317 Dundas St. W. (McCaul St.), Chinatown, 416-968-3456, www.bell.ca/cinematheque

Housed in the basement of the Art Gallery of Ontario, but operating independent of the gallery exhibits, the Cinematheque offers an ambitious program of screenings of independent and avant-garde art, vintage, and foreign films. Programs include traveling screenings, often with the artist or director in attendance. The comfortable and intimate screening room is modern in design, with two screenings nightly throughout the week (typically around 6 and 8:30 p.m.) and an added matinee on Saturdays that often focuses on visual art. The programs, which sometimes include lively pre- and post-screening discussions and lectures, are well attended by locals. *Screenings daily approximately 6 p.m. & 8 p.m.; Sat. matinee 2 p.m.; check listings for specific event details.* $

Distillery District
55 Mill St. (Parliament St.), Distillery District, www.thedistillerydistrict.om
Best Only-in-Toronto Attractions

If you've seen *Chicago*, you may just recognize the Distillery District locations used extensively in the Oscar-winning movie. The Gooderham & Worts Distillery opened in 1832 at this locale east of downtown and for a time was the largest distillery in the British Empire. In the early twenty-first century, entrepreneurs saw a future of a different kind for the deteriorating neighborhood, and invested in a renovation of the area that turned it into Toronto's newest center for the arts. Between frequent location shoots, the District is known for outdoor jazz in the summer, and houses over 20 commercial galleries, artist studios, and workshops. At Pikto (www.pikto.ca), a gallery devoted to the photographic arts, you can sip cappuccino on a couch while you browse photography books and magazines. In fact, the whole enterprise has been such a success that the whole neighborhood is now on the rise as a result. *Hours depend on the venue.*

Elgin/Winter Garden Theatre
189 Yonge St. (Queen St.), Downtown/Yonge, 416-314-2871, www.heritagefdn.on.ca

The imposing arches and marble columns at the entrance stand in stark contrast to the modern glass-and-steel edifices on either side, and provide a taste of the last-century charm that waits to be explored inside. This unique double-decker theater complex was hopping in the vaudeville era, and may just be the most beautiful theater in existence today. Lovingly restored, it still operates as two separate theater halls with separate performance schedules. Ninety-minute tours are offered year-round Saturday mornings at 11 a.m. and include a visit backstage, as well as a viewing of the fascinating collection of original vaudeville costumes and props found during restoration. *Tours offered every Thurs. at 5 p.m. and Sat. at 11 a.m.* $

Elizabeth Milan Day Spa
Fairmont Royal York, 100 Front St. W. (York St.), Entertainment District, 416-350-7500, www.elizabethmilanspa.com
Best Spas

The privately owned Elizabeth Milan Spa is located in suitable splendor in the Royal York Hotel. Here, the rich and famous from the Duchess of York to Queen Latifah have enjoyed the attentive service and unique signature offerings that have made the spa a star in its own right. Along with a full range of skin, hair, and nail treatments, Elizabeth Milan's signature services include the decadent Chocolate Body Indulgence, featuring a chocolate mousse bath, chocolate French-kiss lip treatment, and much more. Ask for the VIP Royal Vault for the ultimate in exclusive pampering. Reservations are recommended at all times. *Open Mon.–Wed. 9 a.m.–7 p.m.; Thurs.–Fri. 8:30 a.m.–8 p.m.; Sat. 8:30 a.m.–7 p.m.* $$$$

Gardiner Museum of Ceramic Art
111 Queen's Park (Bloor St.), University of Toronto, 416-586-8080, www.gardinermuseum.on.ca
Best Chic Museums

Until the Queen's Park location re-opens in a newly renovated building in the fall of 2005, the Gardiner's shop, school, and temporary exhibits are open for visitors in other locations nearby. There's no need to lower your expectations—temporary traveling shows are taking place in handsome University of Toronto spaces—but just be sure to check listings for details and exact location. The permanent collection (which will re-open with the building in 2005) includes over 2,700 pieces that document the history and sheer versatility of ceramics as an art form, concentrating on works from the ancient Americas, Italian Renaissance pieces, seventeenth-century English pottery, and eighteenth-century European porcelain. Traveling exhibits have included the ceramic art of Picasso, among many others. *Open daily 10 a.m.–6 p.m.; Fri. 10 a.m.–9 p.m.* $$

Harbourfront Centre
235 Queen's Quay W. (York St.), Harbourfront, 416-973-4000, www.harbourfrontcentre.com

There's always something going on at the Harbourfront Centre, whether it's shows at the York Quay galleries, a literary reading, dance, or a theatrical performance. Offerings often focus on a central theme and typically have an international flavor, such as the well-attended Danish Festival that featured visual arts, dance, and films. Exhibits and performances take place both indoors and outdoors, weather permitting. A craft studio and shop feature cool ceramics, textile art, and other unique items. In the winter, join the fun at the Natrel outdoor skating rink. *Galleries open Tues.–Sat. noon–5 p.m.; check listings for details on other venues and events.* $

Lionhead Golf & Country Club
8525 Mississauga Rd., Brampton, 905-455-8400, www.golflionhead.com

If you like your golf game to be challenging, you'll find two 18-hole courses, Legends and Masters, to test your mettle at Lionhead. Legends, considered one of the most difficult courses in Canada, has a slope rating of 153 and water on 13 holes. The Masters offers more lush surroundings, with forests and ravines, and the fifth hole is 411 yards and a par four. A snazzy clubhouse awaits after you're done. $$$

Spadina House
285 Spadina Rd. (Davenport St.), Uptown, 416-392-6910
Best Historic Buildings

Built by wealthy Torontonian James Austin in 1866, this lovely restored Victorian house began as a country estate and saw the city grow up around it. Featuring design elements from the Victorian to Edwardian periods, the regal estate reflects four generations of the Austin family's exquisite tastes. In addition to the meticulously landscaped gardens and furnishings of historic interest, however, the original decorations chronicle the Toronto arts scene of the nineteenth and twentieth centuries. *Open Sept. 4 to Dec. 31: Tues.–Fri. noon–4 p.m.; Sat.–Sun. and holidays noon–5 p.m. Open May 1 to Labor Day: Tues.–Sun. noon–5 p.m.* $

Toronto Antique Centre
276 King St. W. (Beverley St.), Entertainment District, 416-345-9941, www.torontoantiquectr.com

The famed former Harbourfront Antique Market has taken its show indoors to a large and suitably historic building in the Entertainment District. Here you'll find 30 dealers carrying specialty antiques ranging from art and furniture to housewares, wood cabinetry, maps and prints, and militaria, along with more-exotic items like Tibetan jewelry and authentic vintage clothing and accessories. Whether you're buying or not, the bright and pleasant surroundings make it great for browsing, and you may just net that truly unique find. *Open Tues.–Sun. 10 a.m.–6 p.m.*

Hipster Toronto

Toronto's West End has long been the epicenter of cool. It's a magnet for artists, designers, and creative types of all disciplines, creating a community of downtown dwellers who have the reputation of living—and playing—on the cutting edge of every trend. It's no accident that Queen Street West, where you'll find most of the city's art galleries, is also home to some of the coolest clubs and lounges, the most inventive little restaurants, the hippest cafes. You'll find that Toronto can show you a world-class experience in hipness. So prepare to steep yourself in some serious attitude, some funky art, and some great tunes in some of the city's most eclectic spaces.

Hipster Toronto: The Itinerary

Our Hotel Choice: The Drake Hotel, because this has become mecca for the über-hip, whether they are looking to stay, drink, or dine.

Prime Time: Thurs.–Sat.

Day 1

Morning: Fuel up for a day of cool at the tongue-in-cheek **Beaver Cafe**, and soak up the Queen West vibe along with artists and other locals.

In decent weather, a walk east down Queen to the Entertainment District, through the *artsy 'hood* that is Queen West, to the **National Film Board/Mediatheque** located at the corner of Richmond and John will give you a good feel for the funky character of the neighborhood. Hunker down in space-age surroundings to browse a huge catalog of award-winning films, all while scoping out this busy corner of the Entertainment District. Then head into a private viewing station to watch your selections.

Lunch: Take a walk back west on Queen Street to **Bar One** for fresh Italian cuisine in slick modern surroundings. If Bar One is too new and strictly upscale for you, then consider a veteran of *the good old days*, the **Gypsy Co-Op**, which boasts an eclectic menu and slightly mad décor, complete with an old-fashioned candy store.

Afternoon: No self-respecting independent artist—or gallery owner—is seen before noon, so don't head out until the afternoon to explore the up-and-coming area called **West Queen West** and its many *art galleries*. More than 20 independent and commercial art galleries await your perusal, including the Museum of Contemporary Canadian Art in its new location at number 952. While you're at it, don't miss the hip designer boutiques, vintage clothing stores, or Queen Video, with its astronomical collection of hard-to-find films (it includes Quentin Tarantino among its members). For an afternoon drink in lively company, head a few blocks south to the popular **Liberty Bistro/Bar**.

Dinner: Funky and hip doesn't mean down-market, and dinner in Hip Central offers plenty of variety too. Sample the inventive *Canadian cuisine* at the **Drake Dining Room and Raw Bar**. Just down the street, mollusk lovers will adore **Oyster Boy**, where a real Maritimer serves up more than 20 varieties, along with other seafood that's scrupulously fresh. Or for an unusual culinary adventure—and most likely a few additions to your dining vocabulary—**Caju** is a *bright and warm destination* restaurant offering Brazilian fare.

Nighttime: No real hipster can leave Toronto without a visit to the **Drake Lounge**, where you'll find the martinis tasty and the scene fashionably artsy. Or, mingle with the local arts community, and try your hand at the city's best karaoke at the **Gladstone Hotel**. A mere block away from the Drake, the Glad has no fewer than three venues for your evening's pleasure. For upscale lounging, **Habitat Lounge** is a popular restaurant and lounge just a few blocks away. After midnight, *spontaneous jams* have been known to take place at the **Stones Place** (where you can occasionally even expect to find Mick himself if he's in town).

Day 2

Morning: Either walk it or cab it along King Street to just a few blocks east of Yonge, where you can sink into the glittery green vinyl chairs and observe a very mixed crowd of downtown locals at **Le Petit Déjeuner** as you order your *morning eggs*.

From there it's a short walk to the Financial District, and *a cool museum* in the former home of the Toronto Stock Exchange. But don't worry—when the financial types moved out, the artistic types moved in and completely revamped it, creating the **Design Exchange**, which is dedicated to chronicling the principles of twentieth-century design. And don't neglect your own fine self just because you're traveling. Even if you've always hated the soft-palate-and-feng-shui-fountains kinds of spas, there's a treat in store for you at **iodine & arsenic**, a place that bills itself as an "anti-spa," back on Queen West. Or check out the schedule and drop in for a class of "hot" yoga at **moksha yoga west town**, where everyone's always welcome.

Lunch: Join the cool downtowners at **Babur** for a lunch of authentic Northern Indian cuisine, and don't be afraid to ask your friendly server for help with the extensive menu. Or, for a *really fun lunch option*, check out **Zelda's** on Church Street in the heart of Toronto's Gay Village, where good food has tongue-in-cheek appeal.

HIPSTER • ITINERARY

Afternoon: Feeling artsy? It's a short stroll down Dundas Street to the **Ontario College of Art & Design** (OCAD) and the **Toronto School of Art Gallery** nearby. Both are premier art schools, featuring galleries lined with student and faculty work, large facilities, and the opportunity to network with creative professionals. Check the website for live interviews, concerts, and assorted alt-rock mayhem at radio station **102.1 the Edge**, which has a storefront studio on Yonge Street. For something completely different, walk the catwalks on a tour of Toronto's *coolest boutique brewery*, the **Steam Whistle Brewing Company**, in the shadow of the CN Tower. If the notion of a refreshing brew tempts, head to the **Beer Bistro**, where you'll order your suds by taste.

Dinner: Let your tastebuds be your guide tonight. For swanky steak and seafood and a long and *creative martini list*, **Byzantium** has been serving it up in the Gay Village for years. If your mood runs more to chic continental style, try **Toba** on King East, and if you're hankering for Asian food among stylish downtowners, **Spring Rolls** on Front Street is a perennial favorite.

Nighttime: Head back west for clubbing with a difference. On College Street, yet another home of the trendy, join the creative classes at **Revival** for a musician-friendly vibe and the odd celebrity sighting. Otherwise, check the listings for what's lined up at the **Mod Club Theatre** just down the street—it's known as one of the city's premier live venues. Alternative types will find an instant spiritual home at the **Velvet Underground**. For *late-night dancing*, the chick DJs at the **Bovine Sex Club** pump out the tunes with lots of style and energy. Right next door, the doors hardly ever close at the diner **Shanghai Cowgirl**, where clubbers and other denizens of cool congregate late night to refuel.

Day 3

Morning: Divine *baked goods* await fragrantly at **Vienna Home Bakery & Cafe** on Queen. Let the locals wonder how you discovered this excellent neighborhood secret.

Leave yourself a little room for tasting, though, and take a leisurely walk from Queen West to the Old Town, centered around **St. Lawrence Market**. Enjoy a tempting and visually enticing stroll through one of the world's top markets. Or, if you want to get get your morning off to a more energetic start, get your *adrenaline rush* at **Joe Rockhead's.** Call ahead to line up a rock-climbing adventure right in the heart of the city.

Lunch: The **Esplanade Bier Markt,** a cross between Belgian brasserie and slick club, is just two blocks from St. Lawrence Market. For more eclectic treats, the venerable **Rivoli** offers global cuisine in the Entertainment District.

Afternoon: After lunch, make your way down to the harbourfront, where *contemporary art* is on display in cool digs at the **Power Plant Gallery.** Another option is to check out the slew of galleries and arts organizations that are housed at **401 Richmond** in a huge renovated industrial complex. A leisurely option is to check the Saturday matinee listings and relax with a drink and an art-house film at the **Camera Bar and Media Gallery** in the late afternoon. One of art's purposes is to provoke discussion, so join the hipsters on College at the **Cafe Diplomatico** for an afternoon cappuccino or snack.

Dinner: Stay in Little Italy for—what else?—classic and updated Italian cuisine at **Bar Italia**, or innovative cafe fare at the perennially bustling little **Kalendar.** If more *exotic flavors* and colors are to your taste, make your way back to the Entertainment District for tantalizing Moroccan cuisine in fabulous surroundings at **Fez Batik.**

Nighttime: Distinctive clubbing beckons in *colorful Polynesian* flavors at the **Sutra Lounge**. Later on you can catch the drag-queen shows at **El Convento Rico**. Back in Clubland, the **Crystal Room** offers a stylishly hip experience—then end the night at posh **This Is London,** an exclusive and edgy nightspot. If you just want straight-up music, check out the listings and head east to the **Phoenix Concert Theatre.**

The Day After: Join the line-up at **Mildred Pierce** for a divine brunch, where any dish with eggs is highly recommended. Afterward, take a walk around the corner to Gladstone to view the Group of Seven paintings at **St. Anne's Anglican Church**. In fine weather, it's not much farther west (or a short cab ride) to **High Park**, to stroll in the woods or along the water and work off the excesses of your Toronto experience.

Hipster Toronto: The Hotels

The Drake Hotel
1150 Queen St. W. (Beaconsfield St.), Parkdale, 416-531-5042 / 866-372-5386, www.thedrakehotel.ca

Once a dive best known for draft beer in dirty glasses, the Drake Hotel underwent a stunning multimillion-dollar renovation and reopened in 2004 as the haunt of the über-hip on artsy Queen Street West. Attention to detail extends to every corner of the hotel, from the dance cave to the "Crash Pads" that combine antique elements and high-end modern design with a dash of the eccentric. The 385-square-foot luxe suite features dark hardwood floors against white walls, with contemporary furnishings in bold green and blue tones, and a striking bathroom with a glass shower stall. The other rooms are all different and feature restored antiques, DVD and CD players, and queen-size beds. Ask for the Salon Room, which has charcoal-colored hardwood floors and 200 square feet of luxurious designer space. The work of local artists is on display throughout the hotel—one of the owners is himself a working artist. The staff are young and attractive, friendly and delightfully attitude-free. Amenities include several meal options from breakfast to sushi to late night, along with a lounge, dance bar, and Yoga Den all located on site. $$$

The Gladstone Hotel
1214 Queen St. W. (Gladstone Ave.), Parkdale, 416-531-4635, www.gladstonehotel.ca

Where the Drake went contemporary high style, the Gladstone has taken a different approach to renovating its once historically seedy space. The Glad retained and restored old architectural features like its big wooden beams, the heavy wood bars and trim, and gorgeous baroque moldings and spiffed them up with cool touches of contemporary luxury like stainless-steel plumbing against exposed brick. Fifteen of the 52 newly refurbished guest room were designed by both famous and emerging artists who entered their proposals in a competition. As a result, each is unique, ranging in style from high-end to designer to arts-and-crafts. All include flatscreen TVs, internet access, and down duvets, and are accessible either by the grand staircase or Toronto's last surviving Victorian hand-operated elevator. High white ceilings arch over wooden plank floors that gleam with TLC. The hip and artsy congregate at this veritable institution in the arts community, and especially at the bar, which is the oldest continuously operating tavern in Toronto. Three bars on three floors host entertaining events from cabaret to film screenings to fashion shows. $$$

The Madison Manor
20 Madison Ave. (Bloor St.), Bloor/Yorkville,
416-922-5579 / 877-561-7048, www.madisonavenuepub.com

The Madison is old Yorkville with a youthful vibe, a Victorian mansion on a quiet leafy street just blocks from the monied classes shopping at Avenue and Bloor, with a patio that rocks until the wee hours in the summer. The houses that make up the Madison were built in 1892, and the Madison wears its age with good humor. Inside, the labyrinthine hallways are elegant, immaculate, with ornate and polished dark wood trim set against pale walls and dark green carpets. The décor includes a creative blend of authentic antique fixtures—lights, furniture—and modern amenities like satellite TV and cable. Ask for a room facing Madison Avenue (rather than the patio) for a quieter stay. Room 201 is a particular favorite—a charming mini-suite with oak armoire, sitting area with gas fireplace, and stained-glass window. The pub features an antique piano player and fireplace along with the patio, and as in the rest of the Madison, the mood is young and hip, with classy antique accents. $$$

The SoHo Metropolitan
318 Wellington St. W. (Blue Jays Way), Entertainment District,
416-599-8800 / 866-764-6638, www.sohomet.com

Featuring gleaming Art Deco style with luxurious appointments, the SoHo Met has spared no expense to make this a destination hotel, and if illustrious clientele are any measure of success, the investment's been sound. The gleaming brown mottled wood, a signature feature of the hotel's design that extends from the elevator to the guest rooms, is imported from Africa. Luxury rooms begin at about 600 square feet, and all include king-size beds, Frette linens, natural down duvets, wireless Internet, marble bathrooms, and heated floors. Ask for the spacious corner room located just above Sen5es Bakery. For real luxury, go where Metallica and Britney Spears have gone, and opt for the 4,000-square-foot, three-story penthouse, complete with its own elevator, three plasma screen televisions, five bathrooms, and a roof-level balcony with gourmet barbecue and eight-person jacuzzi. It's no secret why this hotel has quickly become a favorite of artists at the very high end of the scale. Hotel amenities include a fabulous Art Deco pool and hot tub, an exercise room, and a full-service spa and salon. $$$$

Hipster Toronto: The Restaurants

Babur
273 Queen St. W. (McCaul St.), Entertainment District, 416-599-7720
Best Ethnic Dining

Much acclaimed in the local media, Babur prepares sumptuous Northern Indian food that keeps the downtown crowds coming. An extensive menu of classics, along with tandoori, breads, and plenty of vegetarian choices, are prepared by enthusiastic chefs you can watch in the back. The friendly staff can help even those with no knowledge of Indian fare find mouthwatering fish, chicken, or meats, fiery hot or not. No matter what your choice, you'll find the food fresh and vibrant with the flavors of the subcontinent. In a long room, solid wooden dining-room chairs and white linens are saved from looking sterile by the arched white ceiling and delicate light fixtures. Strains of sitar add atmosphere without being cloying. Especially popular with professionals who work in the area, this is Indian food like you've never experienced it. *Open daily for lunch and dinner 11 a.m.–11:30 p.m.* $$

Bar Italia
582 College St. W. (Manning St.), Little Italy, 416-535-3621, www.bar-italia.ca

A classic of Little Italy, this longstanding institution is responsible for first drawing the chic crowds to this part of town. Characterized by attentive and thoughtful service, Bar Italia offers fresh Italian cuisine with a hip College Street vibe. Dark wood booths and paneling balanced by blue walls and sexy lighting make it a romantic dining experience, and you can then retire to the slick bar and lounge upstairs to continue the evening after dinner. Italian food is popular in Toronto, but it's rare to find it prepared this well, with creations like insalata di salmone with warm wild salmon, and entrées featuring pasta and risotto, steak, seafood, and lamb. A long wine list complements the menu. *Open daily for dinner 5–11 p.m.; open for brunch Sat.–Sun. 9 a.m.–3 p.m.; bar open daily until 2 a.m.* $$$

Bar One
924 Queen St. W. (Shaw St.), Parkdale, 416-535-1655, www.bar-one.com

A relative newcomer to the Queen West scene, Bar One has a glass front that beckons you into a minimalist, chic, and inviting space in yellow and ochre, punctuated by red stools lined up along a slinky bar. The key to the menu is deliciously simple Italian food prepared with a twist, like the ever-popular antipasto Bar One for two, loaded with grilled vegetables, focaccia, and olives, among other delicacies. Along with great food come a hip and black-clad clientele that pack the place from day into night. It takes on a sexy martini-lounge ambience with late-night eats Thursday through Saturday. *Open for lunch and dinner Tues.–Sat. 11:30 a.m.–11 p.m.; open for brunch Sat.–Sun. 9 a.m.–4 p.m.; bar open Tues.–Sat. until 2 a.m.* $$$

Beaver Cafe

1192 Queen St. W. (Northcote St.), Parkdale, 416-537-2768

With a tongue-in-cheek beaver-themed décor and laid-back vibe, the Beaver Cafe is a favorite of local artists and gallery owners. A bright room, friendly service, and a minimalist menu of light fare are a good fit for the leisurely cafe-style ambience. The grilled panini come especially recommended, with fillings like chevre, sun-dried tomatoes, and ham. Offerings are full of pleasant surprises, like the tasty rustic nana (banana) bread. The Beaver is most popular at breakfast time for heaped plates of ham and eggs, house-baked pastries, and lighter fare like granola. *Open daily 8 a.m.–6 p.m.* $$

Beer Bistro

18 King St. E. (Yonge St.), Downtown/Yonge, 416-831-9872, www.beerbistro.com

The goal of the Bistro's owners (a beer writer and a chef) is to spread the word about the wonderful world of beer. A menu of over 100 selections (including craft brews) is classified by taste, not country or name, and includes categories like "crisp," "spicy," or "bold." A whole menu of beer-based continental bistro fare helps the brews go down. Located on a busy downtown corner in a bright, sleekly modern room, Beer Bistro is especially busy with downtown professionals at lunchtime. Its outstanding range of cold brews also makes it a fine escape from the summer heat. *Open for lunch and dinner Mon.–Wed. 11:30 a.m.–1 a.m.; Thurs.–Fri. 11:30 a.m.–2 a.m.; open for dinner Sat. 4 p.m.–2 a.m.* $$$

Byzantium

499 Church St. (Wellesley St.), Gay Village, 416-922-3859

Long considered one of the best martini bars in town, the Byzantium also boasts a fine restaurant in a stylish setting. Green walls contrast with the cushioned orange chairs of the perennially busy bar and lounge, while in the dining room, lush floral arrangements soften the formal tables and seating. The seafood is especially recommended, and the Byzantium Classic is a popular choice of Black Angus strip loin and black tiger shrimp tempura. A long wine list complements the menu, which includes sublime desserts like homemade ice cream and baked-to-order cookies. Service is both playful and efficient, and the overall vibe is upscale but friendly with that special Boystown touch. *Open daily for dinner 5:30–11 p.m.; bar Sun.–Wed. 5:30 p.m.–1 a.m.; Thurs.–Sat. 5:30 p.m.–2 a.m.* $$$

Cafe Diplomatico
594 College St. W. (Clinton St.), Little Italy, 416-534-4637, www.diplomatico.ca

With a simple and casual Italian cafe menu of thin-crust pizza, pasta, and panini, Cafe Diplomatico defies all trendiness and is one of the real veterans of Little Italy. There's a laid-back atmosphere here that has even been known to draw Sophia Loren when she's in town. The interior is nothing special—tile floors and plain white vinyl chairs—but in good weather, the Diplomatico is one of the most popular patios on College to watch the parade of fashionable humanity go by. Unhurried service means you can linger over your latte for hours, and even in bad weather, you'll find a scene of fashionable hipsters and university students doing the same. *Open for breakfast, lunch, and dinner Sun.–Thurs. 8 a.m.–2 a.m.; Fri.–Sat. 8 a.m.–3 a.m.* $$

Caju
922 Queen St. W. (Crawford St.), Parkdale, 416-532-2550, www.caju.ca
Best Ethnic Dining

Modern and minimalist behind its glass storefront, Caju brings the exotica of Brazil to Toronto. Walls of pale blue and green complement a sleek bar and polished wood floors. Further down the long room, rows of tables and tan leather banquettes create an inviting dining area. Expect the unusual—an appetizer of grilled sardines over a corn flan and young greens, a special of grouper rolled in cassava flour, and a host of menu items that will likely expand your vocabulary. Attention to detail—from the Brazilian cherrywood floors, to the bossa nova playing, to the fabulous Caipirinhas (a traditional Brazilian cocktail)—make it a memorable trip south. Caju is open only for dinner and draws a young and eclectic crowd of regulars, along with foodies coming for the latest new tastes. You'll find your servers friendly and knowledgeable, the mood casual and festive. *Open for dinner Tues.–Sat. 5–11 p.m.; Sun. 5–10 p.m.* $$$

Drake Dining Room and Raw Bar
1150 Queen St. W. (Beaconsfield St.), Parkdale, 416-531-5042 / 866-372-5386, www.thedrakehotel.ca
Best Canadian Cuisine

Hipster hub that it is, the Drake is sure to dazzle for dinner in its stylishly offbeat and colorful dining room. This was a high-class renovation taken to the extreme, the hotel—and its dining room—treated as fine art. Insist on a table or booth where you can lounge decadently on the chic green banquettes while you dine and take in the vibe. Twenty-something executive chef David Chrystian is one of the city's rising stars, and the fare will impress with its interpretations of Canadian cuisine that focus on applying classic techniques to local and seasonal ingredients. The results are superb, and include a raw bar with sushi, oysters, and venison tartare, small plates featuring seared scallops and barbecued octopus with creamed parsley, and large plates of cedar-baked organic salmon, all of it prepared with an exquisite attention to detail that creates a happy marriage of form and substance. Film and television types join artists and celebs for dinner in this sociable ambience. Reservations are recommended most days and essential Thursday to Sunday when the line can go out the door. But don't be daunted by the crowds—it's worth wading through the lounge to the dining room. *Dining room is open daily for breakfast, lunch, and dinner 6 a.m.–11 p.m.; Sun. for brunch 10:30 a.m.–2:30 p.m.* $$$$

Esplanade Bier Markt

58 The Esplanade (Church St.), St. Lawrence, 416-862-7575, www.thebiermarkt.com

This block of the Esplanade is home to several pseudo-Celtic pubs, but the Bier Markt draws on Belgium for its brasserie-style brew and menu offerings. The décor is slick and modern, with more traditional brasserie accents like wooden stools at the long bar and rustic wooden chairs and polished brass pillars in the dining room. The extensive beer list includes fruity dessert brews, and the menu features fresh and inventive takes on Belgian brasserie fare like a wurst sampler and gourmet poutine, steak frites, and filet mignon burger. And the mussels are divinely fresh and fragrantly spiced, accompanied by substantial quantities of sourdough bread. This upscale brew pub and dining room turns into a nightclub after dark when yuppie crowds pack the dance floor and hunky staff make sure the festivities are enjoyable. *Open for lunch and dinner Mon.–Wed. 11 a.m.–1 a.m.; Thurs.–Fri. 11 a.m.–2 a.m.; for dinner Sat. 4 p.m.–2 a.m.; Sun. 4 p.m.–midnight.* $$$

Fez Batik

129 Peter St. (Richmond St.), Entertainment District, 416-204-9660

Dining room, lounge, and dance club all in one, Fez Batik is an excellent place to spend an evening. As one might expect from the name, the place is characterized by its exotic, Moroccan-inspired theme of richly colored carpets and harem-style floor cushions. The ambience here is hip and free of attitude, and it's popular with Richmond Street creative types and other adventurous diners and clubbers. The dining room occupies the main floor and overlooks the kitchen. The varied menu is sprinkled with Moroccan influences and makes for an unusual Pan-Global dining experience. The popular lounge has a cozy fireplace indoors and a busy summer patio, and DJs get the crowds moving—watch for urban music events Thursday nights. Try the Fez for fun and exotic dining in a clubby setting, then move on to the lounge and take a turn on the dance floor. *Open for dinner and dancing Thurs.–Sat. 6 p.m.–2 a.m.* $$$

Gypsy Co-Op
817 Queen St. W. (Gore Vale St.), Parkdale, 416-703-5069

The Gypsy Co-Op is what Queen Street is all about. Colorful and eclectic, this longtime queen of Queen West is winning new fans as this up-and-coming neighborhood draws an increasingly hip crowd. Lounge alongside local artsy types and stylish hipsters on well-worn couches, or take a table to sample from an inventive and global menu, featuring everything from honey-glazed calamari to black bean–salsa dip and barbecued strip loin. The dining room is reliably crowded for lunch and dinner most days, and has a lounge and live entertainment stage that really rocks on the weekends. Fun, with a slightly mad bent to both décor and menu—decorated by gypsies raised on Dr. Seuss, if you will. You'll love the full-blown candy store that's part of it. *Open for dinner Mon. 6 p.m.–2 a.m.; open for lunch and dinner Tues.–Sat. noon–2 a.m.* $$$

Kalendar
546 College St. W. (Euclid St.), Little Italy, 416-923-4138, www.kalendar.com

The prettiest little cafe on the College Street strip, and one of the most romantic dinner spots in town, Kalendar has long been a local favorite. Antique chandeliers hover over wooden floors, and there are plenty of booths and corners for quiet conversation, even though it's typically busy, busy, busy with thirty-something yuppies and older hipsters alike. Though the mood is unpretentious, head-to-toe black will never go out of style at Kalendar. With its cozy ambience and hospitable feel, this is a place where you can enjoy casual cafe fare of pizza, pasta, and panini, sip cocktails, and linger over cappuccino very happily. *Open daily for lunch and dinner 11 a.m.–1 a.m.* $$

Le Petit Déjeuner
191 King St. E. (Frederick St.), St. Lawrence, 416-703-1560

The electric-green booths are the first thing you'll notice about this funky eatery on newly yuppified King Street East. Here you'll be served a home-style breakfast and lunch classics prepared simply and well, and eat with a crowd that represents a wide cross-section of urban Toronto—lawyers and construction workers, students and civil servants. Relaxed earthtones and exposed brick complement the glittering green booths. The staff are young and enthusiastic. This welcoming start or boost to the day is a hospitable and welcome find. *Open for breakfast and lunch Tues.–Fri. 8 a.m.–4 p.m.; Sat.–Sun. 9 a.m.–3 p.m.* $$

Liberty Bistro/Bar

25 Liberty St. (Atlantic St.), Parkdale, 416-533-8828

With a cafe menu of appetizers, salads, pastas, and panini, and a busy and friendly vibe, this oasis of casual charm nestled amid converted warehouses and industrial buildings is sure to win you over in no time. The ivy-covered building sports a fine people-watching patio in the summer, but buzzes year-round after work with the creative types and young professionals who work and live in this neighborhood of upscale condos and production and design studios. (Among them is Nelvana Limited animation studios, maker of cartoons that run the gamut from traditional kiddie fare like *Babar* to the edgy *Quads.*) *Open for lunch and dinner Mon.–Thurs. 11 a.m.–11 p.m.; Fri.–Sat. 11 a.m.–1 a.m.* $$

Mildred Pierce

99 Sudbury St. (Dovercourt Rd.), Parkdale, 416-588-5695, www.mildredpierce.com
Best Brunches

The detour to this eatery in a semi-industrial compound off Queen Street West is well worth the effort. Although it's not much to look at from the outside, the cathedral ceilings, white linens, and bay windows within lend a gracious atmosphere to the dining room. The crowds of hip locals, young and old, come not only for the grand room, but for chef Donna Dooher—who tapes her Food Network Canada show, *The Cookworks,* on the premises—and her spectacular gastronomic creations. While Mildred is often bustling, brunch is the perennial favorite, and you can expect lines even if you arrive before 10. Note that brunch is the only time no reservations are accepted, so just be patient, and know that it will be well worth the wait. Dooher serves everything from traditional eggs benedict to an inventive spinach-y green eggs and ham, all of it delicious and beautifully presented. There's no better way to recover from the excesses of the night before than with a bountiful brunch in this lovely setting. *Open for lunch Mon.–Fri. noon–2 p.m.; Sat. 11 a.m.–3 p.m.; dinner Sun.–Thurs. 5:30–10 p.m.; Fri.–Sat. 5:30–11 p.m.; brunch Sun. 10 a.m.–3 p.m.* $$$$

HIPSTER • RESTAURANTS

Oyster Boy
872 Queen St. W. (Crawford St.), Parkdale, 416-534-3432, www.oysterboy.ca

Owned by a real Maritimer, Oyster Boy mixes a variety of mollusks with Queen Street cool for a winning dining experience. The latest addition to Queen's new restaurant row, Oyster Boy is all seafood, all the time, with no respite for the uninitiated and pure heaven for lovers of oysters, mussels, fish, and other delicacies. Congenial service enhances the mood. Don't let the goofy sign and unassuming storefront deceive—the place is packed with the usual West End hipsters, along with a few foodies drawn by glowing reviews. *Open for dinner Mon.–Wed. 5–10 p.m.; Thurs.–Sat. 5–11 p.m.* $$$

Rivoli
332–334 Queen St. W. (Peter St.), Entertainment District, 416-596-1908, www.rivoli.ca

The Rivoli has long defined the groovy ambience of Queen Street West. For many years, it was known mostly for its live music and DJs, but more recently it has drawn crowds for a wider range of events—from comedy nights to literary readings to burlesque—with a more eclectic and upscale crowd in attendance. What's often overlooked, however, is the Rivoli's equally eclectic menu. It's international fusion, with pastas, risottos, and calamari all favorites, and includes everything from burgers to Asian dishes to Caribbean fare. The black-and-white neon bar adds to the funky vibe of this fine institution, where the suits come for a hip lunchtime or after-work escape, and a crowd rich in artists and musicians regularly fills the place for performances and events. *Open daily for lunch and dinner 11:30 a.m.–2 a.m.* $$

Shanghai Cowgirl
538 Queen St. W. (Ryerson St.), Entertainment District, 416-203-6623, www.shanghaicowgirl.com
Late-Night Hangouts

Mix a classic diner with Queen Street hip and a quirky imagination, and you'll have Shanghai Cowgirl. The tongue-in-cheek, over-the-top-diner décor lends the place a fun and casual ambience. Since it's open from 10:30 a.m. and until 4 a.m. on weekends, fashionable hipsters flock here at all hours, especially to carry on the party in the wee hours. The varied menu of Pan-Global offerings includes southern fried chicken, Asian noodle dishes, and Belgian-style mussels, among many other eclectic dishes. If you're in need of sustenance and people-watching after the clubs, the perennially hip Shanghai won't disappoint. *Open Sun.–Thurs. 10:30 a.m.–midnight; Fri.–Sat. 10:30 a.m.–4 a.m.* $$$

Spring Rolls
85 Front St. E. (Market St.), St. Lawrence, 416-365-7655, www.springrollsonline.com

Slick, stylish, and modern describes both the décor and the clientele in this downtown eatery where you'll find it as busy on a Tuesday as on a weekend at both lunch and dinner. Exposed brick walls balance the minimalism of dark wood chairs and stark white tables in the airy room. The plate-glass front, near the St. Lawrence Market, is ideal for people-watching, and there's a small street-side patio in the summer. Spring Rolls features an extensive Pan-Asian menu that's been consistently voted the city's favorite. Dishes are fragrant with the flavors of China, Japan, and Thailand, like the teriyaki salmon that arrives still sizzling with a delicate, spicy crust of sauce. It's a case of superlative cuisine served efficiently to a youthful, fun crowd with a definite downtown buzz. *Open daily 11 a.m.–11 p.m.* $$

Toba
243 King St. E. (Sherbourne St.), St. Lawrence, 416-367-8622, www.toba.ca

Amid the high-end condos and modern furniture showrooms, Toba is an oasis of quiet style and fine dining. The upscale crowd comes for the comfortably hip and chic ambience in a cozy room. Rich, warm colors dominate, with dark red walls balanced by wood furnishings and gleaming stainless-steel lighting. On a bistro-style menu with heavy continental influences, the pan-seared duck breast is especially recommended, and the braised short ribs are second to none. All of the offerings are characterized by freshness and simplicity both in approach and in taste, and get rave reviews in local media. Expect a refined but friendly dining experience that you'll share with hip locals, enhanced by congenial service from the equally hip staff. Note that it's busiest on Fridays at the dinner hour. *Open for lunch Tues.–Fri. 11 a.m.–2 p.m.; dinner Tues.–Fri. 5:30–11 p.m.; brunch Sat.–Sun. 10 a.m.–3 p.m.* $$$

Vienna Home Bakery & Cafe
626 Queen St. W. (Markham St.), Parkdale, 416-703-7278

Simple and unassuming, this bakery and cafe is a magnet for in-the-know locals. It's busy mornings and afternoons with those hungry for the decadent home-baked breads, pastries, and other fare. Watch the gallery and funky shop owners come to break the morning fast with delectable sweets and healthier options. Enjoy the spirit of unpretentious cool in this hip neighborhood gem. *Open for breakfast and lunch Wed.–Sat. 10 a.m.–6 p.m.* $$

Zelda's
542 Church St. (Wellesley St.), Gay Village, 416-922-2526, www.zeldas.ca

Zelda's move to its current address in Toronto's funky Gay Village area was relatively recent, but the club and eatery wasted no time finding its niche and supplying a fun atmosphere for all. An eccentric tongue-in-cheek décor plays up the Gay Village connection with elements of Southern bordello and Indian ashram, although the crowd here represents a broad cross-section of urban cool of all ages, genders, and persuasions. Theme days may feature the hunky staff dressed in drag or military outfits, and don't be surprised if your fellow diners are too—the crowd is half the fun. An open kitchen serves up tasty California-style fare with mixed influences (and a sense of humor) like the I Love Juicy Burger and Wok and Roll Spring Rolls. The dining room dominates until evening, when all attention turns to the lounge. But in good weather, the bright summer patio sees lines down the block. Even standing in line, you'll be entertained by the colorful crowd, and it's well worth the wait to take a seat and nurse a mojito late into the afternoon. *Open for lunch and dinner Mon.–Fri. 11 a.m.–2 a.m.; Sat.–Sun. 10 a.m.–2 a.m.* $$$

Hipster Toronto: The Nightlife

Bar One
924 Queen St. W. (Shaw St.), Parkdale, 416-535-1655, www.bar-one.com

See Hipster Restaurants, p. 131 for description.
Open for lunch and dinner Tues.–Sat. 11:30 a.m.–11 p.m., for brunch Sat.–Sun. 9 a.m.–4 p.m.; bar open Tues.–Sat. until 2 a.m.

Bovine Sex Club
542 Queen St. W. (Ryerson St.), Entertainment District, 416-504-4239, www.bovinesexclub.com

Not nearly as bizarre as the name suggests, the Bovine is home to chick DJs who spin alternative music from retro to glam to punk in a bar with a Dadaist interior design conceived by local artists. In a darkened room with spots of bright colored lights, you'll be hangin' with a crowd that gives new meaning to hip. The throbbing sound system makes it impossible to chat—this is all about the music. Live cutting-edge acts take the stage some nights, so check the listings, or just go with the flow and see what you find. There's always a lively, sexy crowd here ready to party until closing. *Open daily 8:30 p.m.–2 a.m.* $$

Byzantium
499 Church St. (Wellesley St.), Gay Village, 416-922-3859
Best Gay Bars

See Hipster Restaurants, p. 132 for description.
Open daily for dinner 5:30–11 p.m.; bar Sun.–Wed. 5:30 p.m.–1 a.m.; Thurs. –Sat. 5:30 p.m.–2 a.m.

Crystal Room
567 Queen St. W. (Denison St.), Entertainment District, 416-504-1626, www.libertygroup.com/crystalroom
Best Scene Bars

The former Left Bank has gotten a major facelift and has been reborn as an elegant drink and music emporium called the Crystal Room. The old fixtures that gave the Left Bank its artistic character—the carved wooden bar, the baroque moldings and extravagant chandeliers—remain, but the whole has been enhanced with a new gloss of chic. The polished wood floors, ornate

HIPSTER • NIGHTLIFE

white bar (and extensive cocktail list), linen sheers, and beds for private VIP seating all lend the place a contemporary but sumptuous feel. This is upscale clubbing at its finest and the fashionable young trendsetters have taken notice. The Crystal Room is open Friday and Saturday only, and expect a line at the velvet rope after 9 p.m. *Open Fri.–Sat. 9 p.m.–3 a.m. $$*

Drake Lounge
1150 Queen St. W. (Beaconsfield St.), Parkdale,
416-531-5042 / 866-372-5386, www.thedrakehotel.ca

The Drake is a mecca for the city's hip crowd, and the cats who gather here in droves are stylishly funky—like the place itself—with a solid art-school contingent that tends toward the over-thirty demographic. The mood is set by a green-and-bronze-hued room, with warm brown leather furnishings and a wood bar, and artistic wall treatments that look like a Rorschach test. A wide screen plays flicks silently above the fireplace, around which armchairs and a couch invite you to sit and stay a while. Order a martini and take in the ambient groovy setting—you might even be entertained by DJs or performance art. Then head down to the throbbing dance club in the basement. Or check out some of the original art and photography the Drake exhibits each month. The young, good-looking staff are refreshingly helpful and free of attitude. Note that the lines start by 8 p.m. on Friday and Saturday evenings, so come early for dinner in the adjoining dining room and a free pass into the lounge ahead of the line. Weekends can be noisy in the lounge, making the year-round rooftop patio a better bet for more intimate evenings. You won't want to miss this see-and-be-seen spot for the creative classes. *Open daily 11:30 a.m.–2:30 a.m. $$*

El Convento Rico
750 College St. W. (Shaw St.), Little Italy, 416-588-7800,
www.elconventorico.com
Best Late-Night Hangouts

El Convento Rico is known for throbbing merengue and a wild crowd of serious partiers both gay and straight. The retro-glitzy décor is an ode to '70s excesses with colored lighting and lava lamps set against a wood bar, and a lounge area done in minimalist style. Expect sheer dance-club excitement and an over-the-top floor show from both the DJs and the crowd in what is called "Toronto's most mixed bar." The crowd may be diverse, but there's nothing but straight-up Latin music in all its many forms. On Saturdays, the Latino drag-queen show starts at 1 am. *Open Thurs.–Sun. 9 p.m.–3 a.m. $$*

Esplanade Bier Markt
58 The Esplanade (Church St.), St. Lawrence, 416-862-7575,
www.thebiermarkt.com

See Hipster Restaurants, p. 134 for description.
Open for lunch and dinner Mon.–Wed. 11 a.m.–1 a.m.; Thurs.–Fri. 11 a.m.–
2 a.m.; for dinner Sat. 4 p.m.–2 a.m.; Sun. 4 p.m.–midnight.

Fez Batik
129 Peter St. (Richmond St.), Entertainment District, 416-204-9660

See Hipster Restaurants, p. 134 for description.
Open for dinner and dancing Thurs.–Sat. 6 p.m.–2 a.m.

The Gladstone Hotel
1214 Queen St. W. (Gladstone Ave.), Parkdale, 416-531-4635,
www.gladstonehotel.com

The Gladstone offers the latest in cool, housed in lovingly restored historic digs. There are three venues for your pleasure, including the spacious Ballroom, where events including fashion shows, burlesque and vaudeville, live music, and DJs find a home in front of a funky crowd. The Melody Bar is famous for being the city's hottest karaoke spot Thursday through Saturday nights in an attractive room that features its original 1930s Art Deco wood bar and ten-foot ceilings. The smaller and more modern Art Bar hosts poetry readings and various improv events. Join the cool crowd for a raucous night of arty partying, outfitted with—after extensive renovations—arguably the most fabulous men's public bathrooms in town. Expect lines on weekends, especially for the Melody Bar. *Check event listings for special event times.* $$

Gypsy Co-Op
817 Queen St. W. (Gore Vale St.), Parkdale, 416-703-5069

See Hipster Restaurants, p. 135 for description.
Open for dinner Mon. 6 p.m.–2 a.m.; open for lunch and dinner Tues.–Sat.
noon–2 a.m. $$

Habitat Lounge
735 Queen St. W. (Manning St.), Parkdale, 416-860-1551
Best Sexy Lounges

Come to Habitat to mingle with a downtown crowd of creative professionals who work in television and film, fashion, and the arts, along with a smattering of better-dressed corporate types. The bar glows in amber tones against darkly painted wood floors and white leather couches. The restaurant is located at the back of the room, where the white booths and black leather chairs have more seating for the martini-fueled crowd. The menu is eclectic and casual, with pastas and delicious desserts among the favorites. A smaller bar smoulders at the back of the room, where an illuminated panel in fiery orangey red highlights the patrons to dramatic effect. Although it's busiest (and loudest) on weekends, the weeknight crowds are reliably solid and the setting more conducive to conversation. *Open Tues.–Sat. from 6 p.m.* $$

Mod Club Theatre
722 College St. W. (Crawford St.), Little Italy, 416-588-4663, www.themodclub.com
Best Clubs for Live Music

Fueling the city's fetish for Brit-pop cool, the Mod Club gives parties previously held at other venues a permanent home. While the decorations are early '60s-era mod, the scene, with most evenings' agendas event-driven, is new and cutting-edge. The stage is draped in red curtains at one end of the big, long room. The bar is lit up in white along one side of the room, and there's a drink list to satisfy most tastes. Most of the space is given over to the music fans who come to dance or just listen, but there's also a dramatically lit smaller lounge area with tables off to the side. Owner Mark Holmes was once a Canadian pop star, lead singer for '80s hair band Platinum Blonde. He's now known as one of the friendliest club owners in town, and his respect for and in the music industry has made this one of the city's leading live-music venues, with an emphasis on alternative rock and new music. The crowd is hospitable and dresses retro-Brit for Mod Club nights. *Open 9 p.m.–3 a.m. daily, but check concert listings for details.* $$

Phoenix Concert Theatre
410 Sherbourne St. (Carlton St.), St. Lawrence, 416-323-1251, www.libertygroup.com/phoenix/phoenix.html
Best Clubs for Live Music

Host to international acts like the Stones, Metallica, and U2, the Phoenix has been serving up live music, live-to-air DJs, and event programming to the cool masses for decades. With a main floor that includes a dance floor, five bars—including a 50-foot marble bar, a 20-by-30-foot stage, stylish crowds, fab music and fine drinks—there's plenty to keep you partying all night long. There's also a gallery-level Loft that overlooks the Main Room and a Parlour that is quieter and more private, complete with decorative bar and billiards. Check the listings, and join the hepcat crowds for a memorable evening. Opening hours change depending on who's playing. *Check the website for current listings.* $$$

Revival
783 College St. W. (Shaw St.), Little Italy, 416-535-7888, www.revivalbar.com

Housed in what was a Baptist church in the '60s, Revival applies the retro-church theme to its baroquely plush décor. Well-heeled over-thirty hipsters lap up the cocktails and the musician-friendly ambience, where Kid Rock has been known to show up to sing a tune or two. Scarlet crushed-velvet sofas welcome the creative crowds of film, fashion, and music-industry partygoers. The mood is post-modern upscale hip with more fun than pretense in the mix. Friday is blues night here, and the lychee martini is the signature drink. *Open Mon.–Sat. 9 p.m.–3 a.m.; check listings for details; Sun. jazz brunch noon–4 p.m.* $$

Rivoli
332–334 Queen St. W. (Peter St.), Entertainment District, 416-596-1908, www.rivoli.ca

See Hipster Restaurants, p. 137 for description.
Open daily 11:30 a.m.–2 a.m. $$

Shanghai Cowgirl
538 Queen St. W. (Ryerson St.), Entertainment District, 416-203-6623, www.shanghaicowgirl.com
Best Late-Night Hangouts

See Hipster Restaurants, p. 137 for description.
Open Sun.–Thurs. 10:30 a.m.–midnight; Fri.–Sat. 10:30 a.m.–4 a.m.

Stones Place
1225 Queen St. W. (Gwynne St.), Parkdale, 416-536-4242

Smitten with the city's low-key version of hip, the Rolling Stones have opened their last few world tours by rehearsing for a few months in "tdot" (the hipster's term for Toronto), and the Stones Place is vintage Toronto. Mick and the boys have even been known to show up at this Stones-themed haunt. It's all done up as a crazy Old West tavern, and covered in Stones memorabilia. Circular booths at the back feature overstuffed burgundy upholstery and a great view of the stage. Stones Places is known for the cool live bands it draws here and late-night jamming—and a crowd as hip as its Queen Street address. The drink list ranges from basic brews to martinis. It's a favorite with local musicians, and there's sure to be a few in the crowd. *Open Thurs.–Sat. 8 p.m.–3 a.m.* $$

HIPSTER • NIGHTLIFE

Sutra Lounge
612 College St. W. (Clinton St.), Little Italy, 416-537-8755

Up front, the lounge is billed as a classy champagne and oyster bar, the décor a mix of minimalist furnishings and old-grained woods. But in the back, toward the patio, the theme is Polynesian, complete with sand-covered floors, straw umbrellas, and awnings held in place with bamboo stalks. Welcome to Toronto's latest tiki bar! The tiki—or a martiki, featuring plenty of fruit and little umbrellas—is the latest drink of choice, now that cosmopolitans are so yesterday. Its variations come with names like Wicky Wacky Woo (coconut rum, melon liquor, and pineapple juice), and pack a heady punch. Check the listings for Djs, and share an exotic evening in Little Italy with hip College Street types of mixed ages, mostly clustered around the crowded see-and-be-seen bar. *Open Tues.–Sat. 8 p.m.–2 a.m.* $$

This Is London
364 Richmond St. W. (Peter St.), Entertainment District, 416-351-1100, www.thisislondonclub.com
Best Celeb Sightings

Open only Saturday nights and a favorite of over-thirty club kids and A-listers, this is the most exclusive club in town. From the foyer with a flickering fireplace, it's downstairs for dancing or upstairs to the lounge. The décor is Brit-pop Mod, and the upscale crowd dresses for it in retro style. Theme nights set the tone for the music, so check listings to know what to expect. It's tongue in cheek, yet sophisticated, and Room 364—the VIP lounge—is a favorite with celebrities. It has the city's most stylish ladies' rooms, with two stylists on hand to recoiff and revamp your look midway through the evening. This is where the edgiest of the monied classes come to party until 3 a.m. *Open Sat. 10 p.m.–3 a.m.* $$

Velvet Underground
510 Queen St. W. (Portland St.), Parkdale, 416-504-6688, www.libertygroup.com

The venerable Velvet Underground has long seduced with alternative-rock music and a one-of-a-kind design that features found-object sculptures by local artists, pool tables, and a mix of baroque and ultra-modern décor. The crowd too, is "alternative," ranging from dyed-in-the-wool hipsters to those who exchange their weekday suits and yuppie personas for edgier after-hours duds. And when it comes to alt-fashionistas, the competition can be fierce—but great fun to watch. This lush martini lounge and dance bar with an alternative groove often hosts events during the week as well as on weekends, so check listings and come early. *Open Wed.–Sun. 9 p.m.–2 a.m.* $$

Hipster Toronto: The Attractions

Camera Bar and Media Gallery
1028 Queen St. W. (Ossington St.), Parkdale, 416-530-0011, www.camerabar.ca

Owned by acclaimed independent filmmaker Atom Egoyan (*The Sweet Hereafter, Exotica*), the Camera Bar combines hip lounge and cafe society with an art film venue to good effect. Screenings take place in a state-of-the-art digital screening room. Then the cool, artsy crowds congregate to discuss and debate the films around a communal table or comfortable seating in the lounge area. A full bar offers a selection of wines, beers, and cocktails, and a light menu of casual cafe classics is available. Unique in Toronto, the Camera Bar was much talked about when it opened. The initial hype has passed, but the simple contemporary design, innovative screenings, and a community of hip film buffs have kept the atmosphere vibrant and fun. Check the listings for rare films and monthly screenings devoted to shorts. *Lounge open Tues.–Sun.; screenings Tues.–Sun. 7 p.m. & 9 p.m.; Sat. shorts 5 p.m.; check listings for details.* $

Design Exchange
234 Bay St. (Wellington St.), Financial District, 416-363-6121, www.dx.org
Best Chic Museums

Billed as Canada's premier center for design and innovation, the Design Exchange is a cutting-edge museum and educational institution housed in the former home of the Toronto Stock Exchange. In addition to exhibits devoted to fashion, industrial, and household design, some focus on specific materials and other components, such as plastic or wheels. Curators take pains to live up to the principles they espouse, creating displays that are a treat to take in. The sleek retro '50s chairs and cloverleaf nesting tables in the permanent collection are a must-see all on their own. The DX's mandate is to promote design concepts, including accessible design for disabled persons, as well as to commemorate Canadian industrial design. In addition to worthwhile exhibits, the DX offers lectures, workshops, other educational programs, and competitions for design students at a national level. *Open Tues.–Fri. 10 a.m.–6 p.m.; Sat.–Sun. noon–5 p.m.* $$

HIPSTER • ATTRACTIONS

401 Richmond
401 Richmond St. W. (Spadina Ave.), Entertainment District, 416-595-5900, www.401richmond.net
Best Cool Art Spaces

This old industrial building was revamped in 1994 by the owner-architects, who saw the building's possibilities and turned it into the hip downtown home of the arts that it is today. Follow the rabbit warren of hallways through four floors of art galleries and studios, funky fashion retailers and arts organizations. It's home to places like Gallery 44, dedicated to modern photographic art; film festival offices; and dub poets' associations. This is an excellent opportunity to get a look at the local arts scene at street level, and perhaps even network with other creative professionals. The building includes a cafe on the ground floor and a charming rooftop garden patio with a view of busy downtown. *Hours vary according to tenants; special events occur evenings; galleries are typically open Tues.–Sat. noon–5 p.m.*

High Park
1873 Bloor St. W. (High Park Ave.), Parkdale
www.city.toronto.on.ca/parks/parks_gardens/highpark.htm
Best Ways to Enjoy a Sunny Day

At the southwestern edge of metropolitan Toronto, 400 acres of wooded trails and greenery await. A favorite of locals, the park includes a lake along which you can stroll and feed the swans. During the summer months, a fabulous outdoor amphitheater hosts Shakespearean drama and comedy, produced by CanStage. From late June until early July, you can catch Scream in the Park, a hip literary reading series that draws huge crowds. If you need a little break from all the fast-paced urbanity around you, High Park is a lovely retreat on a beautiful day.

iodine & arsenic
867 Queen St. W. (Gore Vale St.), Parkdale, 416-681-0577, www.iodineandarsenic.com

This anti-spa is a place for all who enjoy the self-indulgent benefits of facials, manicures, and other spa treatments, but who don't love that stereotypical spa atmosphere of pale whites and bubbling feng-shui fountains. At Arsenic, the walls are red, the floor is black, and there's just one big room. Since it only caters to one client at a time, appointments are a must at this unique place, which offers a full range of traditional salon services, including manicures and pedicures, skin treatments, massage, and waxing. Specialty treatments include PMS Treatment—billed as "better than chocolate!"—which combines massage, lymphatic drainage, and a seaweed wrap.

Facials involve a line of products using organic ingredients grown in Hungary. The address also includes the O.R. hair studio and body piercing by Tom Brazda (www.tombrazda.com). *Open Mon.–Sat. 11 a.m.–7 p.m.; Sun. noon–5 p.m.* $$$$

Joe Rockhead's

29 Fraser Ave. (Liberty St.), Parkdale, 416-538-7670, www.joerockheads.com

Both experienced and novice rock climbers can find the right course to challenge them here, among the 21,000 square feet of indoor climbing terrains designed by ALF nationally certified course-setters. High standards of training for staff ensure an experience that's both safe and fun. Flexible passes can include equipment rental. Reservations are recommended for lessons, although walk-ins are sometimes accommodated. Take on the challenge of a climb here, and savor a welcome respite from more-intellectual pursuits. *Open May 1–Oct. 31: Mon.–Fri. noon–11 p.m.; Sat.–Sun. 10 a.m.–7 p.m.; open Nov. 1–Apr. 30: Mon.–Fri. noon–11 p.m.; Sat.–Sun 10 a.m.–9 p.m.* $$$

moksha yoga west town

860 Richmond St. W., 3rd Fl. (Strachan St.), Parkdale, 416-361-3033, www.mokshayogawesttown.com

If you can't get through the day without your yoga workout, or even if you just feel like trying something new, the moksha yoga west town studio welcomes expert devotees and rank beginners alike. Moksha yoga is a studio for "hot yoga," practiced at a room temperature of 99 degrees Fahrenheit (37 degrees Celsius) to allow for deep stretching and to promote detoxification. Your body gets a comprehensive workout in a studio designed to meet high environmental standards. A rotating schedule of classes is on offer seven days a week, and drop-ins are always welcome. Just remember to bring your mat! *Classes are offered daily 9:30 a.m.–9:30 p.m., but be sure to check the schedule for each day's time slots.* $$$

National Film Board/Mediatheque

150 John St. (Richmond St.), Entertainment District, 416-973-3012, www.nfb.ca/mediatheque/en

The NFB's Mediatheque is a film-viewing center located in an intriguing contemporary space overlooking the corner of John and Richmond Streets. Currently in the midst of digitizing its phenomenal catalog of thousands of films (including many Oscar-winners), the NFB offers over 1,200 titles for viewing. Single or double viewing stations sport comfortable leatherette recliners. Once comfortably ensconced, you can select from animated shorts and features, documentaries, news programs, dramatic shorts and features,

HIPSTER • ATTRACTIONS

and experimental films, all at your fingertips thanks to cutting-edge touch-screen technology. You get to enjoy the films on a private flat-screen high-definition television, with speakers located in the chair's headrest. It's easy to while away the morning browsing through the astounding catalog, and friendly and enthusiastic staff are always available to answer questions. The Mediatheque hosts groups of various kinds, so a quick call to check for scheduled groups is recommended. *Mon.–Tues. 1 p.m.–7 p.m.; Wed. 10 a.m.–7 p.m.; Thurs.–Sat. 10 a.m.–10 p.m.; Sun. noon–5 p.m.* Free.

102.1 the Edge
228 Yonge St. (Shuter St.), Downtown/Yonge, 416-603-2205, www.edge.ca

Innovative alternative rock radio station 102.1 FM the Edge broadcasts live out of a storefront studio in the middle of busy Yonge Street. Visitors are welcome to come in and check out merchandise and the studio, but check in advance for special events like live tapings and interviews. Indie bands play live in free concerts on Friday and Saturday nights, and draw crowds of young hipsters looking to catch the latest hot sounds. Known for its irreverent post-modern edge and the latest in alternative music, 102.1 is the kind of place where you may bump into your favorite alt-rock idols like the Red Hot Chili Peppers. *Check the website for details about events and interviews.*

Ontario College of Art & Design
100 McCaul St. (Dundas St.), Chinatown, 416-977-6000, www.ocad.on.ca

Known for producing a wide range of working artists—some of Canada's most exciting and innovative among them—the Ontario College of Art & Design is one of Canada's premier art schools. A recent recipient of a multimillion-dollar expansion and renovation, it is now the fourth-largest institution of its kind in North America. Informal visits are possible by calling ahead or checking with the office, and the student gallery is open during business hours for viewing the work of the next generation of up-and-coming Canadian artists. Expect the kind of cutting-edge work only art school can produce—and colored hair and body piercings in abundance among the student body. *Check with the office for an informal visit.*

Power Plant Gallery
231 Queen's Quay W. (York St.), Harbourfront, 416-973-4949, www.thepowerplant.org
Best Cool Art Spaces

As part of the Harbourfront Centre for the Arts, the Power Plant Gallery consists of three rooms of adjustable gallery space roughly 650 square meters in size. Innovative lighting systems create dramatic backdrops and highlight the exhibitions. The Power Plant is devoted to showcasing up-and-coming as well as more established contemporary artists, so expect innovation and originality. Housed in a former trucking garage, the Power Plant opened 16 years ago to much fanfare and has provided a focal point for contemporary art in the city ever since with its full slate of exhibitions, shows, lectures, and educational programs. Check the website to see what's on exhibit when you're in town. *Open Tues.–Sun. noon–6 p.m.; Wed. noon–8 p.m.* $$

St. Anne's Anglican Church
270 Gladstone Ave. (Queen St.), Parkdale, 416-536-3160, www.stannes.on.ca

The only authentic Byzantine church in Canada, and a scale model of St. Sofia in Istanbul, this designated historic site was built in 1908 by Ford Howland and is decorated with 21 paintings on the domed ceiling and walls done by members of the Group of Seven. The Group of Seven painters took modern art and made it Canadian, and their work is considered important in that context, but you won't need to study beforehand to appreciate the talent and colors under the cathedral's dome. *The church welcomes visitors for self-guided tours every Sun. after the 10 a.m. service, or by pre-arranged visit.*

St. Lawrence Market
92 Front St. E. (Jarvis St.), St. Lawrence, 416-392-7219, www.stlawrencemarket.com
Best Historic Buildings

St. Lawrence Market has been feeding Torontonians for two centuries in the spot it still occupies. While the neighborhood's going condo these days, the St. Lawrence hasn't been gentrified. It's still housed in a huge building that looks like an auction house with concrete floors and bright stalls—all scrupulously clean. Two floors beckon with traditional farmers market fare of meats, fish, cheeses, produce, along with international crafts and clothing, and more than a few surprises. Don't miss Caviar Direct, dealing only in caviar and delectable smoked salmon, or the ever-popular Mustachio, which serves up authentic Italian sandwiches to hungry shoppers. Other vendors offer organic produce, fresh roasted coffee, gourmet tofu, and sushi. You'll find a mixed crowd, from students to socialites, gay and straight, and every ethnicity imaginable. A cooking theater, equipped for television tapings, cooking classes, and corporate events, is set to open in summer 2005. *Open Tues.–Thurs. 8 a.m.–6 p.m.; Fri. 8 a.m.–7 p.m.; Sat. 5 a.m.–5 p.m.*

HIPSTER • ATTRACTIONS

Steam Whistle Brewing Company
The Roundhouse, 255 Bremner Blvd. (Blue Jays Way), Harbourfront, 416-362-2337, ext. 246, www.steamwhistle.ca
Best Guided Tours

In the shadow of the CN Tower, this state-of-the-art boutique brewery was started by young up-and-comers who took over the old John Street Roundhouse building in 1999. A pilsner is their signature brew; you'll find it served at most of the hottest clubs in the Entertainment District. Tours along the catwalks through the impressive works, complete with tastings, run every hour in the afternoons. *Open Mon.–Sat. noon–6 p.m.; tours 1–5 p.m. Call ahead in case there's a private function.* $

Toronto School of Art Gallery
410 Adelaide St. W., 3rd Fl. (Spadina Ave.), Chinatown, 416-504-7910, www.tsa-art-ca

The Toronto School of Art was formed in the 1970s as an anti-establishment art school, and left-of-center politics have been part of the artistic landscape here ever since. The political discussions remain, but the school has also developed into a well-respected private institution with a wide range of visual arts programs on offer. A small student gallery here houses the work of the current and future avant-gardists, in addition to faculty exhibits. *Informal visits to the school itself are usually possible, but call ahead to check.*

West Queen West
Between Bathurst and Gladstone, www.westqueenwest.ca

What is today a thriving, upscale, artsy mecca has undergone a great deal of transformation in recent years—from its former heyday as an artists' haunt in the '70s, through falling fortunes, to the resurgence of the independent art scene in the late '90s, and fueled of late by the stunning Drake Hotel renovation that's brought in a whole new era of cool. The result is a surge of historic renovations and an interesting mix of designer and vintage clothing stores; cool modern and retro furniture; specialty shops like Queen Street Video, where 6,000 hard-to-find titles have recruited the likes of Quentin Tarantino, among others; and the art galleries and artists that have always given the street its unique flavor. You'll easily find more black clothing and hair dye per capita here than in any other neighborhood, as well as some unique shopping opps. But the real fun comes in the countless opportunities to hook up with the local hipsters.

Classic Toronto

What was once a prim and proper Victorian city has been transformed by waves of newcomers who have added cosmopolitan European flair, the exotic tastes of Asia, and the rhythms of the Caribbean, among many other influences. This Classic Toronto itinerary reveals the city's many facets—from colorful neighborhoods and a well-established music scene to elegant restaurants and world-class institutions. So get ready to experience the best of this eclectic and fabulous city's offerings.

Classic Toronto: The Itinerary

Our Hotel Choice: The **Fairmont Royal York**, because, with its fine appointments and furnishings, and a commitment to excellence in service, this landmark has a long history of welcoming guests in regal grandeur.

Prime Time: Thurs.–Sat.

Day 1

Morning: Get a *jump start* on the day at the **Bloor Street Diner & Bistro Express** on King and University, and watch the sharply suited Financial District types hurry by as you linger over the hot beverage of your choice.

Begin your exploration of Toronto with a look—a really spectacular look—at the city from above ground. A marvel of modern engineering, the world's tallest freestanding structure, and the lynchpin of the Toronto skyline, the famed **CN Tower** is a fitting way to begin your tour of the town. Once you're back on terra firma, it's a few blocks down Front Street back to Yonge and that shrine to *that most Canadian of sports*, hockey, at the palatial **Hockey Hall of Fame**, where you don't even need to be a diehard fan to enjoy the exhibits.

Lunch: Upscale and elegant, **Avalon**, in the Entertainment District, is a perennial favorite. Enjoy a meal of classic contemporary continental fare among well-heeled locals. If you're hankering for seafood, it's a few blocks down King Street East to **Starfish Oyster Bed & Grill**, a bustling New York–style *oyster bar* and bistro located in a lovely park setting.

Afternoon: After lunch, return to the lakeside for a walk along the Harbourfront to take in the scenery. Boat tours can whisk you off on the sparkling waters of Lake Ontario. Or take one of the ferries to the **Toronto Islands** and explore the "other" Toronto of beaches and gardens and the counterculture vibe of the Islanders. If weather doesn't make a boat trip look appealing, or you want to cap off the experience, **Queen's Quay Terminal** offers upscale souvenir-shopping opportunities in bright and airy surroundings. In the choice of afternoon drinks, let the weather be your guide—make your way to the busy *lakeside patio* at **Lago**, or head to the cozy wood-paneled comfort of the **Library Bar**.

CLASSIC

Dinner: Dress up for dinner downtown at any of the following legendary restaurants. For a swank steakhouse experience, there's none better than **Harbour 60**, located in the posh former home of the Harbour Commission. If you didn't get enough of the view from the CN Tower, or just want to enjoy the sparkling nighttime version, **Canoe Restaurant & Bar** awaits with superb *Canadian cuisine* at the top of the TD Tower. In that same office tower, hidden in the concourse level, **Bymark** lies half-hidden in the concourse level, a sexy slice of the Financial District distinguished by its luxurious décor and soaring views. The dining room is elegant, but the lounge provides superior people-watching opportunities—come early for a drink to catch the movers and shakers playing mating games at the bar.

Nighttime: A day of landmarks deserves a fitting end of clubbing, so let your hair down a little and check out these popular spots. Check out the live music at the eponymous **Healey's**, where the owner, blind blues guitarist Jeff Healey, is a local legend. If jazz is more your style, the best in Canadian and international acts play every night at the venerable **Rex Hotel Jazz & Blues Bar**. Or join the throngs of partying downtowners at **Crocodile Rock**, where classic rock is the soundtrack of choice, and you may just bump into the celebs and pro-sports figures that frequent the joint. Upscale pubbing and a popular patio are the order of the day at Gay Village mainstay **Hair of the Dog**. If hunger pinches in the *late-night hours*, the kitchen at lively pub **C'est What?** is open until 2 a.m.

Day 2

Morning: Head uptown for a *stylish breakfast* in artistic surroundings at the **Studio Cafe** in the Four Seasons.

While you ponder the new day, consider how you'd like to fill the morning. Do the greens call? If so, it's a short drive to Oakville and the home of Tiger Woods' "shot of 2000," **Glen Abbey Golf Club**, for a round of 18 holes. Or perhaps the delayed stresses of travel leave you in need of *celebrity-level pampering* at the renowned **Stillwater Spa**, located nearby in the Park Hyatt. If the neighborhood suits you, then stay uptown and explore Toronto's castle, **Casa Loma**, where imposing nineteenth-century grandeur rises majestically above the modern city.

CLASSIC • ITINERARY

Lunch: **Avenue**, with its neutral-toned décor and *long onyx* bar, is all about muted, sophisticated glamour, and full of fashionable clientele. Or for succulent seafood that impresses even Hollywood types, **Joso's** is nearby, with a patio that overlooks the designer boutiques of Yorkville.

Afternoon: You'll have already noticed the grand and imposing **Royal Ontario Museum** (ROM), but dismiss any notions you might have about stuffy museums—in Toronto, the museums aim to please, fascinate, and entertain as well as educate, so catch the latest blockbuster show or browse the vast permanent collection. Afterward, stop in at the **Tea Room** at the Windsor Arms Hotel for high tea or make a stop at **Caren's Wine and Cheese Bar** for a sampling of fruits of the vine.

Dinner: Tonight return uptown for an evening of luxurious dining. The ultra-posh **Truffles** never fails to seduce its clientele with its high-end continental cuisine and service that's second to none. Or you can choose to go fresh and colorful at the ever-popular **Boba**, where fusion gets a healthy spin in a gorgeous dining room. A short cab ride further north, to fashionable Yonge and Eglinton (called "Young and Eligible" by all the locals), takes you to the famous **North 44°**, a fine-dining estasblishment well-known for its *Mediterranean-inspired masterpieces*.

Nighttime: Stay uptown to check out the nightlife scene above Bloor. **Hemingway's** has an often-packed heated rooftop patio, where the mood is friendly and the celebs have been known to come out to play. Or, for a real piece of Toronto history, head to the **Roof Lounge** at the Park Hyatt, an *upscale watering hole* with a terrific view of the city. You may then want to catch the stylish crowds that congregate at **Wish** for martinis after midnight. When you need a bit of sustenance, **7 West Cafe**, just down the street, has a kitchen that's open 24/7.

Day 3

Morning: **Cafe Supreme** is a fresh way to start to the day, and offers a view of the busy intersection at University and Wellington in the Financial District. Or, if the day is sunny and superb, take a cab to Queen Street East and the Beaches neighborhood. The **Sunset Grill** is a long-standing *Beaches institution* that will welcome you with a bountiful traditional breakfast. Be sure to arrive hungry.

Then head out to either explore the downtown area, or to go for a scenic walk along the Beaches. In town, **Kensington Market** is a feast for the eyes with an eclectic array of shops. For a slice of *laid-back cool*, the **Beaches**, at the bohemian end of town, offers its own collection of shops and curiosities, and the pebbly beaches and clear waters of Lake Ontario.

Lunch: Return downtown for a lunch influenced by Asia. **Bright Pearl Seafood** serves up authentic dim sum, or for a *glamorous experience* in Chinatown and some fine continental cuisine, **One Up Resto/Lounge** beckons from the edge of Bay and Dundas.

Afternoon: Toronto boasts no fewer than five **Chinatowns**, but the downtown hub of Chinese and Asian culture is centered along Spadina. A walk along that avenue is a fine way to explore this fascinating neighborhood of *open-air markets* and more. On your way back, join the late-afternoon crowd for a drink at **Hemispheres** at the Met.

Dinner: This evening's dinner options are especially enticing. In midtown, **Splendido** is sure to impress with its sublime fusion menu and sunny décor. Steeped in old-world glamour, the **Courtyard Cafe** at the Windsor Arms, with its airy room, potted palms, and classic continental menu, will sweep you into a Hollywood frame of mind. Back downtown, above a noisy nightclub is the rarefied sanctuary of a roaring fireplace, rich drapery, and French fare that is called **The Fifth**. Or, for a truly different spin on the evening, hail a cab and head to Greektown—the largest ethnic Greek neighborhood outside the Mediterranean. There you should make it your goal to claim one of the *coveted patio seats* at **Ouzeri**.

Nighttime: **La Rouge Executive Club** is where the execs let down their hair and dance to *groovy tunes*. For either lounging or dancing, head to the sexy and intimate **Up and Down Lounge**, or to the **G-Spot** for a friendly ambience and three floors of cool. If you were in Greektown for dinner, stick around to sample the nightlife. Make your way directly to the stylish **Myth**, or **Lolita's Lust & the Chinchilla Lounge**. When the night wears on and hunger pangs hit, **Bistro 333** serves up Italian fare until 4 a.m.

> **The Morning After:** For brunch, the **Hot House Cafe** has been a mainstay for decades. Sit at one of the window tables and recover in gracious comfort from the excesses of the night before.

Classic Toronto: The Hotels

Fairmont Royal York
100 Front St. W. (York St.), Downtown/Yonge, 416-368-2511, www.fairmont.com/royalyork

You'll be received in grand style from the moment the liveried doorman greets you. From there, you'll walk up the marble staircase to a lobby that is all Waspy elegance, from the ornately tiled floors to the painted inlaid ceiling, to the gilt fixtures, to the crest and Rose of York (one presumes) on the carpeting, and the pseudo-brocade upholstery. Expect to be treated as no less than royalty, but for the ultimate in gilt-edged luxury, ask for one of the specialty suites. The Prime Minister Suite is 850 square feet of sumptuous furnishings, including a full kitchen and dining area, king-size bed, and private ensuite marble bathroom. The Fairmont View Rooms are the best non-suite rooms, which are 250 square feet in size and come with a king-size bed and harbor view. All the specialty suites offer a view of the busy downtown core. Ask about Fairmont Gold, a separate luxury-hotel-within-a-hotel on a separate floor with top-of-the-line amenities. There are many dining options at the Royal York, including the grand, formal dining room at Epic (known for its high tea where a tea sommelier presides to help you order to your taste). Other choices include Benihana Japanese Steakhouse, the posh Library Bar, or the more casual Piper's Bar. $$$

Hilton Toronto
145 Richmond St. W. (University Ave.), Financial District, 416-869-3456 / 800-445-8667, www.hilton.com

After an award-winning $25 million renovation, the Hilton Toronto boasts a sleek contemporary interior. Comfort and attentive service meet here in a convenient downtown location at the heart of the action. The lobby is sober and elegant, with a striking modern décor punctuated by huge columns. Thirty-two floors of guest rooms await, including the prestigious Crowne Suites, located on the 32nd floor with access to a wood-paneled library and living room. The largest Crowne Suite offers 1,812 square feet of elegant furnishings, a fireplace, a stunning city view, and amenities that include high-speed Internet access. For the business crowd, executive-level guests can enjoy a complimentary breakfast, hors d'oeuvres, and other gourmet snacks all day in the Executive Lounge while enjoying a panoramic view of the downtown area. There's a pool and fitness room for your enjoyment, along with several dining options. Tundra offers a menu of Canadian cuisine, while classic steakhouse fare is available at Ruth's Chris Steakhouse. Ovo Cafe provides a more casual menu. $$$$

Park Hyatt Toronto
4 Avenue Rd. (Bloor St.), Bloor/Yorkville, 416-925-1234 / 800-633-7313, www.parktoronto.hyatt.com

The Park Hyatt is more than just another pretty face. Planted firmly at the chic corner of Avenue and Bloor, right in the heart of Yorkville, the Park Hyatt boasts grand hallways with polished wood beams that create the palatial atmosphere of a private estate. Standard deluxe rooms range from 300 to 400 square feet and feature marble bathrooms, plush terry bathrobes, and complimentary high-speed Internet access, along with feather beds in the South Tower rooms. For the ultimate Hyatt experience, ask for the Algonquin Suite, 2,500 square feet on the 15th floor that has a living room with a fully appointed entertainment center, a separate office, and a spectacular carved-wood four-poster bed, among many other features. And don't forget to check out the adjoining Stillwater Spa, to which wealthy Torontonians have been flocking for generations. $$$$

Westin Harbour Castle
1 Harbour Sq. (York St.), Harbourfront, 416-869-1600, www.westin.com/harbourcastle

A twenty-year recipient of the AAA/CAA four-diamond award, this spacious luxury hotel located right on Toronto's waterfront offers far more than just a great view. Solicitous service caters to clients in town on both business and leisure travel, and the signature Westin "Heavenly Bed" is standard in all rooms. Rooms are comfortably appointed in your choice of either contemporary or traditional furnishings—and if you're traveling with Fido, he gets his own Heavenly Bed here. The best rooms, naturally, have a full lakeside view, and include a king-size bed, high-speed Internet access, and a spacious sitting area. Enjoy a massage at the Votre Beauté European Day Spa as you look out over the Toronto Islands. The exercise rooms offer the same gorgeous view, and provide direct access to the sundeck and tennis courts. The Westin Harbour Castle offers several casual dining options, including the Mizzen and the Chartroom Bar & Lounge. For upscale Italian with that million-dollar view, Toula sits atop one of the towers. $$$

Classic Toronto: The Restaurants

Avalon
270 Adelaide St. W. (John St.), Entertainment District, 416-979-9918, www.avalonrestaurant.ca

Avalon once reigned supreme over the Entertainment District, and in a city of fickle diners, it has managed to retain many fans with its emphasis on service and the excellence of chef Chris McDonald's inventive continental-based cuisine. Join the crowd of discerning foodies and upscale locals who love this elegant dining room. Thursday lunches include a solid business crowd, and come weekends, Avalon is a popular pre- or post-theater spot. A marble-and-brushed-steel entrance ushers you upstairs, where white linens and neutral walls contrast with the starkly colored original abstract artwork on the walls. The wine list is exhaustive, the menu offerings of seafood and veal, among others, flavorful and artfully plated. A team approach to service ensures that your every need is met. *Open for lunch Thurs. noon–2 p.m.; dinner Tues.–Sat. 5:30–10 p.m.* $$$$

Avenue
Four Seasons Hotel Toronto, 21 Avenue Rd. (Cumberland St.), Bloor/Yorkville, 416-964-0411, www.fourseasons.com
Best Swanky Hotel Bars

A cosmopolitan hotel lounge and restaurant, dominated by a sleek 20-foot onyx bar that shines against the dark wood railings and set off by white leather furnishings, Avenue is all about style. This is a terrific spot for a fabulous lunch among the beautiful people. Perfect if you're gearing up for or recovering from a Yorkville shopping spree, Avenue also features a "fashion lunch" special that includes a three-course meal and a small bottle of champagne. The menu features creative casual dishes like quesadillas, crab cakes, gourmet pastas, and pizzas. After the dinner hour, it turns into a swank watering hole for well-heeled locals and visiting VIPs. *Open for lunch Mon.–Sat. 11:45 a.m.–3 p.m.; for dinner Mon.–Sat. 3 p.m.–1 a.m.; Sun. 4 p.m.–midnight; brunch Sun. 10:30 a.m.–2:30 p.m.; bar and lounge open Mon-Sat. 11:30 a.m.–1 a.m.; Sun. 11 a.m.–midnight.* $$$$

Bistro 333
333 King St. W. (Widmer St.), Entertainment District, 416-971-3336, www.clubmenage.ca
Best Late-Night Eats

This upscale but casual eatery caters to the clubbing crowds of the Entertainment District with a menu of classics and a kitchen that stays open until 4 a.m. on the weekends. There's a throbbing dance club upstairs, but Bistro 333 is where the club kids go to snack and chat in quieter surroundings. The wood-paneled room is elegant and sports a long carved-wood bar and intimate lighting—and is generally filled with a friendly crowd. The menu offers casual fare like pizza and quesadillas, several pasta selections, and entrées that include steak and seafood. The bar menu is just as long, featuring a long list of wines and martinis, including the After Dinner Martini of vodka, coffee liqueur, Southern Comfort, and crème de cacao. *Open for lunch and dinner Sun.–Wed. 11:30 a.m.–11:30 p.m.; Thurs. 11:30 a.m.–1 a.m.; Fri.–Sat. 11:30 a.m.–4 a.m.* $$$

Bloor Street Diner & Bistro Express
145 King St. W. (University Ave.), Financial District, 416-363-0460, www.bloorstreetdiner.com

The original Bloor Street Diner & Bistro (on Bloor, natch), brought a completely unique concept to Toronto dining—French bistro combined with American diner, in both décor and menu—and the locals came in droves the moment it opened its doors. Now, as part of a small franchise with a handful of locations citywide, the Bistro Express on King West serves hungry downtown white-collar types their fix of java, breakfast, and lunch, and offers both hearty and more delicate fare with a busy, friendly charm. Choose from breakfast classics like pancakes or eggs benedict, or ground sirloin burgers and steak frites later in the day. *Open daily 7 a.m.–5 p.m.* $$

Boba
90 Avenue Rd. (Elgin St.), Bloor/Yorkville, 416-961-2622, www.boba.ca

One of Toronto's finest destination restaurants, Boba offers, quite simply, a lovely dining experience. Located within a converted Victorian townhouse with high ceilings and elegant moldings, Boba is awash in color. Dining here is a refined but friendly experience. This is a favorite spot of well-to-do locals, and the owners are personable and solicitous, which just adds to Boba's charm. A décor in sumptuous red and blue colors is balanced with earthy tones, all brightened by plenty of natural light from the large windows that overlook busy Avenue Road. A healthy and slightly offbeat menu includes exotic fare like Thai steak tartare, and linguine with smoked salmon

CLASSIC • RESTAURANTS

and red onion confit. Boba is known for using only the finest ingredients, including organic produce. *Open Mon.–Sat. 5:45 p.m.–10 p.m. $$$$*

Bright Pearl Seafood
346–348 Spadina Ave. (St. Andrew St.), Chinatown, 416-979-3988, www.brightpearlseafood.com
Best Asian Restaurants

People from all over Toronto—and beyond—come to Bright Pearl to savor its fresh Cantonese cuisine. Known for its all-day dim sum, Bright Pearl offers a delightfully authentic Chinatown experience. Carts are piled high with a selection of the 80 to 100 tantalizing dim sum dishes on offer and served up by friendly and knowledgeable staff. The Peking duck comes highly recommended. Note that the seafood is still swimming in a tank you pass at the entrance. Join the crowds at this bustling Chinatown landmark to experience a taste of Toronto's international scene. *Open daily for breakfast, lunch, and dinner 9 a.m.–11 p.m. $$*

Bymark
66 Wellington St. W., concourse level (Bay St.), Financial District, 416-777-1144, www.bymarkdowntown.com

With a location inside the TD Bank Tower and a suitably imposing design by the superstar team of Yabu Pushelberg (responsible single-handedly for many of the city's high-end haunts of the rich and fabulous), Bymark was designed as a tribute to the masculine vibe of the Financial District. The sober dining room and lounge with dark leather seating definitely make this the spot to impress bosses or colleagues from out of town. Or just come to soak up the high-powered, upscale ambience for the fun of it. Expect nothing but the best in both service and cuisine. The menu choices feature fresh seafood and classic contemporary cooking, rounded out by an extensive wine list and served up by black-clad supermodel types. Or take your business upstairs to the bar and lounge area, a sexy, swank watering hole for movers and shakers. Ingeniously located in the courtyard of the TD Tower, Bymark allows you to sit in luxury gazing at the office towers and stars beyond, watching the hustle of the District as it unfolds around you. *Open for lunch Mon.–Fri. 11:30 a.m.–2:30 p.m.; dinner Mon.–Sat. 5 p.m.–10 p.m.; bar and lounge Mon.–Fri. 11 a.m.–midnight; Sat. 5 p.m.–midnight. $$$$*

Cafe Supreme
40 University Ave. (Wellington St.), Financial District, 416-585-7896

Enjoy a gourmet coffee, latte, or cup of tea and a light breakfast alongside a good cross-section of Bay Street business types and other well-dressed downtowners in a Euro-cafe ambience. The corner of University and Wellington bustles weekday mornings with the people who keep Canada's financial engine humming. The parade on the sidewalk provides ample entertainment, which you can enjoy from one of Supreme's couches or perched on a windowside chair. Pleasant young staff and comfortable surroundings make this a fine way to start the day or stop for a rest later on. *Open daily for breakfast, lunch, and dinner 8 a.m.–6 p.m.* $$

Canoe Restaurant & Bar
66 Wellington St. W., 54th Fl., (Bay St.), Financial District, 416-364-0054, www.canoerestaurant.com
Best Canadian Cuisine

Perched at the top of a skyscraper in Toronto's Financial District, Canoe boasts a breathtaking view that extends beyond the Toronto Islands. Canada was opened up by fur traders in canoes, and Canoe the restaurant takes its inspiration from its iconic name by offering original takes on Canadian cuisine. This is one of Toronto's favorite power-lunch spots, and the crowd here will be rife with expense accounts. The menu uses classical methods in combination with local, seasonal, and other Canadian ingredients like B.C. sablefish, Yarmouth lobster, and Digby clams, among others, to produce exquisite creations. Come early to enjoy the view from the bar—either go with a cocktail or select a glass from the extensive wine list. The modern, minimalist design, all done in pale woods and neutral colors, incorporates a theme of Canadian wilderness, with touches like driftwood and snowshoes on the walls. The overall ambience is open and airy, and clearly dominated by the soaring views. One of the city's most civilized dining experiences, this is classic Toronto at its very best. *Open daily for lunch 11:30 a.m.–2:30 p.m.; for dinner from 5 p.m.; bar open 11 a.m.–1 a.m.* $$$$

Caren's Wine and Cheese Bar
158 Cumberland St. (Avenue Rd.), Bloor/Yorkville, 416-962-5158, www.carenswineandcheese.com

The crowd is stylish, upscale, and uptown, typical of the posh Yorkville neighborhood. People perch at a polished bar or decorate the tables, sipping from a long wine list that includes a bottle for every taste. The menu really delivers—even the small tapas-style nibbles are carefully prepared. Especially popular are the gourmet cheese platters and cheese fondue, which are an excellent foil for the fruits of the vine. Lively and intimate, this is the spot for refined tippling with a polished Yorkville crowd. *Open for lunch and dinner daily noon–2 a.m.* $$$

CLASSIC • RESTAURANTS

C'est What?
67 Front St. E. (Church St.), St. Lawrence, 416-867-9499, www.cestwhat.ca

Located on a busy corner in the Old Town, C'est What? is a perennially popular destination—at all hours of the day and night. It's part lively pub, part restaurant with an "ethno-clectic" menu that features everything from shepherd's pie to chicken satay, and part live music venue that has seen the likes of Jewel and Wilco grace the stage. Crowds of music lovers and downtowners just looking for casual fun fill the popular pub till closing. C'est What? occupies the basement of a historic building, with a wood bar and furnishings to complete the look. The kitchen's open until 2 a.m. daily to accommodate your need for post-midnight sustenance. *Open daily for lunch and dinner 11:30 a.m.–2 a.m.; live music weekends; check listings.* $$$

Courtyard Cafe
Windsor Arms Hotel, 18 St. Thomas St. (Bloor St.), Bloor/Yorkville, 416-971-9666, www.windsorarmshotel.com

Housed in the celeb-rich Windsor Arms, the Courtyard Cafe has a clientele regularly sprinkled with Hollywood greats, rock stars, and supermodels. The dining room is grand in the old Hollywood tradition—think of the era of Bogart and Cagney. Anchored by round upholstered booths in the center, a sprinkling of potted palms, and brightened by Art Deco lighting fixtures and a soaring ceiling, the décor reeks of glamour and style. An award-winning chef prepares a fine selection of continental classics, and you'll also find a lengthy list of wine selections housed in a temperature-controlled wine cellar. The Courtyard Cafe also serves a posh buffet brunch on Sundays. *Open for lunch daily noon–3 p.m.; dinner 5 p.m.–11 p.m.* $$$$

The Fifth
225 Richmond St. W. (Bedford St.), Entertainment District, 416-979-3005, www.easyandthefifth.com

The Fifth is a calm oasis of candlelit elegance. Part of the Fifth is a private supper club, making the atmosphere all the more exclusive. And a glamorous clientele dresses the part. A flickering fireplace casts a glow over the dark wood paneling, softened by white sheers artfully draped over tall windows. Tasting menus are available so that you can sample an exquisite range of the conservative but flawlessly executed French fusion dishes served in these luxe surroundings. An enchanting experience from start to finish, the Fifth serves up a truly memorable meal. Reservations are essential at this destination restaurant. *Dining room is open daily 6 p.m.–2 a.m.* $$$$

Harbour 60
60 Harbour St. (Bay St.), Harbourfront, 416-777-2111, www.harboursixty.com

Housed in the former home of the Toronto Harbour Commission, Harbour 60 is a classic steakhouse that is the very definition of swank. With a grand entrance and opulent dining rooms, Harbour 60 makes it easy to pretend that you've been accepted into an exclusive business club. The furnishings are palatial and feature brocaded upholstery in elegant neutral tones spiced up with royal blue and red accents. Fellow diners are well dressed. The kitchen delivers with a superbly executed menu of classics—appetizers like smoked salmon, Maryland crab cakes, and lobster bisque, mains of seafood and beluga caviar at market prices, and naturally, those divine steaks. This is the ultimate high-end steakhouse experience. *Open for lunch and dinner Mon.–Fri. 11:30 a.m.–1 a.m.; dinner Sat.–Sun. 5 p.m.–1 a.m.* $$$$

Hemispheres
Metropolitan Hotel, 110 Chestnut St. (University Ave.), Chinatown, 416-599-8000, www.metropolitan.com/toronto/hemis/

Visitors and locals alike love this bright, beautiful room. Hemispheres bustles with both business types and lunching ladies from the afternoon to the dinner hour. Rising miles above the typical hotel restaurant-lounge in ambience and quality, Hemispheres takes its Chinatown locale as inspiration. The gorgeous black-and-white plates highlight dishes that put an East-West spin on local ingredients. Many offerings feature seafood with delicate flavorings like lemongrass. If you feel like watching Chinatown in action, ask for a table by one of the windows that face the street. After the dinner hour, Hemispheres becomes a quiet, relaxing lounge. *Open daily for breakfast, lunch, and dinner 7 a.m.–midnight.* $$$

Hot House Cafe
35 Church St. (Front St.), St. Lawrence, 416-366-7800, www.hothousecafe.com

This casual, friendly downtown haunt is a big favorite with locals. The Hot House Cafe has overlooked the busy corner of Front and Church streets for more than a decade. Busy any night of the week with a mixed crowd of students and downtown types, the Hot House offers an extensive menu of classics, from crab cakes and a salad of devilled Brie and poached salmon to main dishes of pastas, pizzette, and veal scallopini. The polished wood floors highlight a slick bar and colorful, artsy dining area that buzzes hospitably at all hours. The popular Sunday brunch is served between 10 a.m. and 3 p.m. to a backdrop of live jazz. Sip your Bloody Mary and watch all of Toronto walk by. *Open for lunch and dinner Mon.–Thurs. 11 a.m.–midnight; Fri.–Sat. 11 a.m.–1 a.m.; Sun. 9:30 a.m.–11 p.m.; brunch Sun. 10 a.m.–3 p.m.* $$

CLASSIC • RESTAURANTS

Joso's
202 Davenport Rd. (Avenue Rd.), Bloor/Yorkville, 416-925-1903
Best Seafood Restaurants

With fish so fresh you'll swear Toronto had moved seaside, Joso's has a reputation for excellence that goes well beyond Canadian borders. Famed Italian director Marcello Mastroianni, in fact, found reasons to work in Toronto just to visit this Yorkville haunt, and you can regularly expect to find a crowd sprinkled with both local and international celebrities. Reservations are a must most evenings, and the dining room can get noisy, but that's made up for by excellent service from staff who bring the catches of the day tableside for you to choose from. The popular and beloved summer patio overlooks the chic designer boutiques of Yorkville, making it the ideal people-watching station. *Open for lunch Mon.–Fri. 11:30 a.m.–2:30 p.m.; for dinner Mon.–Sat. 5:30 p.m.–10:30 p.m.* $$$$

Lolita's Lust & the Chinchilla Lounge
513 Danforth Ave. (Fenwick St.), Greektown, 416-465-1751, www.lolitaslust.ca

See Classic Nightlife, p. 173 for description.
Open daily 5 p.m.–2 a.m. $$$

Myth
417 Danforth Ave. (Chester St.), Greektown, 416-461-8383, www.myth.to

See Classic Nightlife, p. 173 for description.
Open Mon.–Sat. noon–2 a.m. $$$

North 44°
2537 Yonge St. (Eglinton Ave.), Uptown, 416-487-4897, www.north44restaurant.com

North 44° is both Toronto's latitude and star chef Mark McEwan's latest addition to the city's fine-dining repertoire. In the wealthy and stylish neighborhood of Yonge and Eglinton, North 44° tempts the palate with contemporary style. The fare is sumptuous and consistently draws well-heeled locals and the odd traveling celebrity. The menu features appetizers of seared tuna, panfried crab cakes, and white prawn risotto, mains of roasted bison tenderloin with savory rub and truffle risotto, and whole Dover sole in brown butter with caper berries. The space is warmly lit, and punctuated by faux French windows. A black and white exterior reflects the elegant minimalism at work in the décor. However elegant the setting, the crowds really flock here for the superlative food. *Open for dinner Mon.–Sat. 5 p.m.–11 p.m.* $$$$

One Up Resto/Lounge
130 Dundas St. W., 2nd Fl. (Bay St.), Chinatown, 416-340-6349, www.oneup.ca

The décor is an elegant take on its location on the edges of Chinatown, while the equally decorative plates offer a fresh look at continental cuisine. Financial District types love the inventive cuisine in this dining room. With dark red walls set against exposed brick, glowing lights, and black lacquered woods, and a tiled bar and glass wall that create a shimmering effect, One Up has a vibrant, sleek, and gleaming décor that matches its mood. The artfully presented fare beckons too. Start with wild mushroom crostini or seafood tartare, then graduate to pasta with lamb, seafood bouillabaisse, or duck. Stylish professionals flock to the bar and lounge area for after-work cocktails, especially the martini specials on Thursdays. This glamorous new addition to the neighborhood is winning fans who keep the place bustling at all hours, and especially on weekends. *Open for lunch and dinner Mon.–Wed. 11:30 a.m.–10 p.m.; Thurs.–Sat. 11:30 a.m.–2 a.m.* $$$

Ouzeri
500A Danforth Ave. (Logan St.), Greektown, 416-778-0500, www.ouzeri.com
Best Ethnic Dining

Both the menu and the Mediterranean vibe at this busy, classy Greektown restaurant are so authentic that you'll feel like you've stepped right into Athens. Black wrought-iron railings and a striped awning create an attractive European entrance. Come summer, crowds congregate on the patio to people-watch and sample the flavorful cuisine. Start with marinated olives and feta and proceed to main dishes laden with octopus and other seafood or traditional favorites like moussaka. A plate-glass front means you can watch the stylish crowds that take over Greektown in the evening year-round. *Open for lunch and dinner Mon.–Thurs. 11:30 a.m.–midnight; Fri.–Sat. 1:30 a.m.–2 a.m.; Sun. 11:30 a.m.–midnight.* $$$

7 West Cafe
7 Charles St. W. (Yonge St.), Bloor/Yorkville, 416-928-9041
Best Late-Night Eats

Housed in a semi-detached Victorian house, 7 West charms inside with mirrors and twinkling lights, and the work of local artists on exposed brick walls. With the kitchen open 24/7, this is one of the city's late late-night hot spots, good for a romantic post–night-out meal or for noshing with the crowds who flock here from the area's many clubs both before and after hours. The menu offers light cafe fare, and the panini come especially recommended, as do the delectable desserts from Dufflet pastries. *Open daily 24 hours.* $$

Splendido

88 Harbord St. (Sussex Mews), University of Toronto, 416-929-7788, www.splendidoonline.com
Best Canadian Cuisine

Sophisticated but fun at heart, Splendido has won the hearts of Toronto's diners and carved a well-deserved niche in the competitive midtown restaurant scene. Servers cater with quiet efficiency to an upscale and sometimes star-studded clientele while chefs craft meals of Canadian-continental fusion behind a glass wall. The dishes they're preparing are breathtakingly good, highlighting local and regional ingredients in elaborately crafted menus—poached Nova Scotia lobster and egg-yolk ravioli with Charlevoix rabbit and Niagara prosciutto, among others. The menu changes monthly, and is complemented by a wine list with over 700 choices, all made most enjoyable in an elegant room brightened by huge paintings of sunflowers. *Open for dinner Tues.–Sun. 5 p.m.–11 p.m. $$$$*

Starfish Oyster Bed & Grill

100 Adelaide St. E. (Jarvis St.), St. Lawrence, 416-366-7827, www.starfishoysterbed.com
Best Seafood Restaurants

With plenty of seafood restaurants in town to choose from, the competition is fierce. Starfish manages to please consistently, graciously, and with ease. From the chic black awning out front to the sleek interior, Starfish serves up fresh seafood in a room with a New York–style downtown bistro ambience. From lunch through dinner, downtown crowds keep the place humming, and the fragrant smells are a prelude to a delectable menu where mollusks feature prominently: oysters from Malpeque, New Brunswick, and Washington served on ice, an oyster-stuffed omelette. The lamb and other non-seafood items are also popular. A long wine list and large selection of beers complement a menu that changes daily. The dining room offers both table and banquette seating in pleasant neutrals as well as a long gleaming bar. The place is busy with a business crowd at lunch, and caters to a more mixed clientele at dinner. *Open for lunch Mon.–Fri. noon–3 p.m.; for dinner Mon.–Sat. 5 p.m.–11 p.m. $$$*

Studio Cafe
Four Seasons Hotel Toronto, 21 Avenue Rd. (Bloor St.), Bloor/Yorkville, 416-928-7330, www.fourseasons.com

Following the Four Seasons' trademark contemporary elegance, this polished cafe is stylish but casual. Here, you can enjoy your meal in refined yet relaxed surroundings among the hotel's upscale clientele. An artistic look is achieved with white walls, which are separated into sections by glass cases. The cases display works of ceramic and glass art, and black lacquer chairs add to the overall sheen. Breakfast classics are superbly prepared, while the lunch and dinner menus offer casual Italian-Mediterranean options. *Open for breakfast, lunch, and dinner daily 6:30 a.m.–11 p.m.; brunch Sun. 11:30 a.m.–3 p.m.* $$$

Sunset Grill
2006 Queen St. E. (Bellefair St.), The Beaches, 416-690-9985

An authentic diner that has existed in the Beaches area of Toronto for generations, the Sunset is the real deal. A sunny interior and congenial service add to the friendly neighborhood vibe. Breakfast is the king of meals here, served in generous portions, with thick slices of toast and copious coffee refills to wash it down. You will find no post-modern irony here, no tongue-in-cheek design elements, just an unfussy menu and a real taste of laid-back Beaches cool. It's just the fuel you'll need for a walk along Queen or down to the lakeshore. *Open daily for breakfast, lunch, and dinner 7 a.m.–6 p.m.* $

Tea Room
Windsor Arms Hote, 18 St. Thomas St. (Bloor St.), Bloor/Yorkville, 416-971-9666, www.windsorarmshotel.com
Best Ways to Escape a Rainy Day

Venerable and elegant, the Tearoom at the Windsor Arms is an ode to this most civilized of Waspy traditions—the afternoon high tea. Cushions, velvet drapes, silver, and white linens serve as a backdrop to the Chanel- and Gucci-clad society dames taking a respite from shopping in an atmosphere of quiet refinement. Attentive servers bring tiny sandwiches, crumbling scones, and other delicacies, and, of course, a superb cup of tea. Note that there are two seatings, at 1:30 and 3:30 pm. In the evenings, the historic room becomes a champagne and caviar bar for a swank crowd. *High tea served daily 1:30 p.m. & 3:30 p.m.* $$$$

CLASSIC • RESTAURANTS

Truffles

Four Seasons Hotel Toronto, 21 Avenue Rd. (Bloor St.), Bloor/Yorkville, 416-928-7331, www.fourseasons.com

Best Romantic Rendezvous

A wrought-iron gateway ushers you into the reception area. This is the epitome of the impossibly posh dining experience, where ceilings soar over wood-inlaid floors, and the work of local painters and sculptors punctuates the dining rooms. An institution that defies all trends, Truffles is Toronto's premier restaurant. The pace of a meal here is leisurely, allowing you to savor the chef's continental creations. The service is, of course, impeccable, and local movers and shakers appreciate it as much as visiting glitterati. The menu will seduce you, as will the gracious ambience. So prepare to be impressed—and then relax and simply enjoy every flawless moment of this example of special-occasion dining at its finest. *Open for dinner Mon.–Sat. 6 p.m.–10 p.m. $$$$*

Classic Toronto: The Nightlife

Avenue
21 Avenue Rd. (Cumberland St.), Bloor/Yorkville, 416-964-0411, www.fourseasons.com
Best Swanky Hotel Bars

See Classic Restaurants, p. 159 for description. *Open for lunch Mon.–Sat. 11:45 a.m.–3 p.m.; for dinner Mon.–Sat. 3 p.m.–1 a.m.; Sun. 4 p.m.–midnight; brunch Sun. 10:30 a.m.–2:30 p.m.; bar and lounge open Mon–Sat. 11:30 a.m.–1 a.m.; Sun. 11 a.m.–midnight.*

Crocodile Rock
240 Adelaide St. W. (Duncan St.), Entertainment District, 416-599-9751, www.crocrock.ca
Best Meet Markets

This big, loud crocodile-themed bar is packed with an urban thirties-and-up crowd looking to party. Blasting classic-rock standards, Crocodile Rock is something of an anti-hip antidote to Clubland's ultrastylish and ultracool vibe. There's plenty of fun to be had at this multilevel gathering spot where white-collar types let down their hair, and the large main room rocks from after work to late in the evening. Known as a thriving meet market, it's also a good place to bump into pro-sports figures and celebs. When you're ordering, keep in mind that brews are the specialty. *Open Wed.–Fri. 4 p.m.–2 a.m.; Sat. 7 p.m.–2 a.m.*

The Easy
225 Richmond St. W. (Bedford St.), Entertainment District, 416-979-3005, www.easyandthefifth.com
Best Cigar Lounges

A style code is always in effect at Easy, despite the friendly atmosphere. It's strictly upscale at this elegant and fashionable loft-style club, packed with a designer crowd of grown-up clubbers. Polished wood floors reflect sexy lighting, and drapery adds a posh touch. White columns and potted ferns serve to highlight the well-heeled urban types lounging on the overstuffed couches as DJs spin the tunes. In Sidebar, a separately ventilated area with a piano bar, you can enjoy a smoke, cigar, and live jazz. *Sidebar is open Thurs.–Fri. from 5:30 p.m. (menu available Thurs. only), Sat. 9 p.m.–2 a.m.; Main room open Thurs.–Sat. 9 p.m.–2 a.m.* $$

CLASSIC • NIGHTLIFE

G-Spot
296 Richmond St. W. (Widmer St.), Entertainment District, 416-351-7768

One side of this busy and stylish club is made for dancing and for the young and beautiful people and spiffy singles looking to see and be seen. The other side is designed for a more relaxed over-thirty crowd listening to classic rock and top 40 tunes. Amusing décor touches include lip-shaped chairs. The third floor is a busy lounge packed with a mixed crowd with nary an attitude in sight, where local DJs set the mood. Open until 4 a.m., G-Spot boasts a wild after-midnight scene. *Open Wed.–Sun. 10 p.m.–4 a.m.* $$

Hair of the Dog
425 Church St. (Wood St.), Gay Village, 416-964-2708
Best Gay Bars

Hair of the Dog is an upscale pub in the heart of Toronto's Boys' Town, a double-decker experience in imaginative pub fare and expertly mixed drinks (a selection of brews is also on offer). There's a steady stream of upscale gays and a few straights coming in the front door of this hugely popular gay-community mainstay. In the summer, the small patio is packed from opening until closing. The owners double as publishers of *Fab*, a high-end gay-lifestyle mag that has featured Toronto's chief of police as cover boy. A casual menu features vegetarian specials, an extensive wine list, and a delectable martini menu that confirms the impression that this is no average pub. *Open for lunch and dinner Mon.–Fri. 11:30 a.m.–2 a.m.; Sat.–Sun. 10 a.m.–2 a.m.*

Healey's
178 Bathurst St. (Queen St.), Entertainment District, 416-703-5882, www.jeffhealeys.com
Best Clubs for Live Music

If you've seen the 1989 movie *Roadhouse*, you've already seen Toronto-native and blind blues-guitar legend Jeff Healey playing a character close to himself. A favorite of professional musicians and music lovers looking for a party, Healey's is all about the music. The best in live blues and jazz plays live every night, most often performed by or with the musical genius himself. Groove along with hometown crowds and out-of-towners in the know, and if hunger strikes, the menu of bar classics is surprisingly good. *Doors generally open at 8 p.m.; check listings for details; jazz Sat. 4 p.m.–7 p.m.* $$$

Hemingway's
142 Cumberland Ave. (Avenue Rd.), Bloor/Yorkville, 416-968-2828, www.hemingways.to
Best Celeb Sightings

Hemingway's boasts a flowery streetside patio in the summer, but the party doesn't end when the nights get colder. Crowds pack it in at Toronto's only year-round heated rooftop patio. Visiting Hollywood celebs and the usual uptown suspects come to unwind at this perennially popular watering hole in fashionable Yorkville. A menu of roadhouse classics is spiced with Kiwi and other South Pacific influences, but you're not here for the food so much as the friendly pub-style vibe and great drinks. *Open daily 11 a.m.–2 a.m.*

Lago
207 Queen's Quay W. (York St.), Harbourfront, 416-848-0005, www.lagorestaurant.com
Best Summer Patios

One of the finer ways to take advantage of good weather is to head for an outdoor patio, and you can't do better than Lago. Join the summertime crowds at this 120-seat patio at the edge of the sparkling dark blue waters of Lake Ontario. Lago's a hit with locals and travelers alike, with an appeal that goes beyond its fabulous location. Sip a Bloody Mary or martini outside, or perch inside at the wraparound leather bar. *Open May to late Sept. Mon.–Fri. 11 a.m.–11 p.m.; Sat.–Sun. 11 a.m.–midnight.*

La Rouge Executive Club
257 Adelaide St. W. (Duncan St.), Entertainment District, 416-260-5551, www.larougeclub.com
Best Martinis

Join the executive classes who come to party at La Rouge. An over-thirty crowd congregates in the darkly lit VIP lounge, sinking into the dark leather couches as they sip cosmopolitans. Exposed brick, burgundy walls, and heavy wood bookcases make this feel like the exclusive executive hideaway that it is. Upstairs after 10:30 p.m., join the throbbing party of "mature" club kids dancing to Latin and house music. Each floor has a VIP lounge, and access comes with the purchase of a VIP package at $200, $400, or $600. Go for the platinum, which includes valet parking, a private entrance, and your own humidor. *Open Thurs.–Sun. 9 p.m.–3 a.m.* $$

CLASSIC • NIGHTLIFE

Library Bar
Fairmont Royal York, 100 Front St. W. (York St.), Downtown/Yonge, 416-368-2511, www.fairmont.com/royalyork
Best Swanky Hotel Bars

The Library Bar is all sober, Old World elegance. Mahogany paneling, a carved-wood bar, and elegant striped drapes create the feel of your own private library. A favorite of expense accounters and other upscale travelers, it's just the place for a discreet business meeting or contemplative Scotch in the late afternoon as you consider the evening's possibilities. The martinis here change monthly and are considered among the city's best. So order a drink, sink into one of the weighty couches, and watch the business deals going down around you. *Open Mon.–Fri. noon–1 a.m.; Sat. 5:30 p.m.–1 a.m.*

Lolita's Lust & the Chinchilla Lounge
513 Danforth Ave. (Fenwick St.), Greektown, 416-465-1751, www.lolitaslust.ca

This is one of the trendiest restaurant-lounges in Greektown, and the fashionable crowds love to congregate at the shiny tiled bar. Lolita's Lust has an over-the-top sexy Mediterranean appeal that keeps the sometimes-fickle crowds of Greektown partiers coming in droves. Featuring red accents and exotically draped ceilings, the lounge's décor is a perfect backdrop for its stylish clientele. The restaurant is richly colored with green walls against exposed brick and funky green chandeliers. *Open daily 5 p.m.–2 a.m.* $$

Myth
417 Danforth Ave. (Chester St.), Greektown, 416-461-8383, www.myth.to

Myth beckons with big glass doors that usher you into a funky room—the décor mixes Greek temple grandeur with quirky flair. Offering a Greek and Mediterranean-inspired menu, the place goes clubby after dark with a well-dressed crowd of young partiers. Come early for dinner on Friday or Saturday in the baroque dining area that overlooks the bar-lounge-dance floor, and watch the place fill up as you dine. Later, join the crowds on the dance floor. Seats on the coveted summertime patio go quickly, so come by late afternoon to be sure of securing a spot here. *Open Mon.–Sat. noon–2 a.m.* $$

One Up Resto/Lounge
130 Dundas St. W., 2nd Fl. (Bay St.), Chinatown, 416-340-6349, www.oneup.ca

See Classic Restaurants, p. 166 for description.
Open for lunch and dinner Mon.–Wed. 11:30 a.m.–10 p.m.; Thurs.–Sat. 11:30 a.m.–2 a.m.

Rex Hotel Jazz & Blues Bar
194 Queen St. W. (St. Patrick St.), Entertainment District, 416-598-2475
Best Jazz Clubs

Serving up live jazz and blues seven days a week has been the Rex Hotel's raison d'être for many years. This institution opened as a local watering hole in 1951 and is now known as a laid-back place to enjoy the music. The old men have given way to urban jazz lovers and art-school types who pack the place. The vibe is casual, but the crowd takes the music seriously. *Restaurant daily 11 a.m.–midnight; live music Mon.–Tues. 9:30 p.m.–1 a.m.; Wed.–Fri. 6:30–8:30 p.m. & 9:30 p.m.–1 a.m.; Sat. 3:30–6:30 p.m. & 7–9 p.m. & 9:30 p.m.–1 a.m.; Sun. 3:30–6:30 p.m. & 9 p.m.–midnight.* $$$

Roof Lounge
Park Hyatt Toronto, 4 Avenue Rd., 18th Fl. (Bloor St.), Bloor/Yorkville, 416-924-5471, www.parktoronto.hyatt.com
Best Summer Patios

Bartender Joe Gomes has been manning this Toronto institution for 45 years. The Roof Lounge is as busy after work and in the early evening as it is late at night. The summertime patio offers a sparkly view of the city lights. Expert mixology is guaranteed, whether your taste runs to fine Scotch or the signature Mandarin Martini. The walls of this small lounge are covered in blue suede, and the fireplace and leather couches you can sink into allow you to enjoy the view and luxurious ambience. *Open daily 11 a.m.–2 a.m.*

Up and Down Lounge
270 Adelaide St. W. (John St.), Entertainment District, 416-977-4038

This small lounge with an intimate feel mixes art-gallery clientele with Financial District types to make for a fabulous club experience. Downstairs the vibe is younger, more hip-hop oriented; upstairs it's all about glamour. Cheetah rugs serve as a backdrop to the posh crowds sipping delectable martinis. Though there's no dance floor, Up and Down heats up on weekends after 11 p.m. when a DJ spins house music. You'll have to dress to the nines and pose along with the rest to get in. *Open Wed.–Sat. 9 a.m.–3 a.m.* $$

Wish
3 Charles St. E. (Yonge St.), Downtown/Yonge, 416-935-0240

Think South Beach party with Toronto style. Sip an exquisite dry gin martini in luxury surroundings along with the stylish crowd. The patio strikes a funky note with clear plastic chairs and metallic tables, while inside, minimalist wood-and-metal furnishings make a dramatic modern statement against a gleaming bar. *Open daily 11 a.m.–2 a.m.* $$$

Classic Toronto: The Attractions

The Beaches
Queen Street from Coxwell east and south to the lakeshore
Best Ways to Enjoy a Sunny Day

While the waterfront extends both east and west of the city, it's the end furthest east that is officially known as the Beaches. Along the lakeshore from about Coxwell Avenue heading east, the Beaches consists of a few miles of pebbly Lake Ontario beach, and is suitable for sunning, strolling, and swimming (but wait until at least July for the lake to warm up). Farther east along the shoreline are the Scarborough Bluffs, cliffs that make the Beaches a more private area. Along with the natural beauty, the area offers diversion in the form of the mega-entertainment complex the Docks, as well as numerous casual burger joints. The Beaches is also the name given to the funky neighborhood centered around Queen Street East, which is lined with eclectic shops, cafes, and restaurants and has a left-of-center vibe that feels light-years away from downtown's bustle.

Casa Loma
1 Austin Terr. (Davenport Rd.), Uptown, 416-923-1171, www.casaloma.org
Best Historic Buildings

To glimpse a sumptuous bygone era, come visit the castle built for love. Begun in 1911, architect E.J. Lennox's re-creation of a medieval castle took 300 men nearly three years to complete, and was occupied by its original owners—knighted Canadian financier and entrepreneur Sir Henry M. Pellatt and Lady Mary Pellatt—for less than a decade before financial ruin forced them to abandon it. Today it stands overlooking modern-day Toronto as a monument to the sweeping majesty of that era of unbridled riches. The design incorporates elements of Norman, Gothic, and Romanesque style, and the six-acre estate includes several formal and informal gardens, many with fountains and sculptures, ideal for a leisurely stroll. Inside, grandeur and opulence overwhelm every room—from the impressive Great Hall with its oak-beamed ceiling, to the stained-glass dome in the Conservatory. Be sure to check out the view of the city from the turrets. *Open daily 9:30 a.m.–5 p.m. (last entry at 4 p.m.) The Casa Loma Gardens are open daily 9:30 a.m.–4 p.m., May–Oct., and are included with your admission to Casa Loma.* $

Chinatown

Between Spadina, Queen, College, and Bay Streets, Chinatown

There are actually no fewer than five Chinatowns in Toronto—a testament to the truth of Toronto's reputation as a welcoming home to the world—but the downtown area is its bustling core. Here, even the signs are bilingual, and on Saturdays the neighborhood's so busy that the traffic slows to a crawl on Spadina. Come to take in the fresh food markets and the shops of imported clothing and art, gifts, and other curiosities, as well as a wide array of restaurants. You won't doubt the authenticity of this colorful neighborhood.

CN Tower

301 Front St. W. (John St.), Harbourfront, 416-868-6937, www.cntower.ca
Best Views

It may be on every kitschy postcard and souvenir of Toronto, but the fact remains that it is a marvel of the modern world, and at 1,815 feet and 5 inches is still its tallest freestanding structure. Initially developed as a telecommunications tower, it has a uniquely flexible concrete construction that allows it to sway with the strong winds. But there's more to it than just the breathtaking view out over Lake Ontario—or for the brave, the view from 1,112 feet straight down through the glass floor on the Observation Deck—as getting up there is half the fun in a glass-fronted elevator that travels 15 mph. The ubiquitous and friendly staff can answer any questions, and the Tower has several casual cafes both at base level and at the Observation Deck, as well as fine dining at 360, the city's tallest revolving restaurant. *Open daily 10 a.m.–10 p.m. $$*

Glen Abbey Golf Club

1333 Dorval Dr., Oakville, Ontario, 905-844-1811

Designed by golf legend Jack Nicklaus, Glen Abbey has played host to the PGA's Canadian Open for 25 of the last 27 years. Made famous by Tiger Woods' stunning shot of the year 2000 that won the Bell Canada Open victory and completed his triple crown, this highly ranked course is very popular. It's a rewarding and challenging course of 7,112 feet, slope 140 from the black tees, and known for fiendishly deceptive greens. See how you measure up against the greats, and then relax at the luxurious clubhouse facilities, which include the Gallery Grill & Bistro. *Open May–Oct., the Gallery offers fine continental bistro cuisine, as well as Sunday brunch year-round. $$$$*

CLASSIC • ATTRACTIONS

Harbourfront/Mariposa Tours
207 Queen's Quay W. (Bay St.), Harbourfront,
416-203-0178 / 866-627-7672, www.mariposacruises.com
Along a sparkling waterfront where boat lovers can ogle seaworthy crafts both small and large, Toronto's Harbourfront makes for a gorgeous walk on a nice day. The best views of the harbour, though, are to be had from the water. To truly appreciate the picturesque Great Lakes landscape, take a tour or dinner cruise. Cruises are available from various carriers, including Mariposa Tours, a first-class operator with a seven-vessel fleet. Mariposa offers harbour tours five times daily, as well as private charters and specialty cruises like Friday night dancing on the water and Sunday brunch. Torontonians love their waterfront just as much as the visitors do, and flock here to spend the warm summer months by the water. $$$

Hockey Hall of Fame
30 Yonge St. (Front St.), St. Lawrence, 416-360-7765, www.hhof.com

In a country where hockey has iconic status, and a city that was one of the "original six," the Hockey Hall of Fame is a suitably palatial ode to the icy sport. A playful sculpture of hockey players greets you at the entrance. Whether casual or fanatical in your interest, you'll find both the Hall and the exhibits designed to provide maximum entertainment. Several exhibit spaces offer inside details of the sport, as well as interactive games that allow you to test your skills against those of the pros. The centerpiece of the building is a spectacular domed stained-glass ceiling. *July–Labor Day, Mon.–Sat. 9:30 a.m.–6 p.m.; Sun. 10 a.m.–6 p.m.; remainder of the year Mon.–Fri. 10 a.m.–5 p.m.; Sat. 9:30 a.m.–6 p.m.; Sun. 10:30 a.m.–5 p.m.; check for special schedules during the Christmas holidays and spring break.* $$

Kensington Market
Spadina Ave. (College and Dundas Sts.), Chinatown
Best Only-in-Toronto Attractions

Toronto is a city of many ethnicities, and its multicultural heart beats loud and clear in Kensington Market, for 100 years the gateway to Toronto. Today, it's a neighborhood of shops that spill out into the street in the area roughly surrounding the intersection of Baldwin and Augusta. But don't bring your wheels, as this area is best explored on foot. Here, you can buy everything from Ethiopian spices to European linens, funky secondhand clothes and original works of art, and an abundance of fresh food. This is an essential visit for the eclectic shopper, lovers of authentic vintage clothing, or anyone wanting to catch a glimpse of Toronto's multicultural heritage. It's busiest Saturday mornings, with a steady bustle leading up to the weekends.

Queen's Quay Terminal
207 Queen's Quay W. (Bay St.), Harbourfront, 416-203-0510, www.toronto.com/infosite/146662/

A must-see stop on any tour of Toronto's Harbourfront, Queen's Quay Terminal is a shopping and dining extravaganza. Built in 1926, the award-winning building features soaring ceilings that let in plenty of natural light for an airy, open feel. The Terminal has over 30 shops carrying jewelry, gifts, and the largest selection of tasteful Canadiana in Toronto. Waterfront views beckon from Il Fornello, where they can be enjoyed year-round in comfort along with Italian cuisine. Check out authentic Inuit art at the Arctic Nunavut Gallery, or head to Chocolates and Creams if you have a sweet tooth. The Terminal's services also include a currency exchange. *Hours of operation vary, but retail tenants are generally open Mon.–Sat. 10 a.m.–5 p.m.; Sun. noon–5 p.m.*

Royal Ontario Museum
100 Queen's Park (Avenue Rd.), Bloor/Yorkville, 416-586-5549, www.rom.on.ca
Best Ways to Escape a Rainy Day

On a fashionable corner near Yorkville, Canada's largest museum occupies palatial digs, complete with grand arches and high ceilings. The ROM houses an internationally recognized collection of over 5 million pieces. As the country's biggest museum, the ROM also aims to be the best, offering fascinating exhibits from its permanent collection as well as blockbuster traveling shows about the natural and human-made world that aim to both educate and entertain. From biodiversity to decorative arts to textiles and dinosaurs, the ROM is a world-class museum and definitely worth making time for. While undergoing extensive renovations and additions beginning in 2004, the ROM will remain open for business as usual. Exciting new galleries are scheduled to begin opening from late 2005, continuing throughout 2006 and 2007. *Open Mon.–Thurs. 10 a.m.–6 p.m.; Fri. 10 a.m.–9 p.m.; Sat.–Sun. 10 a.m.–6 p.m.* $$

Stillwater Spa
Park Hyatt Toronto, 4 Avenue Rd. (Bloor St.), Bloor/Yorkville, 416-926-2389, www.stillwaterspa.com
Best Spas

This posh spa in the Park Hyatt has been pampering wealthy Torontonians for generations. Stillwater aims to be a relaxed and refined sanctuary from the stresses of the world, and it succeeds beautifully. The entrance alone soothes, bathed in warm neutrals and filled with the sounds of waterfalls and streams. Several treatment rooms offer a range of treatments, including the Stillwater Aqua therapy, during which a therapist uses shiatsu techniques in warm water for the ultimate in relaxation. Choose from massage, manicure and pedicure treatments, or Vichy treatments that incorporate warm cascading water. *Open Mon.–Fri. 9 a.m.–10 p.m.; Sat. 8 a.m.–10 p.m.; Sun. 10 a.m.–5:30 p.m.* $$$$

Toronto Islands

Bay Street (Queen's Quay), Harbourfront,
416-392-8193, ferry information, www.torontoisland.org
Best Ways to Enjoy a Sunny Day

Don't limit your exploration of Toronto's waterfront to the mainland. Take one of the ferries to the Toronto Islands for a real Toronto summer experience. Once the summer playground of the city, the Islands today are home to a fiercely independent community of locals who pride themselves on the natural beauty of their home just minutes from downtown. Ferries leave from the foot of Bay and Queen's Quay (just west of the Westin Harbour Castle), every 30 to 45 minutes for three island destinations. At Hanlan's Point, you can rent bicycles, picnic, or explore the 150-year-old Gibraltar Point Lighthouse. Centre Island has its own amusement park. On Ward's Island, you can rent both bicycles and boats, and the charming Rectory Cafe is only a few minutes' walk from the pier. You can enjoy beaches, gardens, art galleries, and bike paths on all the Islands. This relaxed retreat to the great outdoors also offers a splendid view of the Toronto skyline. *Ferry rides approx. 30 min., check schedules online for details.* $

TORONTO REGION

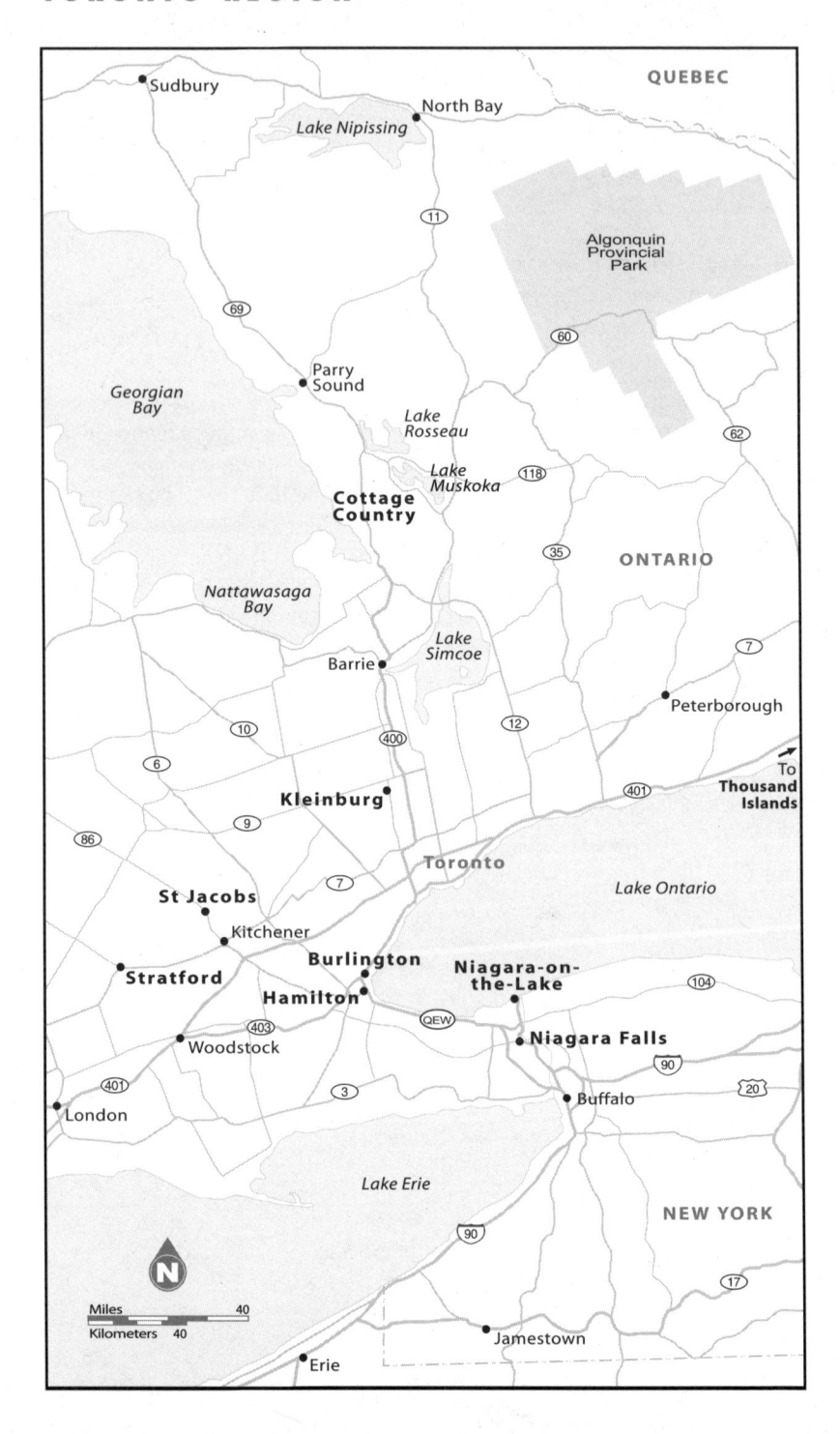

Leaving Toronto

When you've had your fill of urban fun, it's time to head out of town and discover what the area has to offer beyond Toronto. From a trip to Niagara Falls to a tour of Ontario's burgeoning wine country, from a night at exclusive Niagara-on-the-Lake to an evening of gambling in the Thousand Islands region, you have a rich and diverse list of attractions to choose from. You'll find overnight destinations listed first, complete with hotel and nightlife recommendations, followed by day-trip excursions.

Cottage Country

135 miles NE

Prime Time: Huntsville is busiest in the summer, but still popular in the fall and for romantic winter getaways.

Lowdown: "Cottage Country" exists in the Canadian psyche as a near-mythical landscape of woodland and lakes, a pristine wilderness where the silence is broken only by the shrill of the loon or the howl of the wolf.

Cottage Country begins with the area called the "Near North." Upscale Torontonians and a large quotient of wealthy Americans (even Goldie and Kurt) have long been making their summer homes in the Muskoka Lakes area of the province, an area loosely based around Lakes Muskoka, Rosseau, and Joseph, and encompassing over 1,000 freshwater lakes. The nearest towns are Bracebridge, Port Carling, and Huntsville, which has a charming tree-lined downtown of shops and boutiques. The nearby town of Haliburton is central to the Haliburton Highlands region of lakes, woodlands, and rolling hills.

The best accommodations and other facilities here typically are in resort complexes, which offer a wide range of outdoor activities, from boating and fishing to cross-country skiing, along with several dining options, spas, and other luxe touches. Here's how to enjoy the wilderness in high style, without having to give up a soft bed or gourmet meal.

Best Attractions

Aveda Spa at Deerhurst Deerhurst Resort, 1234 Deerhurst Dr., Huntsville, 800-461-4393, www.deerhurstresort.com/spaserv.jsp
Enjoy the luxuries of a spa in a jewel of a setting. Book ahead for a full range of spa services, including the signature Muskoka Maple Body Scrub or Algae Thalasso Wrap.

Echo Valley Observatory Delta Grandview Resort, 939 Hwy. 60, Huntsville, 877-472-6388
The forest is the perfect spot for viewing planets, nebulas, and other galaxies. This observatory is outfitted with cutting-edge equipment.

Golf Packages—SoHo Metropolitan Hotel 318 Wellington St. W., Toronto, 416-599-8800 / 866-764-6368, www.sohomet.com
Golf the incredible Muskoka straight from downtown Toronto with weekend packages at the SoHo Met that include accommodations at the SoHo Met, limousine to the airport, private charter to a day of golfing, and return flight for dinner back downtown.

Hidden Valley Highlands Ski Area 1655 Hidden Valley Rd., Huntsville, 705-789-1773 / 800-398-9555, www.skihiddenvalley.on.ca
Hit the slopes for a day. Over 100 professionals offer lessons. Snowboarding too!

Lady Muskoka Cruises P.O. Box 1327, Bracebridge, 705-646-2628 / 800-263-5239, www.ladymuskoka.com
Take a tour on this 104-foot-long fully furnished vessel, complete with licensed bar.

LEAVING TORONTO • OVERNIGHT

Taboo Golf Course Muskoka Beach Road, R.R. 1, Gravenhurst, 866-982-2669, www.tabooresort.com
Test your game on 2003 Masters Champion Mike Weir's home course, a challenging and exciting 18-hole golf course of 7,123 yards.

Best Hotels

Cedarwood Resort Box 262, Bracebridge/Port Carling, 705-645-8558 / 866-252-0223, www.cedarwoodresort.ca
Luxury suites and stunning cottages right on picturesque Lake Muskoka.

Deerhurst Resort 1235 Deerhurst Dr., Huntsville, 705-789-5204, www.deerhurstresort.com
A landmark resort since 1896 on Peninsula Lake, Deerhurst offers the epitome of the all-inclusive luxury resort experience, including fab accommodations, two challenging golf courses, live entertainment, an Aveda spa, dining options, live entertainment, and much more.

Delta Grandview Resort 939 Hwy. 60, Huntsville, 877-472-6388, www.deltagrandview.ca
Set on the shores of pretty Fairy Lake, this premium luxury resort was built onto an existing historic inn and has two golf courses, an indoor and outdoor pool, an eco-tourism program, an observatory, and upscale furnishings and facilities.

Domain of Killien P.O. Box 810, Haliburton, 705-457-1100 / 800-390-0769, www.domainofkillien.com
This 5,000-acre exclusive and private resort in the Haliburton Highlands offers hiking, biking and swimming (among other activities), with gourmet picnic lunches available.

Taboo Golf & Conference Centre Muskoka Beach Rd., R.R. 1, Gravenhurst, 800-461-0236, www.tabooresort.com
New ultra-posh and high-end modern design complex features deluxe accommodations, fine dining, upscale spa, and golf course.

Windermere House Resort 2508 Windermere Rd., Box 68, Windermere, 888-946-3376, www.windermerehouse.com
Right on the shores of Lake Rosseau, this resort has a real Old Muskoka ambience.

Best Restaurants/Nightlife

Eclipse Restaurant Deerhurst Resort, 1234 Deerhurst Dr., Huntsville, 705-789-5204
A wine list of over 175 selections has earned it a Wine Spectator award for three consecutive years, and eight executive chefs create fusion with international influences. The dining room overlooks Peninsula Lake through a ring of evergreens.

Sherwood Inn Dining Room Delta Sherwood Inn, 1090 Sherwood Rd., Port Carling, 705-765-6668, www.deltahotels.com
Enjoy lunch or dinner in a charming country house in a pastoral setting, with a view from the dining room to lush well-tended gardens.

Tall Trees Restaurant 87 Main St. W., Huntsville, 705-789-9769
Country-style décor and Swiss fare in an intimate country dining room.

> **Getting There:** Huntsville—take the Gardiner Expy. westbound, exiting at Hwy. 427 north. From the 427, exit to Hwy. 401 eastbound to Hwy. 400 north. From Hwy. 400 north, take Hwy. 11 exit and watch for the signs for Huntsville on Hwy. 11.

Niagara Falls

80 miles SW

Prime Time: Fall is appealing because it's less crowded than in the summer. Also popular as a midwinter retreat.

The Lowdown: Gushing over the brink with an awe-inspiring might that transcends all the Honeymoon City retro kitsch, the Falls are always spectacular. From the 1940s and '50s, the moniker of "Honeymoon City" stuck, and to this day you'll see heart-shaped jacuzzis advertised in even the lowliest of motels. A strip of kitschy amusements evolved to cater to honeymooners and nature gawkers—Tussaud's Wax Museum, funhouses.

Casino dollars have transformed the entire area, resulting in new and renovated upscale accommodations and restaurants. One new attraction has been the proliferation of world-class golfing clubs—over 40 public and private—earning it the nickname "Myrtle Beach of the North." And shopping opportunities—from outlet malls to high-end designer boutiques—abound.

In the end, of course, these attractions can't compete with Mother Nature, who remains the star of this show. The Falls are especially pretty in the winter, when the outer fringes of water begin to ice, and the City hosts light shows and fireworks, concerts, and other outdoor events year round.

Best Attractions

Butterfly Conservatory 2405 Niagara River Pkwy., Niagara Falls, 905-356-8119, www.niagaraparks.com
One of North America's largest exhibits of free-flying butterflies, housed year-round in climate-controlled greenhouses that are landscaped to resemble a rain forest.

Casino Niagara 5705 Falls Ave., Niagara Falls, 888-946-3255, www.discoverniagara.com/casino
The first, and still a favorite of gamers, features luxe gaming rooms, 2,400 slots and video poker machines, gaming tables, and 100,000 square feet of lights and action.

Great American Balloon Company 310 Rainbow Blvd. S., Niagara Falls, 716-278-0824 / 716-278-0825
Slip stateside for a ride in the Flight of Angels, an exciting 15-minute ride over Niagara Falls in a helium-filled balloon. Open May to October.

Konica Minolta Tower 6732 Fallsview Blvd., Niagara Falls, 905-356-1501, www.niagaratower.com
See the Falls from an observation deck 25 floors up.

Legends on the Niagara Golf Course 10655 Niagara Pkwy., Niagara Falls, 905-295-4754 / 888-552-9549 www.niagarafallsgolfing.com
Legends is a stunning 700-acre, 5-star, 45-hole course and resort, featuring two 18-hole courses, a 9-hole executive course, and a unique 360-degree practice course.

Niagara Fallsview Casino 6380 Fallsview Blvd., Niagara Falls, 888-325-5883 www.discoverniagara.com/fallsviewcasino

LEAVING TORONTO • OVERNIGHT

Vegas-level glitz and glamour, including a $100,000 fountain and art installation, an 180,000-square-foot facility with 3,000 slot machines, and 150 gaming tables.

The Spa Niagara Fallsview Resort & Casino, 6380 Fallsview Blvd., Niagara Falls, 888-325-5883, ext. 53390, www.discoverniagara.com/fallsview
A European-flavored, full-service spa featuring Vichy treatments.

Whirlpool Jet Tours 61 Melville St., P.O. Box 1215, Niagara-on-the-Lake, 905-468-4800 / 888-438-4444, www.whirlpooljet.com
Get up close and personal with the might of the Falls in a jet boat—you'll go as close as safety allows in the whirlpool just where the water comes rushing down.

Best Hotels

Brock Plaza Hotel 5685 Falls Ave., Niagara Falls, 905-374-4444 / 800-263-7135
This Niagara institution offers access to Casino Niagara with red-carpet service.

Hilton Niagara Falls 6361 Fallsview Blvd., Niagara Falls, 905-354-7887 / 888-370-0700, www.niagarafallshilton.com
A 34-story luxury hotel with over 500 oversize rooms and suites above the Falls. Check out the nine-story atrium lobby with 40-foot trees and a waterfall.

Niagara Fallsview Casino Resort 6380 Fallsview Blvd., Niagara Falls, 888-325-5883, www.discoverniagara.com/fallsviewcasino
The Fallsview offers upscale accommodations, with a view of the Falls from every room.

Best Restaurants/Nightlife

After Hours Bistro & Bar 5470 Victoria Ave., Niagara Falls, 905-357-2503
A friendly, relaxed atmosphere and an eclectic menu. There's a patio deck with barbecue served in the summer, and live music year round.

Millery Dining Room Old Stone Inn, 5425 Robinson St., Niagara Falls, 905-357-1234 / 800-263-6208, www.oldstoneinn.on.ca/dining.html
Enjoy a meal in historic splendor, complete with stone walls, fireplace, and chandeliers.

Penthouse Fallsview Dining Room Sheraton on the Falls Hotel, 5875 Falls Ave., Niagara Falls, 905-374-1077 / 800-618-9059
The home of Niagara's best chef combines gourmet fare and the best view of the Falls.

Pinnacle Restaurant Konica Minolta Tower, 6732 Fallsview Blvd., Niagara Falls, 905-356-1501, www.niagaratower.com
With a dining room that rises 525 feet above the Niagara River, the Pinnacle commands one of the most dramatic views in a town that's built on them.

Queenston Heights 14184 Niagara Pkwy., Niagara Falls, 905-262-4274, www.niagaraparks.com/planavisit/queenstonres.php
Fine dining in period architecture with a view of the Niagara River as it flows into Lake Ontario. Ask about the popular Niagara Grand Dinner Theatre.

Twenty-One Club Casino Niagara (second level), 5705 Falls Ave., Niagara Falls, 888-946-3255
Classic food in elegant simplicity, as well as a lounge and piano bar.

Getting There: Take the Gardiner Expy. westbound to the QEW Hamilton. Stay on the QEW in the direction of Niagara to the Niagara River.

Niagara-on-the-Lake

77 miles SW

Prime Time: Extremely popular in the summer, lovely and quiet in the fall, and a pretty winter escape.

The Lowdown: In 1896, writer William Kirby wrote, "Niagara is as near Heaven as any town whatever," and succeeding generations have continued to vote it one of the prettiest towns in the country. Strict by-laws mean that the main street and older parts of town have retained their lovely nineteenth-century character, and Mother Nature has blessed this area with lush, fertile soil—none of which has escaped the notice of film directors, who have often used the small-town streetscape in movies.

The surrounding lush agricultural lands are mostly planted with soft fruit trees and increasingly vineyards. Some of Canada's finest wines are produced here, and the wineries now cater to visitors with luxury accommodations and gourmet dining. The region is one of the few in the world to produce "ice wines." Watch for festivals and packages.

Together with the Shaw Festival Theatre, the town has become quite an upscale party town, boasting the most expensive hotel rooms in Canada.

Best Attractions

Hillebrand Estates Highway 55, Niagara-on-the-Lake, 800-582-8312, www.hillebrand.com
Visit Canada's leading producer of VQA wines. Tour the vineyards, cellars, and winemaking facilities. Stop at the boutique and acclaimed Hillebrand Vineyard Cafe.

Inniskillin Winery Side Road 66, R.R. 1, Niagara-on-the-Lake, 905-468-3554, www.inniskillin.com
This grand estate winery offers tours year round. Ask about the limited edition tour, which includes private tastings of older vintage and rare premium wines.

Niagara-on-the-Lake Golf Club 143 Front St., Niagara-on-the-Lake, 905-468-3424, www.notlgolf.com
The nine-hole course features lush greens and a newly renovated clubhouse.

Niagara Riding Stables 471 Warner Rd., Niagara-on-the-Lake, 905-262-5101
Ride the scenic trails along the Niagara Escarpment on horseback April to December.

Niagara Wine Tours International 92 Picton St., Niagara-on-the-Lake, 905-468-1300 / 800-680-7006, www.niagaraworldwinetours.com
Explore award-winning wineries with tastings and shopping opportunities along the way.

100 Fountain Spa Pillar & Post Inn, 905-468-2123 / 888-669-5566 www.vintageinns.com
Choose from a full range of European spa treatments in a lavish setting.

Shaw Festival Theatre Niagara-on-the-Lake, 800-511-7429, www.shawfest.com
A highly acclaimed theater festival that runs April to November. Based on the works of George Bernard Shaw, the Festival also includes musicals and classic theater.

LEAVING TORONTO • OVERNIGHT

Steve Bauer Bike Tours 4979 King St., Beamsville, 905-563-8687, www.stevebauer.com
Let Olympic medalist Steve Bauer's team take you on a cycling tour of the region.

Best Hotels

Harbour House Hotel 86 Melville St., Niagara-on-the-Lake, 905-468-4683 / 866-277-6677 www.harbourhousehotel.ca
Bright, airy rooms in this luxury small hotel on the scenic riverfront.

Inn on the Twenty Cave Spring Cellars, 3845 Main St., Jordan, 905-562-5336, 800-701-8074 www.innonthetwenty.com
This Jordan Village winery, inn, and restaurant offers luxury accommodations.

Oban Inn 160 Front St., Niagara-on-the-Lake, 905-468-2165
The twenty-six luxury rooms are furnished in period style, many with canopy beds.

Pillar & Post Inn 48 John St., Niagara-on-the-Lake, 905-468-2123 / 888-669-5566, www.vintageinns.com
A gracious country inn furnished with antiques in a lush garden setting.

Prince of Wales Hotel 6 Picton St., Niagara-on-the-Lake, 905-468-3246 / 888-669-5566, www.vintageinns.com
This palatial landmark property comes complete with liveried doorman.

Queen's Landing 155 Byron St., Niagara-on-the-Lake, 905-468-2195 / 888-669-5566, www.vintageinns.com
A stately Georgian mansion overlooking the Niagara River. Ask about the Lakefront Villa and Waterfront Cottage for an exclusive experience.

Best Restaurants/Nightlife

Escabeche Prince of Wales Hotel, 6 Picton St., Niagara-on-the-Lake, 905-468-3246 / 888-669-5566, www.vintageinns.com
Canadian and regional cuisine, featuring produce grown locally and picked daily.

Olde Angel Inn 224 Regent St., Niagara-on-the-Lake, 905-468-3411, www.angel-inn.com
A casual pub and a more formal room. Popular with locals and actors from the Shaw.

On the Twenty Restaurant Cave Spring Cellars, 3836 Main St., Jordan, 905-562-7313, www.innonthetwenty.com
On the Twenty is the height of country elegance and recipient of the Distinguished Restaurants of North America award.

Restaurant at Peninsula Ridge 5600 King St. W., Beamsville, 905-563-0900, www.peninsularidge.com
Located on the Peninsula Ridge Estates Winery, it offers fine dining with vineyard views.

Ristorante Giardino Gate House Hotel, 142 Queen St., Niagara-on-the-Lake, 905-468-3263, www.gatehouse-niagara.com
This dining room is a bubble of contemporary luxury in this historic town.

Tiara Queen's Landing, 155 Byron St., Niagara-on-the-Lake, 905-468-2195 / 888-669-5566, www.vintageinns.com
An opulent dining room overlooking the Niagara River.

> **Getting There:** Take the Gardiner Expy. westbound to the QEW Hamilton, following it to the QEW Niagara. Once you're over the Garden Skyway Bridge, take the exit for Hwy. 55 and follow it to the end.

Stratford

95 miles W

Prime Time: During the Stratford Festival Season, from April to November.

The Lowdown: In 1828, Stratford was little more than a tavern and a few houses along a small river they called "Little Thames" when the area was first surveyed. In 1832, Thomas Mercer Jones gave a picture of William Shakespeare to William Sargint, the owner of the Shakespeare Hotel. Sargint named the blossoming town Stratford and renamed the river Avon, and the rest, as they say, is history. The first formal Stratford Festival began in 1953, featuring Alec Guinness playing Shakespeare under a temporary tent. A permanent theater, (based on Shakespeare's original theater-in-the-round in England) was built four years later.

The Stratford of today is a thriving small town in the midst of bucolic agricultural lands, focused on theater. The Festival has become an entire industry, with costume and set makers working year round. Another offshoot has been the creation of the prestigious Stratford Chef School, where many of Canada's finest chefs have studied, obviously resulting in a wealth of culinary delights far beyond what you'd expect for a town of this size.

A sweet rural village with inns, restaurants, and a real Ontario country flavor, nearby St. Mary's—a mere 15 minutes west on Hwy. 7—is also worth a visit.

Best Attractions

Birch Farms and Estate Winery 655514 15th Line, R.R. 7, Woodstock, 519-469-3040, www.birtchfarms.com
Balance the intellectual pursuits of high-brow theater with a taste of farmland Ontario at this estate fruit winery and farm a mere 25 minutes south of Stratford.

Gallery Stratford 54 Romeo St., Stratford, 519-271-1642, www.gallerystratford.on.ca
Gallery Stratford houses a permanent collection of over 2,000 works.

Stratford Country Club 53 Romeo St. N., Stratford, 519-271-4212, www.stratfordcountryclub.com
A beautiful, mature 18-hole golf course (par 71) that follows the Avon River for a challenging round in a pastoral setting.

Stratford Festival Theatre 55 Queen St., Stratford, 800-567-1600, www.stratfordfestival.ca
The Festival hosts sophisticated shows of the highest caliber. The playbill is based in Shakespearean plays, but also includes musicals and more modern offerings on stage.

Best Hotels

Annex Inn 38 Albert St., Stratford, 519-271-1407 / 800-361-5322, www.bentleys-annex.com

LEAVING TORONTO • OVERNIGHT

Each room features tasteful furnishings in elegant neutrals, a comfortable sitting area with a gas fireplace, and a large whirlpool tub.

Bentley's Inn 99 Ontario St., Stratford, 519-271-1121 / 800-361-5322, www.bentleys-annex.com
Bentley's offers spacious two-level suites or an upscale loft with exposed brick walls, both with period furnishings and stylish, contemporary touches.

Rundles Morris House, Stratford, 519-271-6442, www.rundlesrestaurant.com/housemain.html
Chosen as a "Record House" by *Architectural Record* magazine, Rundles Morris House features a fireplace and queen-size beds on three floors.

Sally's Place Executive Suites, 28 Waterloo St. and 299 Ontario St., Stratford, 519-272-0022, www.sallysplace.com
This luxury boutique hotel in a Victorian offers stylish self-contained apartment suites in a historic setting.

Best Restaurants/Nightlife

Annex Cafe & Lounge 38 Albert St., Stratford, 519-271-1407 / 800-361-5322, www.bentleys-annex.com
A wood bar, a leather couch, a martini or two, and a nice menu selection of pasta, thin-crust pizza, and more make this a relaxing escape.

Bijou Bakery and Cafe 52 Wellington St., Stratford, 519-273-5486, www.bijourestaurant.com
This relaxed cafe and bakery features artisanal breads, imported cheeses, pastries, and espresso.

Bijou Restaurant 105 Erie St., Stratford, 519-273-5000, www.bijourestaurant.com
The contemporary French menu uses fresh, local ingredients, and is matched by a carefully chosen wine list, all served in a Parisian-style bistro.

The Church Restaurant/The Belfry 70 Brunswick St., Stratford, 519-273-3424, www.churchrestaurant.com
Housed in the vaulted-ceiling splendor of an old church, the Church downstairs is open seasonally with the Festival, while the casual Belfry upstairs is open year-round.

The Old Prune 151 Albert St., Stratford, 519-271-5052, www.oldprune.on.ca
The Old Prune, an Edwardian mansion in a verdant garden setting, offers informed and much-acclaimed service along with superb modern cuisine.

Rundles 9 Cobourg St., Stratford, 519-271-6442, www.rundlesrestaurant.com
Rundles has a longstanding tradition of faultless service and innovative cuisine, thanks to the constant stream of young chefs from the town's fabled Chef School.

Getting There: Take the Gardiner Expy. westbound to Hwy. 427 North, then onto Hwy. 401 westbound. From the 401, take exit 278 Hwy. 8 west toward Kitchener/Waterloo and watch for the signs as Hwy. 8 W merges with Hwy. 7 W, direction Stratford. After about 30 miles, look for the various exits to town.

196 miles E

Thousand Islands

Prime Time: Summer months are the most popular for boating, but visit in early fall for the spectacular foliage.

The Lowdown: Early Native American dwellers called this place, where the St. Lawrence River spills into Lake Ontario and straddles both the Province of Ontario and New York State, "the Garden of the Great Spirit," and you won't question why for a moment. One of the first French explorers to set eyes on this unusually beautiful area enthusiastically declared that there had to be a thousand islands—there's actually over 1,700, but the name remains. In the Gilded Age of the industrial era, this is where the richest families of New York and Toronto came to play in the summer months. Nowadays, it's visitors who can enjoy the splendid Victorian and Edwardian mansions, posh historic accommodations, and equally fine dining.

Tourism in the area is based around two centers, Kingston—a small historic city that's home to the Royal Military College and prestigious Queen's University—and Gananoque. Kingston, located where the Rideau Canal meets Lake Ontario near the St. Lawrence, is the freshwater sailing capital of North America, and you'll soon see that virtually everyone in this area owns a boat. Gananoque is an upscale resort town with a small but pretty public beach and a fabulous marina for boat lovers.

Best Attractions

Bellevue House National Historic Site of Canada 35 Centre St., Kingston, 613-545-8666 / 800-230-0016, www.pc.gc.ca
The Italianate villa where Canada's first Prime Minister—as well known for his flamboyant behavior and copious drinking as his political acumen—lived and worked.

Boldt Castle Heart Island International Region of northern New York State, 800-847-5263, www.boldtcastle.com
A lavish historic home begun by George Boldt, former owner of New York's Waldorf Astoria Hotel, for his wife. Self-guided tours available mid-May through mid-October.

Fex Aviation 900 King St. E., Gananoque, 613-382-1104
For the best view of this scenic area, take to the skies in a helicopter tour of the entire Thousand Islands area that you'll never forget. Open daily.

Gananoque Boat Line Gananoque and Ivy Lea, 613-382-2146, www.ganboatline.com
Cruise on triple-decker boats and marvel at the lavish summer estate islands and the quiet beauty of the scenery and wildlife. Sunset cruises also available.

Spa at the Mill 8 Cataraqui St., Kingston, 613-544-1166 / 877-424-4417, www.spaatthemill.com
A full range of services is on offer at this luxurious spa housed in a renovated mill.

Thousand Islands Charity Casino 380 Hwy. 2, Gananoque, 866-266-8422
This multimillion dollar facility includes 450 slot machines and many gaming tables.

LEAVING TORONTO • OVERNIGHT

Thousand Islands Country Club 46433 County 100, Wellesley Island, 800-928-8422, www.ticountryclub.com
Prestigious golf and country club with a long history of distinguished members.

Thousand Islands Playhouse Box Office 690 Charles St. S., Gananoque, 613-382-7020, www.1000islandsplayhouse.com
Enjoy a professionally produced program of comedies, dramas, and musicals.

Best Hotels

The Gananoque Inn 550 Stone St. S., Gananoque, 613-382-2165 / 800-465-3101, www.gananoqueinn.com
This historic inn with elegant furnishings is set in lush gardens by the water.

Hochelaga Inn 24 Sydenham St., Kingston, 613-549-5534 / 877-933-9433, www.hochelagainn.com
This historic inn has a tower. Rooms are furnished with antiques.

Sleepy Hollow Bed & Breakfast 95 King St. W., Gananoque, 613-382-4377, www.sleepyhollowbb.ca
Stay in a gorgeous three-story mansion, professionally decorated in grand period style.

Victoria Rose Inn 279 King St. W., Gananoque, 613-382-3368 / 888-246-2893, www.victoriaroseinn.com
This Victorian mansion with turret, ornate brickwork, and gingerbread trim has romantic suites on two acres of gardens.

Best Restaurants/Nightlife

Aqua Terra Bistro 1 Johnson St., Kingston, 613-549-8100
This classic steak-and-seafood house is right on the waterfront. Live jazz Fri. and Sat.

Athlone Inn Restaurant 250 King St. W., Gananoque, 613-382-3822 / 888-382-7122
Winner of the Golden Fork Award for seven consecutive years, Athlone serves French and continental cuisine in the romantic ambience of a historic B&B.

Casa Bella Restaurant and B&B 110 Clarence St., Gananoque, 613-382-1618 / 866-382-1618, www.eatatbella.com
Bella serves up imaginative fusion in style in a warm and elegant dining room.

The Gananoque Inn Dining Room 550 Stone St. S., Gananoque, 613-382-2165 / 800-465-3101,, www.gananoqueinn.com
An elegant dining room with a gorgeous view over the water and a menu of updated continental classics; al fresco dining is available when weather permits.

General Wolfe Restaurant 1237 Main St., Wolfe Island, 613-385-2611 / 800-353-1098, www.generalwolfehotel.com
A free 20-minute ferry ride across the scenic St. Lawrence River takes you to Wolfe Island and a 150-year-old dining room that overlooks the storied waterway.

Trinity House Inn 90 Stone St. S., Gananoque, 613-382-8383 / 800-265-4871, www.trinityinn.com
This elegant award-winning restaurant serves an inventive continental menu.

Getting There: From downtown Toronto, take the Gardiner Expy. eastbound. When the Gardiner ends, stay left to merge onto the Don Valley Expy. Exit the Don Valley at Hwy. 401 east, staying on the 401 approximately 2 1/2 hours to exit at either Gananoque or Kingston.

Hamilton and Burlington

45 miles W

Prime Time: Late spring to early fall for the Gardens.

The Lowdown: Hamilton and Burlington share the Royal Botanical Gardens and a location at the head of Lake Ontario. The spectacular Gardens are the region's most popular tourist attraction and straddle the two municipalities almost equally. But that's where the similarities end. Hamilton is a small industrial steel city with a blue-collar feel, while Burlington is its more upscale cousin with parklands and expensive yacht clubs. Together, however, they are ideal for a day visit or refreshing pause along the way to Niagara.

Best Attractions

Art Gallery of Hamilton 123 King St. W., Hamilton, 905-527-6610, www.artgalleryofhamilton.on.ca
Canada's third-largest public art gallery, the AGH houses Canadian art.

Canadian Warplane Heritage Museum 9280 Airport Rd., Hamilton, 905-679-4183
The museum's collection includes aircraft dating from World War II to the present.

Hess Village Hess Street, between Main & King Sts., Hamilton, www.hessvillage.com
A historic area of shops, bars, and restaurants with popular streetside patios.

H.M.C.S. Haida & Marine Discovery Centre 57 Guise St. E., Hamilton, 905-526-0911
Dubbed the "fightingest ship in the Royal Canadian Navy," the saw action in WWII and later wars. Today she is the world's last Tribal Class Destroyer.

Royal Botanical Gardens 680 Plains Rd. W., Hamilton, 905-527-1158, www.rbg.ca
Visit Canada's largest botanical garden at over 2,700 acres in several adjacent sites.

Best Restaurants/Nightlife

The Gardens Cafe 680 Plains Rd. W., Burlington, 905-529-2920
Bright cafe in the midst of the greenhouses of the RBG with a view of the greenery.

Junction Cafe & Lounge 197–199 King William St., Hamilton, 905-528-7245
A lively bistro and jazz lounge housed in a former railway-switching house.

Koi Restaurant & Cocktail Boutique 27 Hess St. S., Hamilton, 905-308-7507
A modern and minimalist high-end Japanese eatery and martini lounge.

Pepperwood Bistro & Brewery 1455 Lakeshore Rd., Burlington, 905-333-6999
An international menu, a long wine list, fresh beer, and a patio overlooking a park.

Rude Native Bistro & Grill 420 Pearl St., Burlington, 905-333-5633
Experience award-winning global cuisine and live entertainment.

> **Getting There:** Take the Gardiner Expy. westbound till it merges with the QEW Hamilton. Take the QEW Niagara, then the Woodward Street exit to reach the east end of Hamilton (*H.M.C.S. Haida*). For other attractions, take Hwy. 403 west and the York Blvd. or Main St. E. exits.

LEAVING TORONTO • DAY TRIP

Kleinburg

25 miles N

Prime Time: Summer is the busiest season, but the foliage is gorgeous in the fall.

The Lowdown: Atop the Humber River Ridge and surrounded by glorious views, this country village just north of Toronto was founded in 1848 by John Kline, a Swiss watchmaker. Early Canadiana lives on here in lovingly restored and tended architecture. Kleinburg is full of city dwellers who came for a visit and decided to stay, as did Robert and Signe McMichael. The wealthy couple were so charmed by the town that they not only stayed, but built an estate that they eventually donated to the Province of Ontario— along with, and most important, their large collection of art by the famed Group of Seven, which eventually became the renowned McMichael Gallery.

The town that's grown around the McMichael is lined with historic streets that offer eclectic shops, galleries, and exhibits with a definite artsy flair.

Best Attractions

Kleinburg Golf & Country Club 115 Putting Green Cr., Kleinburg, 905-893-1900, www.kleinburg-golf.com
There are three different nine-hole courses here, each with its own particular terrain.

Kortright Conservation Centre 9550 Pine Valley Dr., Woodbridge, 905-832-2289, www.kortright.org
Over 16 km of hiking trails through meadows, forests, and across a marsh.

McMichael Gallery 10365 Islington Ave., Kleinburg, 905-893-1121 / 888-213-1121, www.mcmichael.com
The premier collection of Group of Seven paintings.

Best Restaurants/Nightlife

Chartreuse 10512 Islington Ave., Kleinburg, 905-893-0475, www.chartreuserestaurant.com
Two old-fashioned dining rooms and traditional French cuisine.

Doctor's House & Lounge 21 Nashville Rd., Kleinburg, 905-893-1615, www.thedoctorshouse.ca
Continental classics and an extensive wine list. Drinks and casual fare in the lounge.

Dolce Venezia Cafe & Gelato 10519 Islington Ave., Kleinburg, 905-893-0876
Pastries, coffees, and gourmet sandwiches in a chic little room with Euro appeal.

Getting There: Take the Gardiner Expy. eastbound, staying left as it turns into the Don Valley Expy. Exit onto Major Mackenzie Dr., heading west (left) to Islington Ave. Turn north (right) on Islington to reach the village.

82 miles W

St. Jacobs

Prime Time: In the summer months, this region is verdant and fertile and in full swing.

The Lowdown: West of Toronto, the cities become smaller and thin out into pastures and bucolic rolling hills. Tiny and historic St. Jacobs was founded in 1852 as the marketplace for area farmers and developed Ontario's first creamery in 1872. But as far back as the late 1700s, the area was being settled and farmed by Mennonites who traveled there in wagons from Pennsylvania. Today, the area is known as Mennonite country, and you'll see Old Order Mennonites in horse-drawn buggies and traditional dress.

The area has retained its rural charm, and along with the Mennonites and their wares, you'll find a picturesque village and shopping opportunities, with over 100 retailers, including galleries, studios, and an antique market.

Best Attractions

The Mennonite Story—Visitor Centre, 1408 King St. N., St. Jacobs, 519-664-3518
Learn about the history and culture of the Mennonites in a multimedia presentation.

St. Jacobs Antique Market 8 Spring St., St. Jacobs, 519-664-1243
Forty-five antique dealers offering an array of antique furniture and collectibles.

St. Jacobs Farmers and Flea Markets 878 Weber St. N., (2 km south of St. Jacobs), Waterloo, 519-747-1830 / 800-265-3353
Festive farmers market with hundreds of vendors and delicious Mennonite fare. Open Thurs. and Sat. 7 a.m.–3:30 p.m. year round, and Tuesdays during the summer.

Best Restaurants/Nightlife

Benjamin's Restaurant 1430-1 King St. N., St. Jacobs, 519-664-3731
Experience contemporary Canadian cuisine in a refurbished 1852 inn.

Stone Crock 1396 King St. N., St. Jacobs, 519-664-2286
Get a taste of local history with Waterloo County recipes and home-style cooking.

Vidalia's Market Dining 1398 King St. N., St. Jacobs, 519-664-2575
This casual eatery features open kitchens where your food is prepared as you watch.

> **Getting There:** Take the Gardiner Expy. westbound just out of town, then exit to Hwy. 427 north. From 427, get on Hwy. 401 west, (direction London). Take exit 278 to Hwy. 8 west (toward Kitchener-Waterloo). After merging onto Hwy. 8 west, exit to Hwy. 85 toward Waterloo. Follow Hwy. 85 to 15 exit for the Farmers Market. Turn left onto King St. (Rd. 15), then left onto Farmers Market Rd.
>
> For the St. Jacobs, continue on Highway 85. Turn left at the traffic lights onto Sawmill Rd. (Rd. 17) and follow the signs to the Village.

The Toronto Calendar

With our month-by-month calendar of events, there's no excuse to miss a moment of fun in Toronto. We tell you when to be where and why, so you can be sure to be where the action is at the right time. With Toronto's growing reputation as a world-class destination, it's no surprise that some of the world's greatest events—highlighting world-class cinema, food, culture, and the arts, among many others—take place right here. But don't miss out on some of Toronto's smaller neighborhood festivals when the real local flavor shines through.

The Toronto Calendar

January
Toronto International Boat Show

February
Toronto WinterCity Festival

March
Toronto Wine & Cheese Show

April
Hot Docs Canadian International Documentary Festival

May**
Inside Out Annual Lesbian & Gay Film & Video Festival
Toronto Jewish Film Festival

June**
Pride Week*
Toronto Downtown Jazz Festival*

July**
Beaches International Jazz Festival
Festival of Fire
Caribana Festival*
Molson Indy*
Toronto Outdoor Art Exhibition

August**
Canadian National Exhibition
Krinos Taste of the Danforth
Rogers Cup WTA Tennis

September**
Toronto International Film Festival*
Word on the Street

October
Harbourfront International Festival of Authors

November
Royal Agricultural Winter Fair

December
Cavalcade of Lights

* The Fun Seeker's Top Five Events
**High season is from late May through early September.

January

Toronto International Boat Show
National Trade Centre, Exhibition Place, 905-951-0009, www.discoverboating.com/boatshows/toronto/

When: Nine days beginning on a Saturday in mid-January

The Lowdown: There are two ways to cope with winter in the Great White North—cultivate an interest in winter sports, or attend the International Boat Show in January and dream away the weather. Over 100,000 people typically attend this show, which covers 400,000 square feet of exhibition space and features over 1,000 crafts from paddle boats to the latest sport boats and luxury yachts with all the amenities. An indoor lake—the largest in the world—covers 28,000 square feet complete with floating docks and "harborside" dining, and the show features boating and engine repair demonstrations, as well as other educational and entertaining seminars and workshops. This is delightful escapism in the dead of winter.

February

Toronto WinterCity Festival
Various downtown venues, 416-394-0490, www.city.toronto.on.ca/special_events/wintercity/index.htm

When: Two weeks from the end of January to mid-February

The Lowdown: For two weeks in the dead of winter, the city comes out to play, eat, and be entertained in a citywide festival. The Festival includes free outdoor concerts and performances (yes, outdoor!), as well as events that showcase the rich diversity of Toronto's culinary and performing arts scenes. Indoor events include culinary demonstrations and classes. Watch for special Winterlicious menus and special packages at downtown restaurants and hotels. Citywide arts organizations and venues offer a behind-the-scenes tours and special shows. Previous highlights have included a spectacular acrobatic performance in downtown's Eaton Centre.

March

Toronto Wine & Cheese Show
International Centre, 416-229-2060, www.towineandcheese.com

When: Friday to Sunday, between mid-March and early April

The Lowdown: This premier vintners' event is billed as "A world of award-winning wines, beers, single malt whiskies, specialty foods, and cheeses"—in short, a gourmet's dream of samplings and exhibitions. Leading food and wine experts, including the city's hottest chefs, lead more than 20 free seminars and cooking demonstrations in a Gourmet Kitchen Theatre. Preview the latest wines courtesy of the Liquor Control Board of Ontario (LCBO—the province's only liquor retailer and consequently the world's largest buyer of wines and spirits). In addition to the fine wine and food samplings, the show also features a cigar lounge and wine and beer competitions.

April

Hot Docs Canadian International Documentary Festival
Various venues, 416-203-2155, www.hotdocs.ca

When: Ten days toward the end of April

The Lowdown: North America's largest documentary festival screens over 100 works from top-flight Canadian filmmakers and their compatriots from around the world. Programming includes special retrospective screenings honoring a featured artist, as well as an in-depth look at films from a spotlight country. Check out the retrospective galas with the artist in attendance for interviews and Q&A sessions after the screening. For film professionals, there are networking events, seminars, and workshops.

May

Inside Out Annual Lesbian and Gay Film & Video Festival
Various venues, 416-977-6847, www.insideout.on.ca

When: 11 days in mid- to late May

The Lowdown: Canada's largest gay and lesbian film fest, Inside Out presents almost 300 films. Inside Out has grown from humble beginnings to an international showcase that attracts tens of thousands of attendees from all over the globe. In addition to attending the screenings, you can mingle with the film set at parties, panel discussions, director's talks, and meet-and-greets.

Toronto Jewish Film Festival
Various venues, 416-324-9121, www.tjff.com

When: Nine days beginning on a Friday in early to mid-May

The Lowdown: The second-largest Jewish film festival in North America, the TJFF showcases films of all kinds that address themes of Jewish culture and identity. Program offerings have typically included films from up to 20 countries, reflecting the diversity of the Jewish experience and the talent it has produced. Canadian and international filmmakers attend, participating in lectures, discussions, and Q&A sessions. Check out the opening- and closing-night galas to mingle with the film crowd.

June

Pride Week*
Various venues, 416-927-7433, www.pridetoronto.com

When: Beginning on a Friday in the last (full) week of June

The Lowdown: For ten days, Toronto comes out to celebrate its gay community, which is second in size only to San Francisco's. Centered around the Gay Village, the festivities include a three-day multistage arts fest and a weeklong street celebration. Look for specials, events, and entertainment throughout the area. The finale is a bawdy Pride March down Yonge Street on the last Sunday. Not for the prudish or faint of heart, the Parade grows each year to include an increasingly diverse crowd.

THE TORONTO CALENDAR

Toronto Downtown Jazz Festival*
30-plus venues throughout Downtown, 416-928-2033, www.tojazz.com

When: Ten days beginning the last Friday in June

The Lowdown: For ten sultry days in the summer, jazz fever takes over downtown. More than 1,500 world-class Canadian and international musicians are showcased at venues ranging from free outdoor concerts to big-ticket main-stage events, in a line-up that has included greats like Oscar Peterson, Jean-Luc Ponty, and Wynton Marsalis. One of the Festival's perennial highlights is that the luminaries of the jazz world come to some of Toronto's downtown clubs—notably the Rex Hotel or the Montreal Bistro—to let down their hair and jam with the locals.

July

Beaches International Jazz Festival
Various Beaches venues and Distillery District, 416-698-2152, www.beachesjazz.com

When: Eleven days, beginning on a Thursday in mid-July

The Lowdown: Nearly a million people converge on the usually laid-back Beaches neighborhood for this jazz celebration. The music from over 750 bands and solo performers not only includes traditional and experimental forms of the music, but blues, Afro-Canadian influences, world beat, and Latin sounds. And the people come not only for the music, but for the parties, street festivals, dance performances, and workshops. The main stage is outdoors at Kew Gardens, and other area venues participate. Check out the opening party at the Distillery District for a hot start to the Festival.

Canada Day at Ontario Place (Festival of Fire)
Ontario Place (various), 416-314-9933, www.ontarioplace.com

When: July 1 (Festival of Fire is spread over three nights, beginning June 30)

The Lowdown: Join in the celebration of Canada's Confederation by attending any of the events taking place citywide. See the spirit of the True North in concerts and music festivals at the Molson Amphitheatre. Later on, watch a dazzling display of fireworks in the Festival of Fire, a spectacular event that combines music and the work of pyro artists from around the world, fired up into the night sky from a 700-foot lake freighter. Ontario Place is packed with viewers, but note that two of the best vantage points for this extravaganza are the CN Tower and the harbour cruise boats.

Caribana Festival*
Various venues, 416-466-0321, www.caribanafestival.com

When: 18 days beginning on a Friday in mid-July

The Lowdown: Attracting over a million people to a colorful celebration of Caribbean visual and performing arts, this is North America's largest street festival. From the opening King and Queen Xtravaganza at Lamport Stadium, which offers a first glimpse at the eye-popping costumes, to the parade that ends the festivities, it's a feast for the eyes, with lots of steel bands, calypso, and soca to soothe the soul. The parade along Lakeshore Boulevard features thousands of costumed masqueraders and floats. Between the opening and closing parade, there's loads to take in, from free outdoor entertainment to a marketplace and cultural village on Olympic Island.

Molson Indy*
Lakeshore Boulevard and Exhibition Grounds, 416-872-4639, www.molsonindy.com

When: Friday to Sunday, early to mid-July

The Lowdown: Whether you attend the races or not, you'll know when the Indy is in town by the cars roaring up Lakeshore Boulevard and down a route of curving streets throughout the Exhibition Grounds. Stands and bleachers are set up all along the course, with coveted corporate hospitality tents going for up to $100,000. Practice and qualifying runs are held on Friday and Saturday, with the final race, televised live, held on Sunday.

Toronto Outdoor Art Exhibition
Nathan Phillips Square, 416-408-2754, www.torontooutdoorart.org

When: Friday to Sunday, in mid-July

The Lowdown: Over three days, over 100,000 converge on Nathan Phillips Square, rain or shine, for this long-running event (in 2005, entering its 44th year). It's the largest outdoor art exhibition in Canada, and typically features the work of established artists, undiscovered gems, and talented students. As well as presenting an excellent shopping opportunity for art enthusiasts, it's a way of meeting and networking with artists and art dealers.

August

Canadian National Exhibition (CNE)
Exhibition Grounds, 416-263-3800, mmi.theex.com

When: 18 days from mid-August and ending on Labor Day

The Lowdown: Founded in 1879, the "Ex," as it's affectionately known to locals, is one of the continent's biggest fairs, with over 500 attractions, 700 exhibitors, and a fab midway with 65 rides. With 1.4 million visitors in 2004, the festivities include live music on small and midsize stages, a horse show, and the hugely popular Food Building, where you can eat your way through the cultures that make up the city. An onsite casino offers gaming tables and an air-conditioned poker room, along with a pub that features live entertainment. And there's a talent competition to boot.

Krinos Taste of the Danforth
Greektown, 416-469-5634, www.tasteofthedanforth.com

When: Friday to Sunday, in early August

The Lowdown: Over a long weekend in August, blocks of Danforth Avenue are shut down, and Greektown takes to the streets. All the local restaurants are represented at booths with savory Greek culinary delights on offer—from souvlaki to calamari—along with the flavors of other Greektown restaurants, from dim sum to chipotle. There are lots of outdoor concerts and other events, all with a multicultural theme that emphasizes Hellenic heritage. Expect to make a day of it, and stay into the evening too, in the company of over a million other food and entertainment enthusiasts.

Rogers Cup WTA Tennis

Rexall Centre (York University), 416-665-9777, www.rogerscup.com

When: Nine days beginning on a Friday in mid-August (qualifying rounds typically commence the first weekend, with the finals the following weekend)

The Lowdown: Catch an exciting international tennis tournament with top-seeded players like Jennifer Caprioti and Serena Williams. Tennis Canada cosponsors the annual Tennis Championships held in the state-of-the-art facilities on the York University campus. First begun in 1892, this tournament has been around longer than any except Wimbledon and the U.S. Open. Live music and star-gazing (the event is popular among visiting VIPs) round out your experience. Tennis fans purchase tickets up to a year ahead of time, so make your plans well in advance.

September

Toronto International Film Festival*

Various venues, 416-967-7371, www.e.bell.ca/filmfest/

When: Two weeks beginning on a Thursday in early September

The Lowdown: For two weeks, the streets of Toronto are home to the world's glitterati, at the Film Festival, which is second only to Cannes. The international film set are treated to Toronto's own brand of laid-back hospitality and responds in kind. The Festival is a huge fan favorite because the stars come down to earth—staying, eating, and playing on the streets—and they are often accessible to the public. You may bump into Hollywood royalty on the sidewalk, or party with the stars by attending any of the many parties and galas that are open to anyone. If you plan on attending the opening or closing galas, get your tickets to these coveted events early. The film selections are varied but always first-class and a treat for film lovers and stargazers alike. There are too many screenings to catch everything of interest, but you'll have fun trying.

Word on the Street

Queen's Park, 416-504-7241, www.wordonthestreet.ca

When: Saturday in mid- to late September

The Lowdown: Attended by more than 170,000 in 2003, this one-day event takes over Queen's Park for a celebration of the written word. Torontonians are big readers, and they've proven it by making this showcase for independent publishers and booksellers a hugely successful event. The proceedings include over 500 exhibits, readings, book signings, meet-and-greets, and media events. A large selection of books and magazines are for sale, including hard-to-find and out-of-print items.

October

Harbourfront International Festival of Authors
Harbourfront Centre for the Arts, 416-973-4000, www.readings.org

When: 11 days staring on a Wednesday in mid- to late October

The Lowdown: The Harbourfront Centre becomes a hive of literary activity in October. The International Festival of Authors is a well-attended series of author readings, book signings, and social events, attracting a cross-section of book lovers from around the world. Since 1974, over 4,000 authors have participated, including several Nobel Laureates. Authors in 2004 included Russell Banks and Michael Ondaatje, and the organizers produce a stellar line-up of Canadian and internationally recognized artists in a setting with a warm and intimate feel.

November

Royal Agricultural Winter Fair
National Trade Centre, Exhibition Grounds, 416-263-3400, www.royalfair.org

When: Ten days beginning the first Friday in November

The Lowdown: For ten days every November, country comes to the city in a traditional agricultural fair even Martha Stewart loves. This isn't only about pigs and cows and best-in-show, this is the largest combined agricultural, horticultural, canine, and equestrian event in the world. The Royal Horse Show features international-caliber competition in jumping and dressage, as well as carriage-derby racing. The popular Cavalcade of Horses spotlights riding techniques and training. The Celebration of the Dog has also quickly become a crowd favorite, especially the "Raging Jack Russells." There's lots to do and see, including information, shows, and entertaining displays.

December

Cavalcade of Lights
Various venues throughout downtown, 416-395-0490,
www.city.toronto.on.ca/special_events/cavalcade_lights.htm

When: Last weekend in November until New Year's Eve

The Lowdown: The Cavalcade of Lights Festival officially begins with the lighting of a massive Christmas tree, followed by the lighting of the rest of Nathan Phillips Square with over 100,000 lights, and continues throughout the month of December. Begun in 1967, Canada's centennial year, it includes other events such as a popular outdoor skating rink and several shimmering fireworks displays. Throughout the city, various events include light displays, special concerts, neighborhood and historic house tours, and a stunning three-day international ice-sculpting competition. All of it culminates in a huge outdoor New Year's Eve celebration that has traditionally featured hot up-and-coming bands, including the now famous Bare Naked Ladies.

The Toronto Black Book

Where was that hot new Latin dance club I was just reading about? Or that hip cafe that's open 24/7? No one should have to get along without a little black book that contains all the important names and phone numbers at their fingertips. Ours is packed with helpful information, so you can choose your venue by theme, location, or price. It's the best of the city condensed into a few invaluable pages. Don't leave home without it.

The Fun Seeker's Toronto Black Book

Hotels

NAME WEBSITE	ADDRESS (CROSS STREET) PRICE DESCRIPTION	AREA*	PHONE 800 NUMBER	EXPERIENCE PERFECT	PAGE** PAGE
The Drake Hotel www.thedrakehotel.ca	1150 Queen St. W. (Beaconsfield) $$$ A mecca for art and film types.	PD	416-531-5042 866-372-5386	Hipster	125, 129
Fairmont Royal York www.fairmont.com/royalyork	100 Front St. W. (York) $$$$ Old Toronto at its finest.	DT	416-368-2511	Classic	153, 157
Four Seasons Hotel Toronto www.fourseasons.com/toronto	21 Avenue Rd. (Cumberland) $$$$ Upscale home to out-of-town stars.	BY	416-964-0411 800-819-5053	Hot & Cool	75
The Gladstone Hotel www.gladstonehotel.com	1214 Queen St. W. (Gladstone) $$$ Richly renovated old hotel.	PD	416-531-4635	Hipster	129
Hilton Toronto www.hilton.com	145 Richmond St. W. (University) $$$$ Slick and elegant, ideally located.	FD	416-869-3456 800-445-8667	Classic	157
Hotel Le Germain www.germaintoronto.com	30 Mercer St. (Blue Jays) $$$$ Stunning design, popular with celebs.	ED	416-345-4500 866-345-9500	Hot & Cool	71, 75
InterContinental Toronto Centre torontocentre.intercontinental.com	225 Front St. W. (Simcoe) $$$ Airy and modern.	ED	416-597-1400 800-422-7969	Arts & Ent.	103
Le Meridien King Edward Hotel www.toronto.lemeridien.com	37 King St. E. (Victoria) $$$$ Opulence characterizes this historic hotel.	SL	416-863-9700 800-543-4300	Arts & Ent.	99, 103
The Madison Manor www.madisonavenuepub.com	20 Madison Ave. (Bloor) $$$ A historic B&B furnished with antiques.	BY	416-922-5579 877-561-7048	Hipster	130
Metropolitan Hotel www.metropolitan.com/toronto	108 Chestnut St. (University) $$$ Exquisite attention to detail.	CT	416-977-5000 800-668-6600	Arts & Ent.	104
Pantages Hotel Suites www.pantageshotel.com	200 Victoria St. (Shuter) $$$$ Toronto's newest boutique hotel.	DT	416-362-1777 866-852-1777	Hot & Cool	76
Park Hyatt Toronto www.parktoronto.hyatt.com	4 Avenue Rd. (Bloor) $$$$ Elegant, upscale Yorkville institution.	BY	416-925-1234 800-633-7313	Classic	158
The SoHo Metropolitan www.sohomet.com	318 Wellington St. W. (Blue Jays) $$$$ Luxury boutique hotel.	ED	416-599-8800 866-764-6638	Hipster	130
Sutton Place www.toronto.suttonplace.com	955 Bay St. (Gerrard) $$$$ Low-key luxury in a good location.	FD	416-924-2221 866-378-8866	Arts & Ent.	104
Westin Harbour Castle www.westin.com/harbourcastle	1 Harbour Sq. (York) $$$ Contemporary hotel on waterfront.	HF	416-869-1600	Classic	158
Windsor Arms Hotel www.windsorarmshotel.com	18 St. Thomas St. (Bloor) $$$$ Lushly renovated historic hotel.	BY	416-971-9666	Hot & Cool	76

* Area Key Code: BE=Beaches, BV=Bloor/Yorkville, CT=Chinatown, DD=Distillery District, DT=Downtown/Yonge, ED=Entertainment District, FD=Financial District, GT=Greektown, GV=Gay Village, HF=Harbourfront, LI=Little Italy, ON=Ontario, PD=Parkdale, UP=Uptown, UT=University of Toronto, SL=St. Lawrence

** Note regarding page numbers: *Italic* = itinerary listing; Roman = theme chapter listing.

Restaurants

NAME	ADDRESS (CROSS STREET)	AREA	PHONE	EXPERIENCE	PAGE
	PRICE DESCRIPTION			PERFECT	PAGE
Agora	317 Dundas St. W. (McCaul)	CT	416-979-6612	Arts & Ent.	99, 105
(Art Gallery of Ontario)	$$$ Under the high, glassed ceilings of the sculpture atrium at the AGO.				
Auberge du Pommier	4150 Yonge St. (York Mills)	UP	416-222-2220	Arts & Ent.	102, 105
	$$$$ Fabulous French cuisine in a chic uptown neighborhood.			Fine Dining	47
Avalon	270 Adelaide St. W. (John)	ED	416-979-9918	Classic	153, 159
	$$$$ Smooth service and a sophisticated menu.				
Avenue	21 Avenue Rd. (Cumberland)	BY	416-964-0411	Classic	155, 159
(Four Seasons Hotel Toronto)	$$$$ High-end watering hole and lounge in the Four Seasons.				
Azure Restaurant & Bar	225 Front St. W. (Simcoe)	ED	416-597-8142	Arts & Ent.	101, 106
(InterContinental Toronto Centre)	$$$$ Handsome, centrally located spot caters to a white-collar crowd.				
Babur	273 Queen St. W. (McCaul)	ED	416-599-7720	Hipster	126, 131
	$$ Stylish dining room, best in northern Indian cuisine.			Ethnic Dining	46
Balzac's Cafe	55 Mill St. (Parliament)	DD	416-207-1709	Arts & Ent.	101, 106
	$ Cool coffee shop in the Distillery District.				
Banzai Sushi	134 Peter St. (Richmond)	ED	416-341-0404	Hot & Cool	73, 77
	$$$ Japanese cuisine served up in high style in Clubland.			Asian Restaurants	37
Bar Italia	582 College St. W. (Manning)	LI	416-535-3621	Hipster	128, 131
	$$$ Classic Little Italy on College, excellent, efficient service.				
Bar One	924 Queen St. W. (Shaw)	PD	416-535-1655	Hipster	125, 131
	$$$ Clean, bright modern design and a simple Italian menu.				
Beaver Cafe	1192 Queen St. W. (Northcote)	PD	416-537-2768	Hipster	125, 132
	$$ Funky beaver-themed diner that's bright and fun.				
Beer Bistro	18 King St. E. (Yonge)	DT	416-831-9872	Hipster	127, 132
	$$$ Popular downtown restaurant with over 100 brews.				
Biagio Ristorante	111 King St. E. (Jarvis)	SL	416-366-4040	Arts & Ent.	100, 106
	$$$$ Very upscale Italian in the historic St. Lawrence house.				
Biff's	4 Front St. E. (Yonge)	SL	416-860-0086	Arts & Ent.	102, 107
	$$$$ A gleaming bar, good martinis, and imaginative French cuisine.				
Bistro 333	333 King St. W. (Widmer)	ED	416-971-3336	Classic	156, 160
	$$$ Upscale eatery that caters to the clubbing crowds.			Late-Night Eats	53
Bistro 990	990 Bay St. (St. Joseph)	FD	416-921-9990	Hot & Cool	72, 77
	$$$$ Home-style French cooking for movers and shakers.				
Bloor Street Diner	145 King St. W. (University)	FD	416-363-0460	Classic	153, 160
& Bistro Express	$$ Combines American diner with Provençal-style bistro charm.				
Boba	90 Avenue Rd. (Elgin)	BY	416-961-2622	Classic	155, 160
	$$$$ An offbeat, imaginative menu in a Victorian house.				
Brassaii	461 King St. W. (Spadina)	ED	416-598-4730	Hot & Cool	71, 77
	$$$ Sleekly elegant with imaginative gourmet menu.				
Bright Pearl Seafood	346–348 Spadina Ave. (St. Andrew)	CT	416-979-3988	Classic	156, 161
	$$ Best Cantonese in Chinatown, dim sum a specialty.			Asian Restaurants	37
Bymark	66 Wellington St. W., concourse level (Bay)	FD	416-777-1144	Classic	154, 161
	$$$$ Stunning contemporary design, imaginative Canadian cuisine.				
Byzantium	499 Church St. (Wellesley)	GV	416-922-3859	Hipster	127, 132
	$$$ Long a favorite in the Gay Village, with slightly dated décor.				
Cafe Diplomatico	594 College St. W. (Clinton)	LI	416-534-4637	Hipster	128, 133
	$$ Cool and laid-back, longtime people-watching haunt.				
Cafe Supreme	40 University Ave. (Wellington)	FD	416-585-7896	Classic	155, 161
	$$ European cafe that buzzes with activity in the morning.				

Restaurants (cont.)

NAME	ADDRESS (CROSS STREET)	AREA	PHONE	EXPERIENCE	PAGE
	PRICE DESCRIPTION			PERFECT	PAGE
Cafe Victoria (Le Meridien King Edward Hotel)	37 King St. E. (Victoria) $$$$ Ornate dining room with high-end continental menu.	SL	416-863-4125	Arts & Ent. Brunches	*102*, 107 38
Caju	922 Queen St. W. (Crawford) $$$ Warm colors and the flavors of Brazil.	PD	416-532-2550	Hipster Ethnic Dining	*126*, 133 46
Canoe Restaurant & Bar	66 Wellington St. W., 54th Fl. (Bay) $$$$ Excellent Canadian cuisine, stunning view.	FD	416-364-0054	Classic Canadian Cuisine	*154*, 162 39
Caren's Wine and Cheese Bar	158 Cumberland St. (Avenue) $$$ Stylish restaurant/wine bar with notable bistro-style menu.	BY	416-962-5158	Classic	*155*, 162
Casa Cafe	828 Yonge St. (Bloor) $$ Coffee shop with a light menu, exposed brick walls—an oasis of calm.	BY	416-923-3810	Hot & Cool	*72*, 78
Centro Grill & Wine Bar	2472 Yonge St. upper level (Eglinton) $$$$ Haute cuisine in palatial surroundings.	UP	416-483-2211	Arts & Ent.	*102*, 115
C'est What?	67 Front St. E. (Church) $$ Basement pub popular for after-theater snacks and drinks.	SL	416-867-9499	Classic	*154*, 163
Coco Lezzone Grill and Porto Bar	602 College St. W. (Clinton) $$$ Stylish resto/lounge, known for martinis and Cuban cigars.	LI	416-535-1489	Hot & Cool Always-Hot	*74*, 78 36
Courtyard Cafe (Windsor Arms Hotel)	18 St. Thomas St. (Bloor) $$$$ Romantic, stylish dining room, popular with the celebs.	BY	416-971-9666	Classic	*156*, 163
Crepes à Go Go	244 Bloor St. W. (Admiral) $$ French crepes and patisseries with a French cafe ambience.	BY	416-922-6765	Hot & Cool	*71*, 78
Crush Wine Bar	455 King St. W. (Spadina) $$$ Classic French cuisine in this chic bistro dining room.	ED	416-977-1234	Hot & Cool	*74*, 79
Drake Dining Room and Raw Bar	1150 Queen St. W. (Beaconsfield) $$$$ Chef David Chrystian prepares inventive Canadian dishes.	PD	416-531-5042	Hipster Canadian Cuisine	*125*, 133 39
Esplanade Bier Markt	58 The Esplanade (Church) $$$ Classic Belgian brasserie features more than 100 beers and ales.	SL	416-862-7575	Hipster	*128*, 134
Fez Batik	129 Peter St. (Richmond) $$$ Exotic Moroccan-themed resto/lounge popular with creative types.	ED	416-204-9660	Hipster	*128*, 134
The Fifth	225 Richmond St. W. (Bedford) $$$$ A luxurious oasis of candlelight, fireplace, and fusion.	ED	416-979-3005	Classic	*156*, 163
Futures Bakery & Cafe	483 Bloor St. W. (Bathurst) $ Busy bakery and cafe great for Yorkville people-watching.	BY	416-922-5875	Hot & Cool	*71*, 79
Gallery Grill	7 Hart House Circle, 2nd Fl. (Queen's Park) $$$ Open only for lunch in a pretty University of Toronto building.	UT	416-978-2445	Arts & Ent.	*99*, 108
Gamelle	468 College St. W. (Markham) $$$ Cozy and romantic French restaurant and bistro.	LI	416-923-6254	Arts & Ent.	*102*, 108
Gypsy Co-Op	817 Queen St. W. (Gore Vale) $$$ Eclectic, eccentric and chic, it's everything Queen West.	PD	416-703-5069	Hipster	*125*, 135
Harbour 60	60 Harbour St. (Bay) $$$$ A classic steakhouse in an opulent setting.	HF	416-777-2111	Classic	*154*, 164
Hemispheres (Metropolitan Hotel)	110 Chestnut St. (University) $$$ Elegant East-West flavors and setting.	CT	416-599-8000	Classic	*156*, 164

* Area Key Code: BE=Beaches, BV=Bloor/Yorkville, CT=Chinatown, DD=Distillery District, DT=Downtown/Yonge, ED=Entertainment District, FD=Financial District, GT=Greektown, GV=Gay Village, HF=Harbourfront, LI=Little Italy, ON=Ontario, PD=Parkdale, UP=Uptown, UT=University of Toronto, SL=St. Lawrence

** Note regarding page numbers: *Italic* = itinerary listing; Roman = theme chapter listing.

THE TORONTO BLACK BOOK

Restaurants (cont.)

NAME	ADDRESS (CROSS STREET) PRICE DESCRIPTION	AREA	PHONE	EXPERIENCE PERFECT	PAGE PAGE
Holt's Cafe	50 Bloor St. W. (Bay) $$$$ Sleek whites and chromes, fabulously stylish.	BY	416-922-2223	Hot & Cool	73, 79
Hot House Cafe	35 Church St. (Front) $$ A lively eatery with a popular weekend jazz brunch.	SL	416-366-7800	Classic	156, 164
Indian Motorcycle Cafe & Lounge	355 King St. W. (John) $$ Motorcycle-theme bar-resto for a polished downtown crowd.	ED	416-593-6996	Hot & Cool	72, 88
Inspire	491 Church St. (Wellesley) $$$ Hottest gay date spot in the Village.	GV	416-963-0044	Arts & Ent.	100, 116
Joso's	202 Davenport Rd. (Avenue) $$$$ A Yorkville institution, superlative seafood and patio.	BY	416-925-1903	Classic Seafood	155, 165 60
Jump Cafe & Bar	1 Wellington St. W. (Yonge) $$$ Stylish and popular with the movers and shakers, nice wine selection.	FD	416-363-3400	Arts & Ent.	102, 108
Kalendar	546 College St. W. (Euclid) $$ One of Toronto's most romantic dining spots.	LI	416-923-4138	Hipster	128, 135
KitKat2/Club Lucky	117 John St. (Pearl) $$$ Italian eatery with style, open late daily, cigar bar and lounge.	ED	416-977-8890	Arts & Ent.	102, 109
Lai Wah Heen (Metropolitan Hotel)	108 Chestnut St., 2nd Fl. (University) $$$$ The best Cantonese in town, internationally recognized.	CT	416-977-9899	Arts & Ent. Asian Restaurants	101, 109 37
La Maquette	111 King St. E. (Church) $$$ Elegant old-world style with a courtyard patio and a solarium.	SL	416-366-8191	Arts & Ent.	100, 109
Lee	603 King St. W. (Bathurst) $$ Funky and colorful and delicious food from Susur Lee.	ED	416-504-7867	Hot & Cool Trendy Restaurants	71, 80 65
Le Petit Déjeuner	191 King St. E. (Frederick) $$ Intimate little eatery with plenty of hip flair.	SL	416-703-1560	Hipster	126, 135
Le Saint Tropez	315 King St. W. (John) $$ South-of-France feel and cuisine and live French cabaret.	ED	416-591-3600	Arts & Ent.	100, 116
Liberty Bar/Bistro	25 Liberty St. (Atlantic) $$ An unfussy menu and patio popular with design and media types.	PD	416-533-8828	Hipster	125, 136
Lolita's Lust & the Chinchilla Lounge	513 Danforth Ave. (Fenwick) $$$ Greek-international fusion downstairs and cool lounge upstairs.	GT	416-465-1751	Classic	156, 173
Luce (Hotel Le Germain)	30 Mercer St. (Blue Jays) $$$$ Stylish décor and old-school Italian menu for the fabulous crowd.	ED	416-599-5823	Hot & Cool	74, 80
Marché (BCE Place)	42 Yonge St. (King) $$$ A centrally located gourmet cafeteria.	DT	416-366-8986	Arts & Ent.	101, 110
Michelle's Brasserie	162 Cumberland Ave. (Yorkville) $$ Bustling casual restaurant with French bistro menu, open late.	BY	416-944-1504	Hot & Cool	72, 80
Mildred Pierce	99 Sudbury St. (Dovercourt) $$$$ Superb Sunday brunch but be prepared to line up.	PD	416-588-5695	Hipster Brunches	128, 136 38
Mistura	265 Davenport Rd. (Avenue) $$$ Contemporary Italian fare.	BY	416-515-0009	Arts & Ent.	100, 110
Monsoon	100 Simcoe St. (Peter) $$$$ Striking décor, edgy Asian-inspired menu.	ED	416-979-7172	Hot & Cool Trendy Restaurants	71, 81 65
Moonbean Coffee Company	30 St. Andrews St. (Kensington) $ Coffee and light menu in bustling Kensington Market.	CT	416-595-0327	Arts & Ent.	100, 111
Myth	417 Danforth Ave. (Chester) $$$ Refined dining room and opulent upstairs lounge.	GT	416-461-8383	Classic	156, 173
Nanoo Cafe	57 Front St. E. (Church) $$ Busy cafe full of stylish white-collar downtowners.	SL	416-214-1852	Arts & Ent.	99, 111

Restaurants (cont.)

NAME	ADDRESS (CROSS STREET) PRICE DESCRIPTION	AREA	PHONE	EXPERIENCE PERFECT	PAGE PAGE
North 44°	2537 Yonge St. (Eglinton) $$$$ Haute cuisine for an A-list crowd in elegant surroundings.	UP	416-487-4897	Classic	155, 165
One Up Resto/Lounge	130 Dundas St. W. 2nd Fl., (Bay) $$$ Upscale continental cuisine overlooking Dundas Street.	CT	416-340-6349	Classic	156, 166
Opus	37 Prince Arthur Ave. (St. George) $$$$ French continental menu in an elegant townhouse.	BY	416-921-3105	Hot & Cool Fine Dining	71, 81 47
Oro	45 Elm St. (Bay) $$$ Inventive Canadian cuisine and a serious wine list.	FD	416-597-0155	Hot & Cool	72, 81
Ouzeri	500A Danforth Ave. (Logan) $$$ A perennial favorite, especially the summer patio.	GT	416-778-0500	Classic Ethnic Dining	156, 166 46
Oyster Boy	872 Queen St. W. (Crawford) $$$ Good seafood with the requisite Queen Street hip quotient.	PD	416-534-3432	Hipster	125, 137
Pangaea	1221 Bay St. N. (Bloor) $$$$ Fabulous menu and airy dining room.	BY	416-920-2323	Hot & Cool Fine Dining	71, 82 47
Panorama	55 Bloor St. W., 51st Fl. (Bay) $$$$ Dining and drinks with a view of the city from the 51st floor.	BY	416-967-0000	Hot & Cool Views	74, 90 66
Perigee	55 Mill St. (Parliament) $$$$ Four chefs cook in the dining room as you watch.	DD	416-364-1397	Arts & Ent. Trendy Restaurants	101, 111 65
Prego Della Piazza	150 Bloor St. W. (Avenue) $$$$ Summer patio and hopping piano bar in the smoking section.	BY	416-920-9900	Hot & Cool	71, 90
Provence Delices	12 Amelia St. (Parliament) $$$ Warm ambience and Mediterranean décor with a bistro menu.	SL	416-924-9901	Arts & Ent.	101, 112
Pure Spirits Oyster House & Grill	55 Mill St. (Parliament) $$$ Handsomely renovated seafood and oyster bar.	DD	416-361-5859	Arts & Ent. Seafood	101, 112 60
Rain	19 Mercer St. (Blue Jays) $$$$ A beautiful dining room with 15-foot waterfalls and a celebrity-rich crowd.	ED	416-599-7246	Hot & Cool	74, 91
Rivoli	332–334 Queen St. W. (Peter) $$ Landmark club and eclectic restaurant.	ED	416-596-1908	Hipster	128, 137
Room Service/Room 471	471 Richmond St. W. (McDougall) $$$ Stylish supper club that serves Italian fare till 5 am.	ED	416-703-6239	Hot & Cool Late-Night Eats	74, 83 53
Rosewater Supper Club	19 Toronto St. (King) $$$$ Continental cuisine, lounge popular after work.	SL	416-214-5888	Arts & Ent. Romantic	99, 113 58
Sassafraz Cafe	100 Cumberland St. (Bellair) $$$$ Popular celebrity haunt that can be touristy, jazz brunch.	BY	416-964-2222	Hot & Cool Brunches	74, 83 38
Scaramouche	1 Benvenuto Pl. (Edmund) $$$$ Busy stalwart offering fine dining and a view of Toronto.	UP	416-961-8011	Arts & Ent. Views	99, 113 66
Sen5es Bakery & Cafe (The SoHo Metropolitan)	318 Wellington St. W. (Blue Jays) $$$ High-end bakery and cafe in central location.	ED	416-935-0400	Hot & Cool	73, 83
Sen5es Restaurant & Lounge (The SoHo Metropolitan)	318 Wellington St. W. (Blue Jays) $$$$ Sexy dining room, gorgeous lounge, sublime food.	ED	416-935-0400	Hot & Cool Romantic	73, 84 58
7 West Cafe	7 Charles St. W. (Yonge) $$ Artwork, great panini, appetizers, kitchen open 24 hours.	BY	416-928-9041	Classic Late-Night Eats	155, 166 53

* Area Key Code: BE=Beaches, BV=Bloor/Yorkville, CT=Chinatown, DD=Distillery District, DT=Downtown/Yonge, ED=Entertainment District, FD=Financial District, GT=Greektown, GV=Gay Village, HF=Harbourfront, LI=Little Italy, ON=Ontario, PD=Parkdale, UP=Uptown, UT=University of Toronto, SL=St. Lawrence

** Note regarding page numbers: *Italic* = itinerary listing; Roman = theme chapter listing.

THE TORONTO BLACK BOOK

Restaurants (cont.)

NAME	ADDRESS (CROSS STREET)	AREA	PHONE	EXPERIENCE	PAGE
	PRICE DESCRIPTION			PERFECT	PAGE
Shanghai Cowgirl	538 Queen St. W. (Ryerson)	ED	416-203-6623	Hipster	*127*, 137
	$$$ Campy diner-themed restaurant, weekends until 4 a.m.			Late-Night Hang	54
Sotto Sotto Trattoria	116A Avenue Rd. (Tranby)	BY	416-962-0011	Hot & Cool	*71*, 84
	$$$$ Roman trattoria serves old-school Italian classics.				
Splendido	88 Harbord St. (Sussex Mews)	UT	416-929-7788	Classic	*156*, 167
	$$$$ An elegant and popular spot with fabulous cuisine.			Canadian Cuisine	39
Spring Rolls	85 Front St. E. (Market)	SL	416-365-7655	Hipster	*127*, 138
	$$ Hip downtown crowds for superb Pan-Asian cuisine.				
Starfish Oyster Bed & Grill	100 Adelaide St. E. (Jarvis)	SL	416-366-7827	Classic	*153*, 167
	$$$ A New York–style bistro with a bustling atmosphere.			Seafood	60
Studio Cafe	21 Avenue Rd. (Bloor)	BY	416-928-7330	Classic	*154*, 168
(Four Seasons Hotel Toronto)	$$$ Bright gallery-ish décor with original works of art, wide-ranging menu.				
Sunset Grill	2006 Queen St. E. (Bellefair)	BE	416-690-9985	Classic	*155*, 168
	$ An institution in the Beaches, great for breakfast, cash only.				
Sushi Inn	120 Cumberland St. (Hazelton)	BY	416-923-9992	Hot & Cool	*73*, 84
	$$$ Fashionable Yorkville denizens line up at this super-chic sushi bar.				
Susur	601 King St. W. (Bathurst)	ED	416-603-2205	Hot & Cool	*73*, 85
	$$$$ Cool elegance and food artistry from a top chef.			Always-Hot	36
Tea Room	18 St. Thomas St. (Bloor)	BY	416-971-9666	Classic	*155*, 168
(Windsor Arms Hotel)	$$$$ Quiet oasis of gentility; champagne and caviar bar.			Rainy Day	68
Toba	243 King St. E. (Sherbourne)	SL	416-367-8522	Hipster	*127*, 138
	$$$ Chic and fashionable refuge among the condos and furniture showrooms.				
Top o' the Senator	249 Victoria St. (Dundas)	SL	416-364-7517	Arts & Ent.	*101*, 119
	$$ Upscale live-jazz club.				
Trattoria Giancarlo	41 Clinton St. (College)	LI	416-533-9619	Arts & Ent.	*100*, 114
	$$$ Classic Italian in Little Italy.			Celeb Sightings	40
Truffles	21 Avenue Rd. (Bloor)	BY	416-928-7331	Classic	*155*, 169
(Four Seasons Hotel Toronto)	$$$$ Posh French cuisine and pampering service.			Romantic	58
Ultra Supper Club	314 Queen St. W. (Soho)	ED	416-263-0330	Hot & Cool	*74*, 92
	$$$ Beautiful people dance after midnight in this stylish resto-lounge.				
Vienna Home Bakery & Cafe	626 Queen St. W. (Markham)	PD	416-703-7278	Hipster	*127*, 138
	$$ Divine baked goods, notable for breakfast.				
Xacutti	503 College St. W. (Palmerston)	LI	416-323-3957	Hot & Cool	*73*, 85
	$$$$ High-end Indian fusion and a happening crowd.			Always-Hot	36
Zelda's	542 Church St. (Wellesley)	GV	416-922-2526	Hipster	*126*, 138
	$$$ Campy fun in the Gay Village for all ages, genders, and persuasions.				

Nightlife

NAME	ADDRESS (CROSS STREET)	AREA	PHONE	EXPERIENCE	PAGE
	PRICE DESCRIPTION			PERFECT	PAGE
Afterlife Nightclub	250 Adelaide St. W. (Duncan)	ED	416-593-6126	Hot & Cool	*73*, 86
	$$ Three floors of dancing and lounging.			Dance Clubs	45
Avenue	21 Avenue Rd. (Cumberland)	BY	416-964-0411	Classic	*155*, 159
(Four Seasons Hotel Toronto)	- High-end watering hole and lounge.			Swanky Hotel Bars	64
Azure Restaurant & Bar	225 Front St. W. (Simcoe)	ED	416-597-8142	Arts & Ent.	*101*, 106
(InterCont'l. Toronto Centre)	- Handsome, centrally located spot caters to a white-collar crowd.			Swanky Hotel Bars	64

Nightlife (cont.)

NAME	ADDRESS (CROSS STREET) PRICE DESCRIPTION	AREA	PHONE	EXPERIENCE PERFECT	PAGE PAGE
BaBaLu's	136 Yorkville Ave. (Hazelton) $$$ Upscale Latin club known to big-name out-of-towners.	BY	416-515-0587	Hot & Cool Dance Clubs	72, 86 45
Bar One	924 Queen St. W. (Shaw) - Clean, bright modern design, a simple Italian menu.	PD	416-535-1655	Hipster	125, 131
Boiler House	55 Mill St. (Parliament) $$ A long bar with booths built for two and live jazz.	DD	416-203-2121	Arts & Ent.	101, 115
Bovine Sex Club	542 Queen St. W. (Ryerson) $$ Dance club with alt-rock, glam, and disco mix, cutting-edge live acts.	ED	416-504-4239	Hipster	127, 140
Budo Liquid Theatre	137 Peter St. (Queen) $$ Three floors of style, cocktails, and beautiful people.	ED	416-593-1550	Hot & Cool Sexy Lounges	73, 86 61
Byzantium	499 Church St. (Wellesley) - Long a favorite in the Gay Village.	GV	416-922-3859	Hipster Gay Bars	127, 132 48
C-Lounge	456 Wellington St. W. (Draper) $$$ High-end nightclub and lounge with summer deck.	ED	416-260-9393	Hot & Cool Meet Markets	73, 87 56
Centro Grill & Wine Bar	2472 Yonge St., upper level (Eglinton) - Haute cuisine in palatial surroundings.	UP	416-483-2211	Arts & Ent.	102, 115
Club 22 (Windsor Arms Hotel)	18 St. Thomas St. (Bloor) $$ Stylish lounge, piano and live bands, cigar lounge.	BY	416-971-9666	Hot & Cool Cigar Lounges	72, 87 42
Courthouse Chamber Lounge	57 Adelaide St. E. (Yonge) $$ Upscale lounge in an old courthouse with DJ and retro music.	SL	416-214-9379	Arts & Ent.	101, 116
Crocodile Rock	240 Adelaide St. W. (Duncan) - Popular and always busy, retro and classic rock.	ED	416-599-9751	Classic Meet Markets	154, 170 56
Crystal Room	567 Queen St. W. (Denison) $$ Bottle service, leather couches, and beds to lounge on.	ED	416-504-1626	Hipster Scene Bars	128, 140 59
Drake Lounge	1150 Queen St. W. (Beaconsfield) $$ Three floors of modern lounge, dance cave, and seasonal roof patio.	PD	416-531-5042	Hipster	126, 141
The Easy	225 Richmond St. W. (Bedford) $$ Swank lounge that draws a beautiful crowd.	ED	416-979-3005	Classic Cigar Lounges	170 42
El Convento Rico	750 College St. (Shaw) $$ Retro glitzy décor and throbbing merengue.	LI	416-588-7800	Hipster Late-Night Hang	128, 141 54
Esplanade Bier Markt	58 The Esplanade (Church) - Classic Belgian brasserie features more than 100 beers and ales.	SL	416-862-7575	Hipster	128, 134
Fez Batik	129 Peter St. (Richmond) - Exotic Moroccan-themed resto-lounge popular with creative types.	ED	416-204-9660	Hipster	128, 134
5ive Nightclub	5 St. Joseph St. (Yonge) $$$ Gay dance club where the beats are fast and furious.	DT	416-964-8685	Hot & Cool Gay Dance Clubs	73, 87 49
Flow Restaurant + Lounge	133 Yorkville Ave. (Hazelton) - Sleek lounge for Blackberry Lexus types.	BY	416-925-2143	Hot & Cool Martinis	72, 88 55
Fly Nightclub	8 Gloucester St. (Yonge) $$ Hot gay male dance club.	GV	416-410-5426	Hot & Cool Gay Dance Clubs	74, 88 49
The Gladstone Hotel	1214 Queen St. W. (Gladstone) $$ Three rooms of music, performance art, and burlesque shows.	PD	416-531-4635	Hipster	126, 142

* Area Key Code: BE=Beaches, BV=Bloor/Yorkville, CT=Chinatown, DD=Distillery District, DT=Downtown/Yonge, ED=Entertainment District, FD=Financial District, GT=Greektown, GV=Gay Village, HF=Harbourfront, LI=Little Italy, ON=Ontario, PD=Parkdale, UP=Uptown, UT=University of Toronto, SL=St. Lawrence

** Note regarding page numbers: *Italic* = itinerary listing; Roman = theme chapter listing.

THE TORONTO BLACK BOOK

Nightlife (cont.)

NAME	ADDRESS (CROSS STREET)	AREA	PHONE	EXPERIENCE	PAGE
	PRICE DESCRIPTION			PERFECT	PAGE
G-Spot	296 Richmond St. W. (Widmer)	ED	416-351-7768	Classic	156, 171
	$$ Where the beautiful people come to dance.				
Gypsy Co-Op	817 Queen St. W. (Gore Vale)	PD	416-703-5069	Hipster	125, 135
	$$ Eclectic, eccentric and chic, it's everything Queen West.				
Habitat Lounge	735 Queen St. W. (Manning)	PD	416-860-1551	Hipster	126, 142
	$$ Hip and artsy, but sleekly upscale.			Sexy Lounges	61
Hair of the Dog	425 Church St. (Wood)	GV	416-964-2708	Classic	154, 171
	- Double-decker upscale pub and gay community mainstay.			Gay Bars	48
Healey's	178 Bathurst St. (Queen)	ED	416-703-5882	Classic	154, 171
	$$$ Toronto's best live venue.			Live Music	43
Hemingway's	142 Cumberland St. (Avenue)	BY	416-968-2828	Classic	155, 172
	- Toronto's only year-round rooftop bar, friendly atmosphere.			Celeb Sightings	40
Indian Motorcycle Cafe & Lounge	355 King St. W. (John)	ED	416-593-6996	Hot & Cool	72, 88
	- Motorcycle-theme bar-resto for a hip downtown crowd.				
Inspire	491 Church St. (Wellesley)	GV	416-963-0044	Arts & Ent.	100, 116
	- Sleek, straight-friendly resto-lounge in the Gay Village.			Gay Bars	48
Lago	207 Queen's Quay W. (York)	HF	416-848-0005	Classic	153, 172
	- Continental cuisine, a wraparound bar and lakeside patio.			Summer Patios	63
La Rouge Executive Club	257 Adelaide St. W. (Duncan)	ED	416-260-5551	Classic	156, 172
	$$ Three levels include lounge and dance bar.			Martinis	55
Le Saint Tropez	315 King St. W. (John)	ED	416-591-3600	Arts & Ent.	100, 116
	$$ South-of-France feel and cuisine, live French cabaret.				
Library Bar (Fairmont Royal York)	100 Front St. W. (York)	DT	416-368-2511	Classic	153, 173
	- Posh hotel bar-lounge for those with expense accounts.			Swanky Hotel Bars	64
Lobby	192 Bloor St. W. (Avenue)	BY	416-929-7169	Hot & Cool	72, 89
	$$ Chichi club modeled after the lobby of a boutique hotel.			Scene Bars	59
Lolita's Lust & the Chinchilla Lounge	513 Danforth Ave. (Fenwick)	GT	416-465-1751	Classic	156, 173
	$$ Greek-international fusion downstairs and cool lounge upstairs.				
Lüb Lounge	487 Church St. (Wellesley)	GV	416-323-1489	Hot & Cool	72, 89
	$$ One of the latest lounge-bars, cool décor and a hot crowd.			Gay Dance Clubs	49
Mod Club Theatre	722 College St. W. (Crawford)	LI	416-588-4663	Hipster	127, 143
	$$ Fueling the fetish for Brit-pop cool.			Live Music	43
Monsoon	100 Simcoe St. (Peter)	ED	416-979-7172	Hot & Cool	71, 81
	- . Striking décor and edgy Asian-inspired menu.				
Montreal Bistro & Jazz Club	65 Sherbourne St. (Adelaide)	SL	416-363-0179	Arts & Ent.	101, 117
	$$ Bistro menu and sultry jazz club for music aficionados.			Jazz Clubs	52
My Apartment	81 Peter St. (Adelaide)	ED	416-348-9884	Arts & Ent.	102, 117
	$$ Recently renovated dance club popular with the downtown set.				
Myth	417 Danforth Rd. (Chester)	GT	416-461-8383	Classic	156, 173
	$$ A refined dining room and an opulent upstairs lounge.				
N'awlins	299 King St. W. (John)	ED	416-595-1958	Arts & Ent.	102, 117
	$$$ Cajun cooking and hot live jazz.				
One Up Resto/Lounge	130 Dundas St. W., 2nd Fl. (Bay)	CT	416-340-6349	Classic	156, 166
	- Upscale continental cuisine overlooking Dundas Street.				
Panorama	55 Bloor St. W., 51st Fl. (Bay)	BY	416-967-0000	Hot & Cool	74, 90
	- Dining and drinks with a view of the city.			Views	66
Phoenix Concert Theatre	410 Sherbourne St. (Carlton)	SL	416-323-1251	Hipster	128, 143
	$$$ Five bars, three rooms, and big-name live acts.			Live Music	43

Nightlife (cont.)

NAME	ADDRESS (CROSS STREET) PRICE DESCRIPTION	AREA	PHONE	EXPERIENCE PERFECT	PAGE PAGE
Pravda Vodka Bar	36 Wellington St. E. (Victoria) $$ Elegant black-and-white vodka bar with Russian theme and cuisine.	SL	416-306-2433	Arts & Ent.	100, 118
Prego Della Piazza	150 Bloor St. W. (Avenue) - Menu of steaks and seafood, summer patio, and hopping piano bar.	BY	416-920-9900	Hot & Cool	71, 90
Rain	19 Mercer St. (Blue Jays) - A beautiful dining room with 15-foot waterfalls.	ED	416-599-7246	Hot & Cool Martinis	74, 91 55
Reservoir Lounge	52 Wellington St. E. (Victoria) $$ Live swing jazz plays here every night of the week.	SL	416-955-0877	Arts & Ent.	100, 118
Revival	783 College St. W. (Shaw) $$ Over-thirty crowd full of film, fashion, and music industry pros.	LI	416-535-7888	Hipster	127, 144
Rex Hotel Jazz & Blues Bar	194 Queen St. W. (St. Patrick) $$$ Venerable jazz and blues bar with live music nightly.	ED	416-598-2475	Classic Jazz Clubs	154, 174 52
Rivoli	332–334 Queen St. W. (Peter) $$ Landmark club and eclectic restaurant.	ED	416-596-1908	Hipster	128, 137
Roof Lounge (Park Hyatt Toronto)	4 Avenue Rd., 18th Fl. (Bloor) - Friendly vibe and great patio.	BY	416-924-5471	Classic Summer Patios	155, 174 63
Rosewater Supper Club	19 Toronto St. (King) - Continental cuisine, lounge popular with after-work crowds.	SL	416-214-5888	Arts & Ent.	99, 113
Sen5es Restaurant & Lounge (The SoHo Metropolitan)	318 Wellington St. W. (Blue Jays) - Sexy dining room, gorgeous lounge, sublime food.	ED	416-935-0400	Hot & Cool	73, 91
Shanghai Cowgirl	538 Queen St. W. (Ryerson) - Campy diner-theme, open until 4 a.m. weekends.	ED	416-203-6623	Hipster Late-Night Hang	127, 137 54
Sky Bar	132 Queen's Quay E. (Lower Jarvis) $$ Toronto's swankiest rooftop lounge, with view.	HF	416-869-0045	Hot & Cool Summer Patios	74, 91 63
Stones Place	1225 Queen St. W. (Gwynne) $$ Rolling Stones theme bar that showcases live acts.	PD	416-536-4242	Hipster	126, 144
Sugar Club	57 Duncan St. (Richmond) $$ Fun club for dancing to hip-hop and R&B.	SL	416-597-0202	Arts & Ent. Dance Clubs	100, 119 45
Sutra Lounge	612 College St. W. (Clinton) $$ Exotic drink bar with sand-covered floors and straw umbrellas.	LI	416-537-8755	Hipster	128, 145
Therapy Ultra Lounge	203 Richmond St. W. (Bedford) $$ High-end lounge, home to a fashionable crowd.	ED	416-977-3089	Hot & Cool Sexy Lounges	74, 92 61
This Is London	364 Richmond St. W. (Peter) $$ Exclusive club for trendy over-thirty club kids.	ED	416-351-1100	Hipster Celeb Sightings	128, 145 40
Top o' the Senator	253 Victoria St. (Dundas) $$$ Upscale live jazz club.	SL	416-364-7517	Arts & Ent. Jazz Clubs	101, 119 52
2 Cats Cocktail Lounge	569 King St. W. (Portland) $$ Cigar and cocktail lounge, popular late-night spot.	ED	416-204-6261	Hot & Cool Cigar Lounges	73, 92 42
Ultra Supper Club	314 Queen St. W. (Soho) $$ Beautiful people flock to this stylish resto-lounge.	ED	416-263-0330	Hot & Cool Late-Night Hang	74, 92 54
Up and Down Lounge	270 Adelaide St. W. (John) $$ Mixed crowd of exec and artsy types.	ED	416-977-4038	Classic	156, 174

* Area Key Code: BE=Beaches, BV=Bloor/Yorkville, CT=Chinatown, DD=Distillery District, DT=Downtown/Yonge, ED=Entertainment District, FD=Financial District, GT=Greektown, GV=Gay Village, HF=Harbourfront, LI=Little Italy, ON=Ontario, PD=Parkdale, UP=Uptown, UT=University of Toronto, SL=St. Lawrence

** Note regarding page numbers: *Italic* = itinerary listing; Roman = theme chapter listing.

THE TORONTO BLACK BOOK

Nightlife (cont.)

NAME	ADDRESS (CROSS STREET)	AREA	PHONE	EXPERIENCE	PAGE
	PRICE DESCRIPTION			PERFECT	PAGE
Velvet Underground	510 Queen St. W. (Portland)	PD	416-504-6688	Hipster	127, 145
	$$ Alternative rock club known for live music.				
West Lounge	510 King St. W. (Bathurst)	ED	416-361-9004	Hot & Cool	73, 93
	$$ Exclusive club high on design and beautiful people.			Meet Markets	56
Wish	3 Charles St. E. (Yonge)	DT	416-935-0240	Classic	155, 174
	$$$ Ultra-hip and coastal cool, popular after midnight spot.				
YYZ Restaurant & Wine Bar	345 Adelaide St. W. (Charlotte)	ED	416-599-3399	Hot & Cool	74, 93
	- Stylish resto-lounge popular with a fashionable crowd.			Scene Bars	59

Attractions

NAME	ADDRESS (CROSS STREET)	AREA	PHONE	EXPERIENCE	PAGE
	PRICE DESCRIPTION			PERFECT	PAGE
Allan Gardens Conservatory	19 Horticultural Ave. (Jarvis)	SL	416-392-1111	Hot & Cool	73, 94
	- Six greenhouses, Edwardian garden in the heart of Toronto.			Rainy Day	68
Art Gallery of Ontario	317 Dundas St. W. (McCaul)	CT	416-979-6648	Arts & Ent.	99, 120
	$$ One of the largest art museums in North America.			Cool Art Spaces	44
Artinsite			416-979-5704	Arts & Ent.	102, 120
	$$ Art experts lead studio and gallery tours, custom tours.			Guided Tours	50
Bata Shoe Museum	327 Bloor St. W. (St. George)	BY	416-979-7799	Hot & Cool	71, 94
	$ A collection of shoes through the ages.			Chic Museums	41
The Beaches		BE		Classic	156, 175
	- A laid-back hippie-ish vibe along Queen Street East.			Sunny Day	67
Camera Bar and Media Gallery	1028 Queen St. W. (Ossington)	PD	416-530-0011	Hipster	128, 146
	$ Small indie art film theater meets cocktail bar.				
Casa Loma	1 Austin Terr. (Davenport)	UP	416-923-1171	Classic	154, 175
	$ Toronto's own castle, with 98 rooms, extensive gardens.			Historic Buildings	51
Chinatown	Between Spadina, Queen, College, & Bay St.	CT		Classic	156, 176
	- Chinese restaurants, an open-air farmers market, and specialty shops.				
CHUM/Citytv Building	299 Queen St. W. (John)	ED	416-591-5757	Hot & Cool	71, 94
	$ Independent media empire with open concept studios.			Guided Tours	50
Cinematheque Ontario (Art Gallery of Ontario)	317 Dundas St. W. (McCaul)	CT	416-968-3456	Arts & Ent.	102, 120
	$ Screening room dedicated to the world of cinema; daily screenings.				
CN Tower	301 Front St. W. (John)	HF	416-868-6937	Classic	153, 176
	$$ Breathtaking views.			Views	66
Design Exchange	234 Bay St. (Wellington)	FD	416-363-6121	Hipster	126, 146
	$ Galleries and exhibits that examine the role of design.			Chic Museums	41
Distillery District	55 Mill St. (Parliament)	DD		Arts & Ent.	101, 121
	- Renovated area with art galleries, restaurants, shops.			Only-in-Toronto	57
Elgin/Winter Garden Theatre	189 Yonge St. (Queen)	DT	416-314-2871	Arts & Ent.	101, 121
	$ Roof-garden theater and double-decker theater.				
401 Richmond	401 Richmond St. W. (Spadina)	ED	416-595-5900	Hipster	128, 147
	- Dozens of art galleries and arts organizations.			Cool Art Spaces	44
Gardiner Museum of Ceramic Art	111 Queen's Park (Bloor)	UT	416-586-8080	Arts & Ent.	101, 122
	$$ Museum of amazing ceramic art.			Chic Museums	41
Harbourfront Centre	235 Queen's Quay W. (York)	HF	416-973-4000	Arts & Ent.	99, 122
	$ Center devoted to contemporary culture.				

Attractions (cont.)

NAME	ADDRESS (CROSS STREET) PRICE DESCRIPTION	AREA	PHONE	EXPERIENCE PERFECT	PAGE PAGE
Harbourfront/Mariposa Tours	207 Queen's Quay W. (Bay) $$$ Ferry rides that take you to the Toronto Islands.	HF	416-203-0178	Classic	177
High Park	1873 Bloor St. W. (High Park) - Toronto's biggest inner-city park.	PD		Hipster Sunny Day	128, 147 67
Hockey Hall of Fame	30 Yonge St. (Front) $$ Major trophies, interactive exhibits, and other displays, beautiful building.	SL	416-360-7765	Classic	153, 177
Kensington Market	Spadina Ave. (College and Dundas) - An eclectic mix of wares is on display here.	CT		Classic Only-in-Toronto	156, 177 57
Museum of Television	277 Queen St. W. (McCaul) $ Exhibits that celebrate North American culture of the 20th century.	ED	416-599-7339	Hot & Cool	71, 95
National Film Board/Mediatheque	150 John St. (Richmond) - A library of films with personal viewing stations.	ED	416-973-3012	Hipster	125, 148
102.1 the Edge	228 Yonge St. (Shuter) - Alternative-rock radio station with unique storefront concept.	DT	416-603-2205	Hipster	127, 149
Ontario College of Art & Design	100 McCaul St. (Dundas) - A small gallery featuring innovative student works.	CT	416-977-6000	Hipster	127, 149
Power Plant Gallery	231 Queen's Quay W. (York) $ Prominent showcase for contemporary art.	HF	416-973-4949	Hipster Cool Art Spaces	128, 149 44
Royal Ontario Museum	100 Queen's Park (Avenue) $$ Collections span natural history and human civilization.	BY	416-586-5549	Classic Rainy Day	155, 178 68
St. Anne's Anglican Church	270 Gladstone Ave. (Queen) - Canada's only Byzantine-style church, a designated historic site.	PD	416-536-3160	Hipster	128, 150
SkyDome Tour	1 Blue Jays Way (Front) $ Sports and entertainment venue, with a unique retractable roof.	ED	416-341-2770	Hot & Cool	73, 96
Spadina House	285 Spadina Rd. (Davenport) $ Lovingly restored Victorian house and gardens.	UP	416-392-6910	Arts & Ent. Historic Buildings	100, 123 51
Steam Whistle Brewing Co. (The Roundhouse)	255 Bremner Blvd. (Blue Jays) $ Funky craft brewery.	HF	416-362-2337	Hipster Guided Tours	127, 151 50
Textile Museum of Canada	55 Centre Ave. (Dundas) $ Bright and beautiful exhibits of textile art from around the world.	CT	416-599-5321	Hot & Cool	72, 96
Toronto Islands	Queen's Quay (Bay) $ Ferries to Toronto Islands, and a view of the city skyline.	HF	416-392-8193	Classic Sunny Day	153, 179 67
Toronto School of Art Gallery	410 Adelaide St. W., 3rd Fl. (Spadina) - Gallery featuring work of students at this alternative art school.	CT	416-504-7910	Hipster	127, 151
Toronto Stock Exchange Media Centre	130 King St. W. (York) - Media broadcast center.	FD	416-947-4676	Hot & Cool	72, 97

* Area Key Code: BE=Beaches, BV=Bloor/Yorkville, CT=Chinatown, DD=Distillery District, DT=Downtown/Yonge, ED=Entertainment District, FD=Financial District, GT=Greektown, GV=Gay Village, HF=Harbourfront, LI=Little Italy, ON=Ontario, PD=Parkdale, UP=Uptown, UT=University of Toronto, SL=St. Lawrence

** Note regarding page numbers: *Italic* = itinerary listing; Roman = theme chapter listing.

Golf

NAME	ADDRESS (CROSS STREET)	AREA	PHONE	EXPERIENCE	PAGE
	PRICE DESCRIPTION			PERFECT	PAGE
Eagles Nest Golf Club	10000 Dufferin St. (Maple)	ON	905-417-2300	Hot & Cool	72, 95
	$$$$ Course designed by Doug Carrick features sand dunes, clubhouse, 18 holes.				
Glen Abbey Golf Club	1333 Dorval Dr. (Oakville)	ON	905-844-1811	Classic	154, 176
	$$$$ This challenging course has hosted many Canadian Opens.				
Lionhead Golf & Country Club	8525 Mississauga Rd. (Brampton)	ON	905-455-8400	Arts & Ent.	101, 123
	$$$ Two 18-hole championship courses, one among the most difficult in Canada.				

Spas and Fitness

NAME	ADDRESS (CROSS STREET)	AREA	PHONE	EXPERIENCE	PAGE
	PRICE DESCRIPTION			PERFECT	PAGE
Elizabeth Milan Day Spa (Fairmont Royal York)	100 Front St. W. (York)	ED	416-350-7500	Arts & Ent. / Spas	99, 122 / 62
	$$$$ High-end day spa to the stars.				
iodine & arsenic	867 Queen St. W. (Gore Vale)	PD	416-681-0577	Hipster	126, 147
	$$$ The anti-spa, serving clients one at a time in trendy style.				
Joe Rockhead's	29 Fraser Ave. (Liberty)	PD	416-538-7630	Hipster	128, 148
	$$$ 21,000 sq. feet of rock climbing for novice and advance level alike.				
moksha yoga west town	860 Richmond St. W., 3rd Fl. (Strachan)	PD	416-361-3033	Hipster	126, 148
	$$$ Trendy hot yoga studio in the West End, drop-ins welcome.				
Pantages Anti-Aging & Longevity Spa (Pantages Hotel Suites)	200 Victoria St. (Shuter)	DT	416-367-1888	Hot & Cool / Spas	73, 96 / 62
	$$$$ The latest in anti-aging and longevity treatments.				
Stillwater Spa (Park Hyatt Toronto)	4 Avenue Rd. (Bloor)	BY	416-926-2389	Classic / Spas	154, 178 / 62
	$$$$ A wide range of treatments, including aqua therapy.				

Services and Shops

NAME	ADDRESS (CROSS STREET)	AREA	PHONE	EXPERIENCE	PAGE
	PRICE DESCRIPTION			PERFECT	PAGE
King Street East Furniture Dist.	Jarvis and Parliament	SL		Hot & Cool	72, 95
	- High-end furniture shops.				
Queen's Quay Terminal	207 Queen's Quay W. (Bay)	HF	416-203-0510	Classic	153, 178
	- Specialty shopping on the waterfront.				
St. Lawrence Market	92 Front St. E. (Jarvis)	SL	416-392-7219	Hipster / Historic Buildings	127, 150 / 51
	- Offers a wide range of food and specialty products.				
Toronto Antique Centre	276 King St. W. (Beverley)	ED	416-345-9941	Arts & Ent.	100, 123
	- 28 antique dealers all under one roof.				
West Queen West	Between Bathurst and Gladstone	PD		Hipster	125, 151
	- Home to the highest density of art galleries in Toronto.				
Yorkville Shopping District	Around Bloor and Avenue Rd.	BY		Hot & Cool / Only-in-Toronto	74, 97 / 57
	- Canada's priciest shopping district.				

Notes

Notes

The Fun Seeker's Toronto Black Book by Best Category

Always-Hot Restaurants
Coco Lezzone Grill and Porto Bar
Susur
Xacutti

Asian Restaurants
Banzai Sushi
Bright Pearl Seafood
Lai Wah Heen

Brunches
Cafe Victoria
Mildred Pierce
Sassafraz Cafe

Canadian Cuisine
Canoe Restaurant & Bar
Drake Dining Room and Raw Bar
Splendido

Celeb Sightings
Hemingway's
This Is London
Trattoria Giancarlo

Chic Museums
Bata Shoe Museum
Design Exchange
Gardiner Museum of Ceramic Art

Cigar Lounges
Club 22
The Easy
2 Cats Cocktail Lounge

Clubs for Live Music
Healey's
Mod Club Theatre
Phoenix Concert Theatre

Cool Art Spaces
Art Gallery of Ontario
401 Richmond
Power Plant Gallery

Dance Clubs
Afterlife Nightclub
BaBaLu's
Sugar Club

Ethnic Dining
Babur
Caju
Ouzeri

Fine Dining
Auberge du Pommier
Opus
Pangaea

Gay Bars
Byzantium
Hair of the Dog
Inspire

Gay Dance Clubs
5ive Nightclub
Fly Nightclub
Lüb Lounge

Guided Tours
Artinsite
CHUM/Citytv Building
Steam Whistle Brewing Company

Historic Buildings
Casa Loma
St. Lawrence Market
Spadina House

Jazz Clubs
Montreal Bistro & Jazz Club
Rex Hotel Jazz & Blues Bar
Top o' the Senator

Late-Night Eats
Bistro 333
Room Service/Room 471
7 West Cafe

Late-Night Hangouts
El Convento Rico
Shanghai Cowgirl
Ultra Supper Club

Martinis
Flow Restaurant + Lounge
La Rouge Executive Club
Rain

Meet Markets
C-Lounge
Crocodile Rock
West Lounge

Only-in-Toronto Attractions
Distillery District
Kensington Market
Yorkville Shopping District

The Fun Seeker's Toronto Black Book by Best Category (cont.)

Romantic Rendezvous
Rosewater Supper Club
Sen5es Restaurant & Lounge
Truffles

Scene Bars
Crystal Room
Lobby
YYZ Restaurant & Wine Bar

Seafood Restaurants
Joso's
Pure Spirits Oyster House & Grill
Starfish Oyster Bed & Grill

Sexy Lounges
Budo Liquid Theatre
Habitat Lounge
Therapy Ultra Lounge

Spas
Elizabeth Milan Day Spa
Pantages Anti-Aging & Longevity Spa
Stillwater Spa

Summer Patios
Lago
Roof Lounge
Sky Bar

Swanky Hotel Bars
Avenue
Azure Restaurant & Bar
Library Bar

Trendy Restaurants
Lee
Monsoon
Perigee

Views
CN Tower
Panorama
Scaramouche

Ways to Enjoy a Sunny Day
The Beaches
High Park
Toronto Islands

Ways to Escape a Rainy Day
Allan Gardens Conservatory
Royal Ontario Museum
Tea Room

The Fun Seeker's Toronto Black Book by Neighborhood

Beaches (BE)
Restaurants
Sunset Grill
Attractions
The Beaches

Bloor/Yorkville (BY)
Hotels
Four Seasons Hotel Toronto
The Madison Manor
Park Hyatt Toronto
Windsor Arms Hotel
Restaurants
Avenue
Boba
Caren's Wine and Cheese Bar
Casa Cafe
Courtyard Cafe
Crepes à Go Go
Futures Bakery & Cafe
Holt's Cafe
Joso's
Michelle's Brasserie
Mistura
Opus
Pangaea
Panorama
Prego Della Piazza
Sassafraz Cafe
7 West Cafe
Sotto Sotto Trattoria
Studio Cafe
Sushi Inn
Tea Room
Truffles
Nightlife
Avenue
BaBaLu's
Club 22
Flow Restaurant + Lounge
Hemingway's
Lobby
Panorama
Prego Della Piazza
Roof Lounge
Attractions
Bata Shoe Museum
Royal Ontario Museum
Services
Yorkville Shopping District
Spa
Stillwater Spa

Chinatown (CT)
Hotels
Metropolitan Hotel
Restaurants
Agora
Bright Pearl Seafood
Hemispheres
Lai Wah Heen
Moonbean Coffee Company
One Up Resto/Lounge
Nightlife
One Up Resto/Lounge
Attractions
Art Gallery of Ontario
Chinatown
Cinematheque Ontario
Kensington Market
Ontario College of Art & Design
Textile Museum of Canada
Toronto School of Art Gallery

Distillery District (DD)
Restaurants
Balzac's Cafe
Perigee
Pure Spirits Oyster House & Grill
Nightlife
Boiler House
Attractions
Distillery District

Dowtown/Yonge (DT)
Hotels
Fairmont Royal York
Pantages Hotel Suites
Restaurants
Beer Bistro
Marché
Nightlife
5ive Nightclub
Library Bar
Wish
Attractions
Elgin/Winter Garden Theatre
102.1 the Edge
Spa
Pantages Anti-Aging & Longevity Spa

Entertainment District (ED)
Hotels
Hotel Le Germain
InterContinental Toronto Centre
The SoHo Metropolitan
Restaurants
Avalon
Azure Restaurant & Bar
Babur
Banzai Sushi
Bistro 333
Brassaii
Crush Wine Bar
Fez Batik
The Fifth
Indian Motorcycle Cafe & Lounge
KitKat2/Club Lucky

The Fun Seeker's Toronto Black Book by Neighborhood (cont.)

Lee
Le Saint Tropez
Luce
Monsoon
Rain
Rivoli
Room Service/Room 471
Sen5es Bakery & Cafe
Sen5es Restaurant
 & Lounge
Shanghai Cowgirl
Susur
Ultra Supper Club

Nightlife
Afterlife Nightclub
Azure Restaurant & Bar
Bovine Sex Club
Budo Liquid Theatre
C-Lounge
Crocodile Rock
Crystal Room
The Easy
Fez Batik
G-Spot
Healey's
Indian Motorcycle
 Cafe & Lounge
La Rouge Executive Club
Le Saint Tropez
Monsoon
My Apartment
N'awlins
Rain
Rex Hotel Jazz &
 Blues Bar
Rivoli
Sen5es Restaurant
 & Lounge
Shanghai Cowgirl
Sugar Club
Therapy Ultra Lounge
This Is London
2 Cats Cocktail Lounge
Ultra Supper Club
Up and Down Lounge

West Lounge
YYZ Restaurant &
 Wine Bar

Attractions
CHUM/Citytv Building
401 Richmond
Museum of Television
National Film
 Board/Mediatheque
SkyDome Tour

Services
Toronto Antique Centre

Spa
Elizabeth Milan Day Spa

Financial District (FD)

Hotels
Hilton Toronto
Sutton Place

Restaurants
Bistro 990
Bloor Street Diner
 & Bistro Express
Bymark
Cafe Supreme
Canoe Restaurant & Bar
Jump Cafe & Bar
Oro

Attractions
Design Exchange
Toronto Stock Exchange
 Media Centre

Gay Village (GV)

Restaurants
Byzantium
Inspire
Zelda's

Nightlife
Byzantium
Fly Nightclub
Hair of the Dog
Inspire
Lüb Lounge

Greektown (GT)

Restaurants
Lolita's Lust & the
 Chinchilla Lounge
Myth
Ouzeri

Nightlife
Lolita's Lust & the
 Chinchilla Lounge
Myth

Harbourfront (HF)

Hotels
Westin Harbour Castle

Restaurants
Harbour 60

Nightlife
Lago
Sky Bar

Attractions
CN Tower
Harbourfront Centre
Harbourfront/Mariposa
 Tours
Power Plant Gallery
Steam Whistle Brewing
 Company
Toronto Islands

Services
Queen's Quay Terminal

Little Italy (LI)

Restaurants
Bar Italia
Cafe Diplomatico
Coco Lezzone Grill
 and Porto Bar
Gamelle
Kalendar
Trattoria Giancarlo
Xacutti

Nightlife
El Convento Rico
Mod Club Theatre

The Fun Seeker's Toronto Black Book by Neighborhood (cont.)

Revival
Sutra Lounge

Ontario (ON)
Golf
Lionhead Golf & Country Club
Eagles Nest Golf Club
Glen Abbey Golf Club

Parkdale (PD)
Hotels
The Drake Hotel
The Gladstone Hotel
Restaurants
Bar One
Beaver Cafe
Caju
Drake Dining Room and Raw Bar
Gypsy Co-Op
Liberty Bistro/Bar
Mildred Pierce
Oyster Boy
Vienna Home Bakery & Cafe
Nightlife
Bar One
Drake Lounge
The Gladstone Hotel
Gypsy Co-Op
Habitat Lounge
Stones Place
Velvet Underground
Attractions
Camera Bar and Media Gallery
High Park
iodine & arsenic
Joe Rockhead's
moksha yoga west town
St. Anne's Anglican Church
Services
West Queen West

St. Lawrence (SL)
Hotels
Le Meridien King Edward Hotel
Restaurants
Biagio Ristorante
Biff's
Cafe Victoria
C'est What?
Esplanade Bier Markt
Hot House Cafe
La Maquette
Le Petit Déjeuner
Nanoo Cafe
Provence Delices
Rosewater Supper Club
Spring Rolls
Starfish Oyster Bed & Grill
Toba
Top o' the Senator
Nightlife
Courthouse Chamber Lounge
Esplanade Bier Markt
Montreal Bistro & Jazz Club
Phoenix Concert Theatre
Pravda Vodka Bar
Reservoir Lounge
Rosewater Supper Club
Top o' the Senator
Attractions
Allan Gardens Conservatory
Hockey Hall of Fame
Services
King Street East Furniture District
St. Lawrence Market

Uptown (UP)
Restaurants
Auberge du Pommier
Centro Grill & Wine Bar
North 44°
Scaramouche
Nightlife
Centro Grill & Wine Bar
Attractions
Casa Loma
Spadina House

University of Toronto (UT)
Restaurants
Gallery Grill
Splendido
Attractions
Gardiner Museum of Ceramic Art

TORONTO AREA

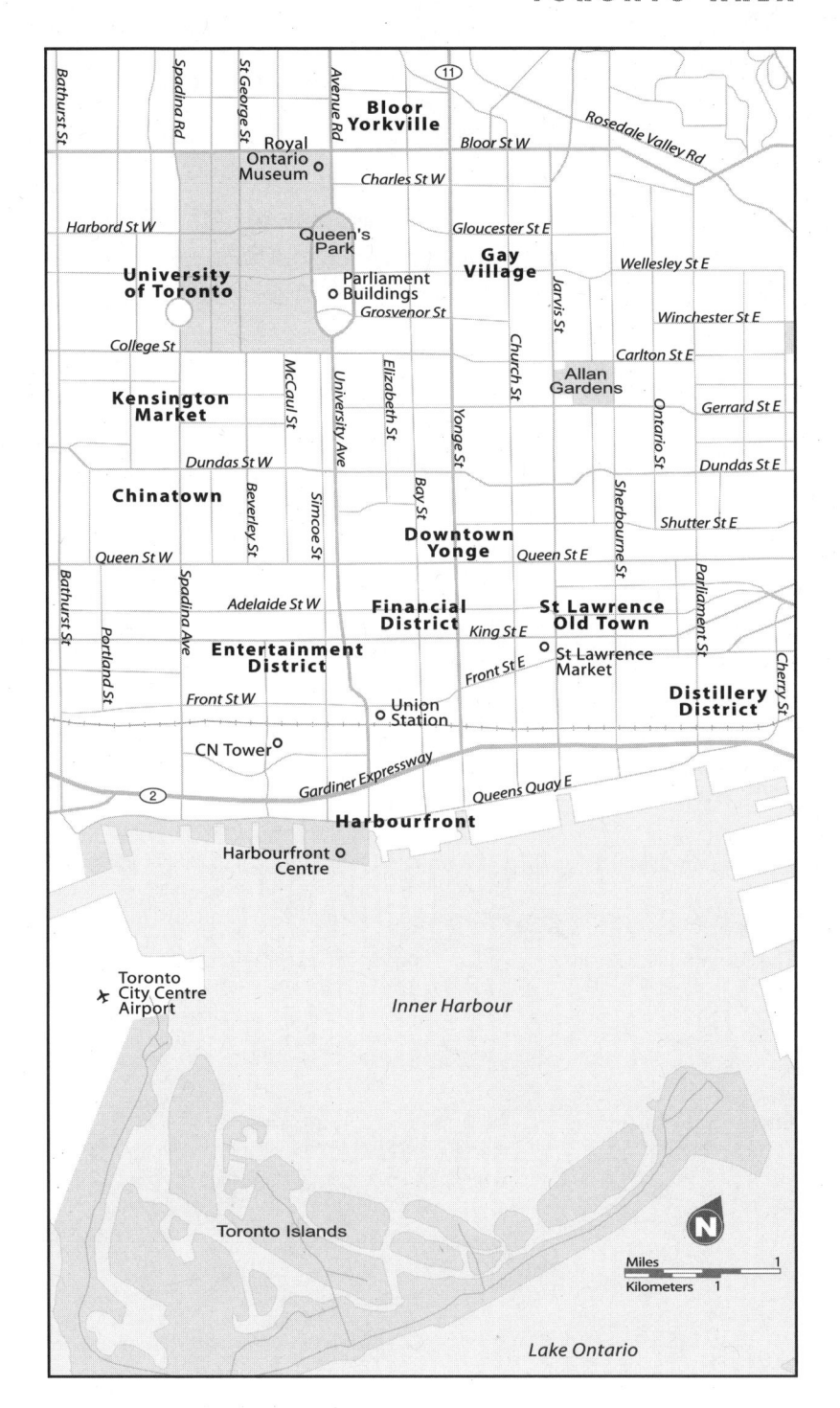

What makes *The Fun Seeker's Toronto* the *ultimate* guide to one of the world's hottest cities?

- **Information that puts you in the right place at the right time**
- **best restaurants, nightlife, attractions, and hotels**
- **great attention to detail • insider tips • easy-to-use format**

Hit the Ground Running — From how to get around to what to wear, find all the **logistical information** you need to plan a successful vacation. (p. 15)

The Perfect Toronto — With detailed descriptions and insider tips, select from the **best of the best** in 33 categories—such as Best Summer Patios, Best Jazz Clubs, and Best Trendy Restaurants—to create your own fabulous vacation. (p. 35)

The Toronto Experience — Choose the experience (Hot & Cool, Arts & Entertainment, Hipster, or Classic) that suits you best with four unique theme-based **three-day itineraries** followed by descriptions of all related venues. (p. 69)

Leaving Toronto — When you need a break from the city, head out to one of these **day trips** or **overnight** destinations. (p. 181)

The Toronto Calendar — For even more fun, time your vacation around a selection of the best **world-class events** and local festivals. (p. 195)

The Toronto Black Book — Quickly find all important information, including phone numbers, addresses, and brief descriptions, in the most **complete and accurate list** of what is cool, hip, funky, classic, and chic. (p. 203)

MAPS
Greater Toronto — View the entire city. (p. 14)
Toronto Region — Pinpoint each *Leaving Toronto* destination. (p. 180)
Toronto Area — Zoom in on key streets in frequented areas. (p. 223)